Aspects Yellowing Darkly

Also by Peter McCormick

Poverty among Immigrant Children in Europe (co-author)

Eco-ethics and Contemporary Philosophical Reflection: The Technological Conjuncture and Modern Rationality

Eco-ethics and an Ethics of Suffering: Ethical Innovation and the Situation of the Destitute

The Negative Sublime: Ethics, Warfare, and the Dark Borders of Reason

When Famine Returns: Ethics, Identity, and the Deep Pathos of Things

Modernity, Aesthetics, and the Bounds of Art

Fictions, Philosophies, and the Problems of Poetics

Heidegger and the Language of the World

Roman Ingarden: Über das Wesen (editor)

Starmaking: Realism, Anti-realism, and Irrealism (editor)

The Aesthetics of Roman Ingarden (editor)

Contemporary Essays on Roman Ingarden (co-editor)

Art and its Reasons (editor)

Husserl: Shorter Works (co-editor)

Husserl: Expositions and Appraisals (co-editor)

Contemporary Japanese Philosophy (director): 4 vols to date

Gabriel Marcel: Tragic Wisdom and Beyond (translator)

Peter McCormick

Aspects Darkly

Ethics, Intuition, and the European High Modernist Poetry of Suffering and Passage

Jagiellonian University Press

The publication of this volume was financed by the Institute of European Studies (MA in Euroculture Programme) at the Jagiellonian University.

MANAGING EDITOR
Krzysztof Kowalski

EDITOR IN CHIEF
Mirosław Ruszkiewicz

COVER DESIGN
Rafał Bartkowicz

COVER PHOTOGRAPH
Hélène Bessière

PROOFREADER
Magdalena Buchta

TYPESETTER
Katarzyna Mróz

First edition, Kraków 2010

ISBN 978-83-233-2980-0

WYDAWNICTWO UNIWERSYTETU JAGIELLOŃSKIEGO

www.wuj.pl

Jagiellonian University Press
ul. Michałowskiego 9/2, 31-126 Kraków
phone: +48 12-631-18-81, +48 12-631-18-82, fax: +48 12-631-18-83
Sales: phone: +48 12-631-01-97, +48 506-006-674, fax: +48 12-631-01-98
e-mail: sprzedaz@wuj.pl

For Juliette Puech, Guillaume and Xavier Critchlow

Gloria del disteso mezzogiorno
quand'ombra non rendono gli alberi,
e piu e piu si mostrano d'attorno
per troppa luce, le parvenze, falbe.

Glory of the spread out midday
when shade is not rendered by the trees,
and more and more all around appear,
in too much light, aspects darkly yellowing.

Eugenio Montale (1925)

CONTENTS

PREFACE

This meditative essay in philosophy and literature is the much expanded and revised version of three invited seminar lectures and discussions that I was privileged to present and direct at the Institute of European Studies of the Jagiellonian University in Cracow during the last week of May, 2009. The main theme was moral intuitionisms and emerging European reflection on principled bases for an eventual common European social policy.

I am very grateful to the Director of the Institute, Professor Zdzisław Mach, and to Professor Czesław Porębski for their invitation, and to Dr. Krzysztof Kowalski and Dr. Martin Galent for their hospitality and their encouragements. I thank Łukasz Kocój, Director of the Jagiellonian University Press, for accepting the book manuscript, and his professional colleagues for their preparation of the manuscript for publication. I owe particular thanks to the participants in the seminars for their lively interventions, and especially to Professor Czesław Porębski for his comments and criticisms of the manuscript, and for his long and patient friendship.

As the numerous billboards next to the Barbakan Fortress behind the medieval Florian's Gate insisted at the time, the immediate contexts of these Cracow Seminars were the European elections that were to be held the following week on June 7, 2009. The global contexts were those of a continuing and historically unprecedented financial and economic crisis together with increasing geopolitical tensions, especially between the European Union (EU) and Iran, the EU and Russia, and even the EU and China. And the national contexts both in France and in Poland were troubled, especially socially.

For even in the relatively affluent new Europe and not just in the already deeply impoverished countries of many parts of Africa and Asia, many persons were beginning to suffer again from deep-seated fears about a threatening inflation, widespread unemployment, and a growing and yet strangely familiar sense of helplessness. Grandparents' memories were returning from the past with so many of their desperate images from the lean years that had slowly built up to the terrifying outbreak and then to the horrific cataclysms, catastrophes, and consequences of the Second World War and its prolonged aftermaths.

The imminent European elections were quite important because much was at stake. Partly at stake was trying to resolve further the fundamental division between those who see the new Europe as a mainly liberal federation of independent states, an intergovernmental entity, and others who see the new Europe as a mainly socialized union of member states, a single unified entity only. At stake was Europe's geopolitical, economic, and environmental future. And partly at stake, too, was the newly shaky consensus about the shared moral and ethical values informing generous European social policies at a time when increasing immigration, health costs, poverty, and generally hard times had already started to revive the old demons of European nationalisms.

In particular, many thoughtful younger European persons were concerned about how the still emerging new Europe would be able to deal effectively with the challenges of new European political and social thinking in the near future. How could they ever reach consensus on such difficult matters as the profoundly ethical issues necessarily at the bases of any common and harmonized European social policy? Among other matters, they had in mind future candidacies to the EU, Croatia and Macedonia from the still unsettled Balkan states, Ukraine, and Turkey. Could such candidates fully subscribe to the many exigencies of EU membership? Could they participate fully, for example, not just in a common EU immigration policy, but in a whole range of common EU policies on defense, energy, environment, law, education? And could they participate in an eventual harmonized EU social policy? The coming European elections were indeed an important moment in Europe's ongoing attempts to reinvent itself in very complicated, even dangerous times.

And yet when viewed at least from France, which is the quite limited standpoint whence this essay is written, these important elections also seemed obscure, disquieting, and at times pointless. They seemed obscure because few thoughtful persons apparently had sufficiently clear ideas about just what the central issues were in these elections, and especially about just what really needs to matter in the emerging Europe today. The elections also seemed disquieting because many thoughtful persons were aware that at least French political parties, and perhaps several Polish political parties as well, had put forward all too many candidates – in France there were 3000 candidates for 72 seats – who were evidently ignorant of many of Europe's current problems and whose readiness to work hard in the European Parliament could have been rightfully questioned.

And these important elections seemed at times even pointless. For many thoughtful young persons, for example in France, apparently had lost confidence in the capacities of at least many French politicians to contribute positively enough to promoting not just French interests. How much more EU money should go to French farmers? – but also to institutionalizing common European moral values and ethical ideals? And how much money and effort ought to go towards harmonizing still seriously deficient EU social policies and programmes? For example, should there be the same minimum salary in at least all euro country members of the EU?

In fact, these elections seemed to require making new occasions for winning a sustainable and effective clarity. That is, the EU elections at the time seemed to require making occasions where competing political, economic, social, and intellectual projects, and especially their underlying moral and ethical presuppositions, might be carefully laid out, studied, debated, and finally voted on. But as I began the seminars in Cracow, signs of such occasions materializing before these elections were very few.

Today, with the European Parliament now elected for better or for worse, with the Lisbon Treaty now signed although not without much difficulty by all twenty-seven EU states, and with for the first time a President of the European Union's Council in office, the Cracow seminars were, in retrospect and perhaps sadly, not one of those required occasions. Taking place just before the European elections, the seminars turned out to be with, I am afraid to say, all too little ambition, no more than "a momentary stay against confusion." No more, but perhaps no less either.

In general, the objective was to promote further informed critical discussion about how to articulate less unsatisfactorily what moral requirements and ethical ideals Europe might continue to stand for and which might even serve as eventual signposts for the elaboration of a common European social policy. Similar discussions were already well underway in many places including notably in the distinguished and characteristically interdisciplinary European Studies Programme founded in 1999 in Cracow. And these discussions continue today as a highly motivated and quite gifted younger generation of scholars from many countries complete their graduate training before seeking permanent positions in the still expanding higher European civil service.

That initial general objective remains the same for this philosophical essay. For one of the issues repeatedly under consideration in Cracow, and not just in the universities, is, perhaps surprisingly, philosophical. That issue is just how do we come to know properly just what are those genuine moral requirements and ethical ideals we would hope to further through individual and communal political commitment and social action in Europe today and tomorrow.

In short, the Cracow seminars were designed to offer a modest but serious occasion for investigation and critical discussion together of what roles our most basic intuitions about what is morally right and what is ethically good might play in such ongoing reflection about knowing how to act thoughtfully enough in today's complex and newly emerging Europe.

May this philosophical and meditative essay offer a similar occasion!

Peter McCormick
Paris, December 8, 2009

ORIENTATIONS

Moral Intuitionisms and the Emerging Europe

In this introductory chapter we begin with a specific problem among the many that are facing the European Union (EU) today after the long-awaited approval of the Lisbon Treaty at last in the late autumn of 2009. Some of the main lines of force in this specific problem will then enable us to see more easily just what our main objective is in this extended essay. Consider then briefly some initial reflections on one only of the several quite serious social problems facing the EU today, the problem of European immigration.[1]

Immigrants in Europe

Do the basic human rights of immigrants from economically less developed countries include the freedom to migrate to more developed European countries where they have far better chances for leading lives of greater fundamental well-being?[2]

The very different and regularly changing immigration policies of most of the twenty-seven EU states testify to the large differences of opinion as to how such an important question is to be answered.[3] Yet any eventual consensus about a harmonized European social policy[4] cannot avoid including as an essential element not only a common European policy on access to health, education, and many other shared areas of central concern, but also a common policy on immigration.[5]

Achieving such a consensus will necessarily involve protracted debate among various stakeholders about what social, moral, and ethical principles should form the bases of such a unified European social policy. Ultimately, many of those debates will come to focus on just how we may properly be said to come to know such principles.[6] Given the nature of such issues, some philosophers need to play a modest but continuing role in these debates. And

EU parliamentarians, who already include among their numbers several philosophers, need to keep studying some current political and social philosophy.

One distinguished contemporary English philosopher, Sir Michael Dummett, has argued that the basic human rights of persons do include the right to what he calls "first class citizenship." "The truth within the principle of national self-determination," he writes, "is that everyone has the right to live in a country in which he and others of a group to which he belongs are not persecuted, oppressed or discriminated against, in which his religion, language, race and culture are not reviled or held up to contempt and in which he can fully identify himself with the state under whose sovereignty that country falls. Whether that holds good of where he is living depends in part upon the conduct of that state, and in part on the behaviour of its people: it is ultimately decided by whether that individual feels that he fully belongs. This may be called the right to be a first-class citizen."[7]

But however applicable such a notion of first-class citizenship might prove to be for those immigrants who for cogent reasons are seeking asylum, some critics of an eventual harmonization of European immigration laws as an element in a common European social policy would quickly register a counter claim. Their retort would be that this notion does not apply to the majority of immigrants seeking entry to EU countries today on economic grounds only. Further considerations than merely a so-called "right to first-class citizenship," they would insist, are surely in order.

Dummett himself goes on to address a related question about European immigration today. "[W]hat duties and what rights," he asks, "does a state have towards individuals seeking to enter the land over which it rules?" And he continues, "The initial answer has to be that it must deal with them justly: it must give them their due."[8] That is, if immigrants have certain rights, some states have certain duties, and conversely. But, again, critics might well reply that this assertion, while not incorrect, remains too general.

In another passage, however, Dummett offers a more particular version of his earlier and perhaps overly general claim. "To refuse help to others suffering from or threatened by injustice," including those suffering from the economic injustices of what he describes as "savage inequalities of wealth and opportunity," is, he claims, "to collaborate with that injustice, and so incur part of the responsibility for it."[9] But making this claim is to move from strictly individual to communal concerns. And that move from the individual to the communal, especially in this particular case, remains controversial.

The underlying issue in these kinds of ongoing debates today in the EU parliament about immigration is twofold. The first aspect of the immigration issue is whether some persons have a basic human right to immigrate to a place of their own choosing, whether that place be in Europe or elsewhere. And the second aspect of this issue is whether at least all member states of the

EU should recognize EU member states as having not just a legal but a moral obligation to honour that right even when the grounds for that assertion are economic only.

Dummett's own position is clear. "[I]f an individual has a duty to give help to those in need when they ask him for it," Dummett observes, "he also has a duty not to deny them the opportunity to ask. The same applies to states. They have an internationally recognised duty towards refugees: they therefore have a duty to do nothing to prevent refugees from reaching their borders."[10] Fine for refugees, someone might object, but what about economic immigrants?

Similarly, many EU parliamentarians today could argue effectively against such a position on at least three kinds of grounds. First, the determination of the precise relationships between natural rights and human rights still eludes professional consensus.[11] Moreover, any consensus about what constitutes the basic principles of distributive justice at the level of nation states remains elusive.[12] Furthermore, the nature of the responsibilities of nation states with respect to international justice is unclear.[13]

Now one of the most fundamental challenges here is to find the appropriate verbal resources for rearticulating less unsatisfactorily common ethical intuitions in EU societies about the principled bases of an eventually harmonized EU social policy in such ways as to achieve consensus more advisedly and more readily. What would such "principled bases" look like?

By way of example only, since our main concern is not with what those bases might be but with how they might come to be properly known, consider briefly only the suggestiveness in our contexts of a list of intermediate moral and ethical intuitionist principles such as those that the American philosopher, Robert Audi, has recently elaborated in other contexts. Some much revised version of these kinds of middle-level principles, which derive from very general principles of moral rightness and ethical goodness and from which in turn many subordinate principles can be derived, might make up what we are calling here the "principled bases for an eventual common European social policy."

Without making room now for any philosophical comment or for the necessary work of transposing something like these principles from the individual to the social realm, here are ten such principles that we may keep in mind throughout this essay whenever we make use of our quite abbreviated expression, "principled bases for an eventual common European social policy."

1. "Prohibition of injury and harm. We should not injure or harm people [or member states]."
2. "Veracity. We should not lie."
3. "Promissory fidelity. We should keep our promises."
4. "Justice. We should not treat people unjustly and should contribute to rectifying injustice and to preventing future injustice."

5. "Reparation. We should make amends for our wrong-doing."
6. "Beneficence. We should contribute to the good (roughly, the well-being) of other people [and member states]."
7. "Gratitude. We should express gratitude, in deed or at least in words of thanks, in a way that befits good things done for us by other people [and member states], where, other things being equal, our obligation is stronger if what was done for us was not owed to us."
8. "Self-improvement. We should develop or at least sustain our distinctively human capacities."
9. "Enhancement and preservation of freedom. We should contribute to increasing or at least preserving the freedom of persons, giving priority to removing restraints over enhancing opportunities."
10. "Respectfulness. We should, in the manner of our relations with other people [and member states], treat them respectfully."[14]

In short, the European Union (EU) today, with its now twenty-seven member states working under the now approved Lisbon constitutional treaty that became effective on December 1, 2009 and with several candidate states anticipating entry soon, faces many difficult challenges in the actual international geopolitical, economic, and social contexts. One of these challenges is forging a common EU immigration policy. And one of the EU's basic tasks today, and it is an urgent one, is that of constructing a common European social policy for all persons living in the member states now and in the future that would include not just immigration policy but other social issues as well, such as health, poverty, and so on.[15]

But an eventual common EU social policy must have principled bases. And reaching consensus about such principled bases requires clarity about just how one may properly come to know such principled bases. One source of such knowledge, many would agree today as we will see, is moral and ethical intuition. In order to sidestep recurring disagreements about such intuitions, however, further reflection such as that we are proposing to pursue here is necessary.

Among the key factors that make this difficult task urgent are the rapidly accelerating levels and different degrees of social and individual suffering.[16] For since the middle of the 1980's, many European states have already showed continuing increases in social inequalities in comparison with other states in the Organisation for Economic Cooperation and Development (OECD).[17] What makes this task so challenging is the simple fact that no such harmonized social policy is possible[18] without achieving some consensus about the moral and ethical values that must lie at the basis of such policies.[19]

But, as the distressing, sometimes tragic, and continuing incapacities of the United Nations and other international organizations have demonstrated repeatedly, achieving even partial consensus in ethical matters is extremely difficult. For, among other things, our common moral and ethical intuitions about the nature of these values all too often differ appreciably.

We will need to return to some of these issues later in this essay in both the "Interlude" and in the concluding "Envoi." For now, however, we should not overlook some recent suggestions of a general nature that may be of help.

In a recent review, suggestively entitled for those who would reflect further today on the demanding challenges of the newly emerging Europe, "How England Became Modern: A Revolutionary View," the distinguished historian, Bernard Bailyn, has offered some helpful general observations. "[O]ne of the deepest tendencies of late-twentieth-century historiography," he writes, "[is] the impulse to expand the range of inquiry, to rescale major events and trends into larger settings, and to seek heightened understanding at a more elevated and generalized plane. In every sphere of historical study – intellectual, cultural, political – the scope of inquiry has broadened."[20]

Faced with the very difficult problem of achieving consensus among 27 different countries about not just the details but also about reliable means for coming to know the principled bases of an eventual common European social policy that would appreciably diminish the growing social and individual[21] suffering of many persons especially in the Eastern parts of Europe, perhaps a modest but sustained effort both to rescale the problem, to expand the scope of inquiry, and to seek understanding at a more general plan might not prove unhelpful.

One highly pertinent way of doing so is philosophical. That is, one might examine freshly at least one of the main ways for coming to know principled bases for such an eventual social policy by critical reconsidering one of the most important sources of knowledge of these principled bases, namely our moral and ethical intuitions. And a closely related way of fruitfully rescaling the continuing debates in the new EU about those principled bases might be to suggest shifting the focus of some such discussions from the often overly narrow terms of much traditional philosophical talk about moral and ethical intuitions to the now mostly overlooked verbal and conceptual suggestiveness within the enormously rich moral and ethical idiom of what may be called "the distinctive European high modernist poetry of suffering."

The key issue in reaching agreement for an emerging common European social policy is how to forge broad enough and especially clear enough consensus for reasonable agreement. This is not just a matter of effective diplomacy. More fundamentally, achieving consensus in such matters is also a matter of finding sufficiently nuanced and yet still substantive verbal articulation. And one major resource for achieving such nuanced articulation is the richness of the still largely neglected linguistic innovations on hand in much of the European high modernist poetry of suffering and passage.

This richness of language, we will be trying to appreciate in what follows, comprises fresh and powerful resources for rearticulating many of those disparate viewpoints about the reliability of many of our moral and ethical intuitions about principled bases for a common European social policy.[22] Such intuitions have to do primarily for both individuals and communities with our moral obligations and duties on the one hand, and on the other with our ethical values and ideals.

Moral Intuitionism

Close to the centre of renewed reflection on Europe today on the possibility of a common European social policy are, perhaps surprisingly, philosophical questions about knowing how to act rightly, about right action both at the individual and at the communal level. In particular, some reflective persons wanting to know[23] what acting rightly comes to[24] in many of our newly complex ethical situations in Europe today are investigating anew the still controversial merits of what is called "moral intuitionism."

Moral intuitionism was one of the important general philosophical accounts that dominated much European ethical discussion from the eighteenth through the first third of the twentieth century. In general, moral intuitionism may not unfairly be understood as the view that persons come to know at least some basic objective moral truths not indirectly through, say, a species of inference but directly by immediate awareness.

Such a general view, however, is not without its difficulties. For example, when intuition is understood as immediate awareness alone, difficult issues arise about the reliability of such awareness and especially about its vulnerability to different kinds of self-deception. Yet after much thorough criticism through most of the twentieth century, moral intuitionism today has again become the focus of renewed, and constructive, investigation.[25]

Even when taken rather particularly as the view that some persons reliably come to know some basic objective moral truths not indirectly through inference but directly by an immediate awareness, moral intuitionism has a complicated history. That history includes its protracted discussion and argument in very different forms, not just in the work of Plotinus and Augustine, Aquinas and Ockham, but especially in its eighteenth-century elaborations in Fichte and the early Schelling during the transitions from Kant's overly suspicious views to Hegel's perhaps overly enthusiastic ones.[26]

Over the last century or so the most important instances of moral intuitionism in English-language philosophy were to be found in the works of Henry Sidgwick (1838–1900), especially the seventh edition of *The Methods of Ethics* (first published in 1874), G.E. Moore (1873–1958), especially *Prin-*

cipia Ethica (1903), H.A. Prichard (1871–1947), *Duty and Interest* (1928), C.D. Broad (1887–1971), *Five Types of Ethical Theories* (1930), and W.D. Ross (1877–1971), especially *The Right and the Good* (1930).[27] Although each of these English-language philosophers made several still important contributions to other areas of philosophy, arguably each also made a particularly important contribution to moral intuitionism.[28]

If we leave aside their other contributions and much of the necessary nuance for precisely detailing their contributions to moral philosophy today, we can perhaps summarize very roughly at least one major element in each of these philosophers' contributions to our main theme of moral intuitionism. This summary will then serve to motivate our focussing critical attention in the chapters that follow on three aspects only of moral intuitionism – moral discourses, moral knowledge, and moral motivations.

Thus, Sidgwick[29] argued that, besides utilitarianism and egoism, intuitionism as an investigation of intuitively self-evident principles as "absolute practical principles" for action was one of the three fundamental methods for establishing rational bases for moral action. For his part, Moore[30] argued that, although some moral intuitions may allow us to grasp an intrinsic moral goodness in certain actions, goodness itself including moral goodness is apparently indefinable.

In these contexts, Prichard[31] emphasized that not only was the moral goodness of those morally obligating actions that presented themselves intuitively to persons indefinable; moral goodness was also – to use Moore's own cardinal term – "unanalysable."[32] While working mainly outside ethics, Broad[33] nonetheless suggested that moral situations like any others engaged perceptions on the part of the moral subject, processes in which what he called "*sensa*" are presented to our intuitive capacities as the effects of a specifically mental kind of causation.

Ross went back to Sidgwick. Ross[34] argued that Sidgwick had been mistaken in taking the intuitively grasped moral rightness of an action to be equivalent to the maximization of its moral goodness. He argued that there are other so called *prima-facie* moral obligations that in some cases are more basic than and take priority over such a maximization.

Today, many of these seminal reflections continue to generate further critical consideration.[35] But when we reflect even briefly on these summary remarks, we can notice right away the pertinence for reconsidering moral intuitionism of focussing renewed inquiry on at least three selected themes, namely those of moral discourse, moral knowledge, and moral motivations. For language, perception, and freedom are among the most central issues for understanding moral intuitionism.[36]

Many of these instructive historical and contemporary perspectives, however, risk remaining too technical for many thoughtful persons today. Moreover, considered ethical reflection today continues to neglect some of the most suggestive representations of ethical intuition not just in professional philosophical discussions but in literary works of art. Such suggestive literary representations are especially on view in what I have suggested elsewhere may be called "the twentieth-century's distinctive modernist poetry of suffering."[37]

Accordingly, this philosophical and meditative essay is an attempt to put on exhibit some of these extraordinary linguistic resources against the backgrounds of such ongoing EU discussions as the construction of an eventual unified European social policy, in the general contexts of literature and philosophy,[38] and from the particular perspectives of contemporary English-language moral philosophy[39] and European high modernist poetry. The focus is on the important notion of ethical intuitions about the sense and significance of the still insufficiently appropriated legacy of our most recent and tragic pasts, the different kinds of human suffering so much in evidence throughout the last century of European history and culture.

The main objective is to call renewed attention to such linguistic and conceptual resources in the high modernist European poetry of suffering for imagining and partly rearticulating a more broadly construed account of moral intuitionism, perhaps a more accessible one for all those interested in Europe today. Such an account usefully focuses on three central aspects of moral intuitionism and different kinds of human suffering on view respectively in the poetry of T.S. Eliot (1888–1965), Paul Valéry (1871–1945), and Eugenio Montale (1896–1981).

Ethical Intuitions

One central consideration in ethical reflection today, then, both in Europe and elsewhere, is the specific nature of moral and ethical intuition. These are not necessarily the same. But just what is intuition?

In general, the notion of "intuition" is difficult to pin down. Dictionaries do not help enough. For example, the latest *Oxford Dictionary of English* definition of intuition unhelpfully appeals to "instinct" and to the unclear distinction between the "conscious" and the unconscious: "intuition = the ability to understand something instinctively, without the need for conscious reasoning."[40]

Intuition evidently is more than one thing. Many psychologists, for example, understand intuition generally as a capacity for "arriving at [reliable] decisions or conclusions without explicit or conscious processes of reasoned thinking."[41] For most philosophers writing in English, intuition is understood more particularly as "an alleged direct relation, analogous to visual seeing, between the mind and something abstract and so not accessible to the senses."[42] And in particular most moral philosophers writing in English take ethical intuition as the direct awareness of basic moral truths expressed in propositions arising from judgments whose contents are unlike any empirical or other kind of judgment (e.g., mathematical) and which are objectively true or false.[43]

Each of such general views, however, requires close critical scrutiny. For talk about "conscious processes," analogies with "visual seeing," and unique judgmental "contents" remains quite misleading. As for a distinction between moral and ethical intuitions, some philosophers often understand the first expression, "moral intuition," to refer mainly to intuitions about moral obligations and moral duties, whereas they understand the second, "ethical intuition," to refer mainly to intuitions about ethical values and ethical principles. Other philosophers largely use these expressions interchangeably, except where argument may require more precision.

Interestingly, some rather recent philosophical work has taken up freshly many of the traditional problems affecting different philosophical notions of intuition. Attention has focussed especially on at least one important strain of philosophical ethics. A good sense of this recent work on moral intuitionism emerges from what may not unfairly be taken as representative summary remarks such as the following:

> Moral intuition has an authority of its own; but it can be refined, and must sometimes be corrected, by theoretical reflection. Intuition must also respond both to the pressure of obligation [i.e., what we might call hereafter "moral intuitionism"] and to the incentive of ideals [i.e., what we might call hereafter "ethical intuitionism"]. Our obligations require us to reach certain destinations on life's journey, and they prohibit others; our ideals call us to take harder paths and to go further than we must. Along the way, the manner of our actions – their style, their timing, their sensitivity to others – is also governed by obligations and ideals that reflect the value of persons. A sound moral theory integrates these two kinds of normative sources, the obligatory and the ideal. It guides moral judgment, it stimulates moral imagination, and it clarifies the values that we seek to fulfil. In these and other ways, it can help us to achieve the good in doing the right.[44]

Our central concern in this essay lies in exploring some of these relations between ethical intuitions as "just seeing" moral obligations and ethical values, and such intuitions as also requiring "corrective reflection."[45] And yet our approach to these relations between intuiting moral obligations and ethical values as just seeing them and reflecting on what one intuitively sees may seem to some unconventional. For we would like to proceed by way of examining several earlier high modernist poetic articulations of particular ethical ideals as cardinal instances of the distinctive twentieth century poetry of personal suffering. And with respect to at least the two kinds of normative sources mentioned above, we want to stress not so much the morally obligatory but the ethically ideal.

In particular, we would hope to elucidate at least several of the recurring conceptual tensions between what some moral philosophers have criticized as the supposed "self-evidence" of certain ethical intuitions of values, and what some other moral philosophers have criticized as the insufficiently general character of ethical reflection on values that is based on examples only.

Moral and Ethical Situations

Many genuine and important connections between art and life seem somehow evident yet remain deeply puzzling. That is, both reasonably evaluating one's appreciative understandings of what several literary works of poetic art may represent and rationally making use of such representations in leading one's everyday life more satisfactorily – in more completely doing what is right and good – seems problematic.[46]

On the one hand, social and cultural history continues to show how some literary representations, for example, representations of several Victorian fictional models for what counts as leading an exemplary young woman's life, indeed connect strongly with some Victorian young women actually having relied on such fictional models for leading their exemplary lives. But on the other hand, specifying just what kinds of sense and significance thoughtful readers may properly come to see in fictional representations of particular literary states of affairs and then act on remains elusive.

Perhaps someone may indeed act reasonably in choosing to imitate in her own life some of the admirable moral ideas and ethical ideals she has intuited in the actions of certain fictional characters on exhibit in some novels, poems, and plays. Today, we would probably also have to add: on exhibit in some popular songs and especially in films too. But is it also reasonable for her to believe that what she has seen as morally and ethically exemplary in these fictional representations is indeed objectively the case?[47]

This kind of question arises in acute form when what is at issue is dealing rationally and reasonably with different types of avoidable personal suffering. For here, perhaps more than anywhere else, our grasp of what is at stake for us as persons in such suffering is necessarily undermined by our unreliable capacities to act on such apprehensions – our fragility, our vulnerability, our absences, our uncertainties – in a word, our contingency.[48] This basic point about the essential contingency of personhood will be one of the assumptions in what follows. A brief overview of some similar assumptions we will be working with may now prove helpful.

Much of the twentieth-century's distinctive European poetry of suffering and passage, what I have called elsewhere the poetry of "a negative sublime" – think of some of the work of Celan, Mandelstam, Herbert, or, earlier, of Rilke,

Akhmatova, Miłosz – present thoughtful readers with, among other things, a deeply meditative evocation of the almost unbearable burdens even today of recent European history. More simply, this work presents its persistent readers with poetic and hence essentially verbal representations of what we might call generally a particular kind of moral state of affairs, one that specifically insists on a personal response on the part of its readers. But what makes a state of affairs moral?

Generally, most persons already have a good idea of what makes an actual state of affairs moral. For, while perhaps not being able to define such situations, most persons can readily give examples of them – my seeing a child falling into a river, your hearing a pregnant woman at the supermarket crying out for help against an assailant, some situations on view in documentary films about still unmastered but today still all too ominously insistent past evils.[49]

What seems to make such states of affairs moral, some philosophers would argue, is the presence of certain salient intrinsic and objective moral elements.[50] Franz Brentano (1838–1917), the teacher of both Kazimierz Twardowski (1866–1938) who was the founder of the Lvov–Warsaw school of Polish analytical philosophy, and of Roman Ingarden (1893–1970), the founder of Polish realist phenomenology, termed such moral objective and intrinsic moral elements "moral substances."[51] When taken generally and not just in its technical Aristotelian senses, such talk of moral substance here proves helpful. Modern Polish philosophy, we should recall here, contributed greatly to providing a more nuanced understanding not just of moral substance but of value theory generally, and continues to do so today.[52]

But how do we grasp what it is that makes such states of affairs moral? Some moral philosophers have argued that we grasp such moral substances, such objective intrinsic moral values, by directly and immediately intuiting them. Insight, as it were, enables persons to "see into" such states of affairs and, as it were, see their moral substance.

This already partly classical view (Brentano was both a distinguished Aristotelian scholar as well as a major figure in phenomenological psychology and ethics[53]) derives today mainly from eighteenth-century British work, especially by Francis Hutcheson (1694–1746), Adam Smith (1723–1790), and David Hume (1711–1776), on the so-called "moral sense."[54] According to the moral sense view, thanks to an inner capacity[55] some persons usually come to admire and then to judge certain states of affairs as virtuous and morally good and to despise and then to judge certain other states of affairs as vicious and morally bad. That is, most persons have the capacity to feel some things to be good or bad, whether the feeling be well-founded or not, rather than just to reason to a conclusion that these things are indeed good or bad.

Note that, in any particular case, the feelings of such a moral sense are well-founded when they arise from so-called "disinterested" reflection on the morally good or morally bad tendencies of things. And note too that the moral "sense" is not to be understood as analogous to any physical sense like the sense of vision or the sense of hearing that deliver particular sensations. Rather the moral "sense" is said to be like, say, a sense of propriety or a sense of tact that result not in particular sensations but in particular attitudes that accommodate formulation as propositions.[56]

Not all moral states of affairs are like the examples we just considered. For some moral states of affairs while genuinely incorporating objective intrinsic moral values require no particular response on the part of those persons who are said actually to intuit these values. I recognize and respect the value of the life of a child anywhere without necessarily that value always imposing itself on me in a special way, as it does in the case of a child falling into a river, as requiring of me an immediate response on my part to safeguard that value. So how does a person determine just when a moral state of affairs requires such an immediate response?

Some would reply: by properly describing and then elucidating the situation at issue. These descriptions and elucidations can be direct and contemporaneous, or they may be indirect and after the fact. By way of situating our later reflections on poetic representations of moral states of affairs, we need to distinguish these different cases briefly.

Consider an example. In the case, let us say, of my neighbour's child, Rachel, falling from her tricycle on the grassy path into the Vistula streaked with light at sundown, I may call out immediately for help, say, to a policeman standing nearby. I cry out "Help! Save the child who just fell into the river!" And the policeman jumps into the river and tries to save the child from drowning. That is, I don't just wordlessly gesticulate towards the drowning child: I describe the situation verbally – a child has just fallen into the river. And I don't just exclaim "Help!" I also elucidate the situation verbally – I call out to the policeman in just such a way as clearly to imply that a child will lose its life unnecessarily by drowning if no one tries to rescue the child and preserve her life. And so on. This is the contemporaneous and direct case.

Perhaps the policeman in fact succeeds in saving Rachel's life. Back at home after the dramatic event let us say that I try to explain to myself why I believed that the policeman was the one to attempt that rescue rather than me. I write down my confused thoughts. I describe the situation as best and as plainly as I remember it. I spell out clearly what seemed so pressing in the situation. I distinctly separate my reaction from that of the policeman. And, besides describing the situation distinctly, clearly, and plainly, I also try to elucidate just what intrinsic and objective aspects of the child's situation seemed to impose themselves on me as requiring an immediate response such that I would have imperatively felt obliged to jump in after the child myself if no policeman had been on hand. And so on. This is the indirect and after the fact case.

Consider now a complication. After trying to put my confused thoughts in order, both to describe and to elucidate just those salient features of the dramatic situation that made it a moral situation of such an obliging nature as to require some kind of immediate action at least on my part, I fail to satisfy myself that I have succeeded in capturing what was essential in the situation. Some days later I am still thinking of the situation and my continuing complicated reactions to it. I decide to try to capture what in retrospect seemed essential in salient features of that situation imposing themselves on me in such a way that it was not morally permissible for me to disregard them and not to act accordingly in some way. I write a poem about my complicated experience. And I call the poem, "Latvian Autumn" (after the poem of that name by Johannes Bobrowski which I cite and discuss at the very end of this essay in the concluding section, "Envoi").

On often re-reading my poem later, I come to see that my poem certainly included many descriptive elements. Remarkably, however, I chose to describe Rachel's almost drowning only very briefly. But I also described many other things as well – a candle's flame, and so on. I come to see too that my poem also included elucidative elements. Notably, I drew on simile, metaphor, and symbol to evoke what I apparently had come to apprehend in retrospect about this deeply affecting incident of the child's threatened life, a candle's reddish flame like light on dark crumbling and ruined walls, like light snaking through the dark waters of a river, like light falling on the dark hair of a Jewish child. And then I think of Rachel and her children, and I remember myself holding a candle at dusk near the darkening creek in the overgrown fields outside the crumbling walls of Oświęcim.

Here we have an indirect, after the fact case. Unlike the previous case, however, the moral situation here is not represented as factual but as fictional although life-like. The poem presents the situation with verisimilitude. The poetically represented state of affairs is not literally true; nonetheless, the represented situation gives the appearance of being true in the sense of being plausible. As described, the poetically represented situation never occurred. But as elucidated, it is not implausible that some actual situation – say, a particular state of mind – could very well have occurred in the past, a situation that could reoccur in the minds of its readers in the present and in the future.

An Overview

In the following chapters we will be focussing particular attention on similarly poetically represented moral states of affairs. One issue we will look at in detail is whether all moral states of affairs can be satisfactorily represented plainly, in literal uses of language, or whether some moral states of affairs can only be satisfactorily represented figuratively or symbolically, in non-literal uses of language. We will argue the latter case. We will refer to this first issue as "an aspect of moral discourse." Another issue will be whether all moral states of affairs can be said to be properly known directly, or whether some such states can only be said to be properly known indirectly. Again, we will argue the latter. And we will refer to this issue here as "an aspect of moral knowledge." A final issue will be whether apprehending some poetically represented moral states of affairs can be properly taken as personally liberating. We will argue affirmatively. And here we will call this issue "an aspect of moral motivation."

At the outset of these meditative reflections we need to note that it is no part of the intention here to attempt anything so pretentious as trying to work out elements for a "theory" of ethics that might have some special significance for Europeans today. Nor is there any intention here to put on view some particular "theory" of philosophical ethics in the sense in which contemporary moral intuitionism might be taken as an ethical theory elaborating the philosophical view that "there is an irreducible plurality of moral principles that are non-inferentially and intuitively knowable."[57] "Theory" is far too strong a word for what we hope to be able merely to suggest here for further much more sustained reflection on the part of our betters.

Nor can it be it any part of the intention here either to offer some chapters of a "moral philosophy" in the sense of some systematic account of a particular set of basic ethical principles and moral standards – say, those governing "*liberté, égalité, et fraternité*," or those governing "veracity, fidelity, justice, beneficence, reparation, and much more"[58] – that both appear in and apply to the ordinary lives of persons living in Europe today. "A moral philosophy" is far too comprehensive an expression for designating the few suggestions that will be emerging here.

Rather, the hope here is to call reflective attention to what in fact are the extraordinarily rich linguistic representations of genuinely ethical dimensions of personal suffering in some only of the twentieth century's high modernist European poetry of suffering. And, in particular, the hope is that the conceptual resourcefulness on view in some of these linguistic representations may assist some European policy makers to do greater intellectual justice to these still mostly overlooked powerful philosophical and poetic representations of insights into the complicated twofold nature of some intuited ethical ideals.

Accordingly, the main working assumption throughout will be that some of such abstract suppositions and insights about the still unthought immensities of innocent suffering and moral evil in Europe that we find suggested in such profoundly challenging work as some of the high modernist European poetry of Montale, Valéry, and Eliot in particular may help some thoughtful persons today in a historical European moment of particular complexity and confusion, a moment not just of economic and financial breakdown but even of "ethical rupture" with the past.[59] These insights may even help provide some of these thoughtful persons with some still largely overlooked linguistic and conceptual recourses for articulating kinds of moral intuitions that make possible the presentation of ethical ideals that lie beyond the borders, the limits, the boundaries of many of even our most successful scientific worldviews.

These are the kinds of intuitions that, once grasped, enable us both to break through and then, perhaps, actually to accomplish that passage from one universe of thought essentially constructed in terms of the limits of both language and thought to other universes of thought where the very notion of limit would seem to disappear. Looking out from here onto these worlds we do seem to discover limits that seem ultimate; looking back from other worlds onto our own we may come to realize that many if not all of those limits are but mirages.

Dealing sensibly with such overly general questions here as how some poetic utterances in literary works of art might give rise to forming rational beliefs for acting rightly when confronting the innumerable faces of suffering depends on thinking more particularly about whether some fictional utterances may rationally be understood in literal ways only.[60] We will take up that first issue shortly. First, however, we need now to specify briefly just what the following chapters are intended to be about and how they connect with our social contexts in Europe today.

The general concern of the first and eighth chapters is to put on exhibit some of the different kinds of philosophical reflection about the elusive notion of modernity. These reflections are designed to show the philosophical interest for a better understanding of moral intuitionism of enlarging what is often the overly narrow scope of much work in moral epistemology today.

The main task of the second and seventh chapter is to try to elucidate the first of at least three central and still problematic aspects of our general subject of moral intuitionism, the theme of moral discourse, of just how we are to talk both less imprecisely and more fruitfully of our moral intuitions. We will do so with the help of a first reading of figurative expressions of moral intuition and moral suffering in a cardinal section of T.S. Eliot's modernist masterpiece, *The Waste Land* (1922). And, as with the initial reflections on some of Paul Valéry's and Eugenio Montale's work, we will then return for second thoughts on Eliot's expressions in a parallel later chapter that will benefit from the initial investigation in the earlier one. Our considered views on moral discourse will turn out to be based firmly on what has recently been described as "the Simple View" about the contents of thought and talk.[61]

We will proceed by formulating an informal working hypothesis about the usefulness for better articulating moral discourse about moral intuitions today by taking critical account of figurative uses of language in some literary works of art and not just of mainly literal uses of language in some philosophical theories. Against the controversial background of the distinction between literal and the non-literal uses of language, we will then explore the details of some central uses of figurative language in a representative section of Eliot's poetry of suffering. We will conclude tentatively with a formulation of several interim conclusions.

The general concern of the third and sixth chapter on moral intuitionism and suffering is to investigate further the nature of moral intuitionism by focussing our critical attention now on the character of perception and moral knowledge in moral intuitionism. We will again set out an informal working hypothesis for a renewed critical reading of some European high modernist poetic representations of moral suffering, this time with respect to moral knowledge and visual perception of suffering in Paul Valéry's very extensive poetic journals, his *Cahiers*.

Our informal working hypothesis here will be that some attentive readings of Valéry's figurative representations of varied interactions between world, body, and mind in the poetic prose of his *Cahiers* may open up further fruitful perspectives on the nature and the kinds of perception peculiar to acquiring genuine moral knowledge through moral intuitions. Our guideline here, however, will be of a different sort than in our second chapter. For here we will try to look especially at Valéry's reflections on his own poetic practices of articulating moral intuitions rather than, as in the case of Eliot, at a poetic practice as such. And, again, with our initial tentative results in hand we will make time for a second reflection on Valéry in a companion chapter.

To sharpen our understanding of what his literary work seems to be representing only indirectly and while looking at Valéry's work broadly rather than narrowly as in the previous case study of Eliot's poetry, we will draw on the eighteenth-century Scottish philosopher Thomas Reid's (1710–1796) still often overlooked analyses of non-inferential perceptions. These analyses will yield several promising suggestions for further development of suitably weakened forms of so-called direct realist accounts of perception in moral philosophy. Our second thoughts on Valéry in chapter six will conclude with several summary formulations, this time of the variety of non-inferential perceptions on hand for parsing in more detail the usually overly general talk of moral intuitionism.

Finally, the objective of the fourth and fifth chapter will be to continue our efforts to elucidate the connections between moral intuitionism and suffering as partially represented in the high modernist poetry of Eugenio Montale's *Ossi de seppia* (*Cuttlefish Bones*, 1925), this time under the heading of our final theme, moral motivation and ethical emancipation from suffering.

Our informal working hypothesis here will go as follows. Some attentive readings of Eugenio Montale's poetic representations of various moral situations in his early high modernist poetry of an abstract spiritual suffering may provide access to a novel standpoint on the nature of both moral motivation and ethical emancipation from suffering. Taking this standpoint may sometimes yield fresh understanding of the nature of moral intuitions of external objective moral values.

In our second thoughts on Montale's poetry in chapter five, we will consider how taking a particular standpoint on moral motivation may also sometimes result in both ethical emancipations from some overly constrained moral frameworks for understanding personal suffering and ethical emancipation for receiving genuine spiritual freedoms through such suffering. Our guidelines here will be Montale's repeated variations on the passage through some improperly restrictive moral frameworks out onto some re-vivifying ethical horizons.

Between the first set of chapters on modernity Eliot, Valéry, and Montale and the second set of chapters on second thoughts about Montale, Valéry, Eliot, and modernity, we will recall some of these opening remarks in "Orientations" and try to articulate an interim report on our preliminary findings. Then at the end of these inquiries, in a final "Envoi," we will offer some concluding reflections on the pertinence both of our main theme of moral and ethical intuitionism and of our three minor themes of moral discourse, moral knowledge, and moral motivation and ethical emancipation with respect to the continuing challenges within the EU today of finding consensus about the principled bases for an eventual harmonized European social policy.

The "Envoi" will also provide us with an opportunity to conclude with a brief retrospective on an understanding of moral intuitionism in Europe today that need not be limited to the examination of strictly technical philosophical concerns only. Rather we will summarize how such an understanding of moral intuitionism might also make articulate use of linguistic and conceptual resources in several of the often still overlooked poetic masterpieces of European high modernist works of literary art.

By way of anticipating a general conclusion to this philosophical and meditative essay we may note already that the two sets of reflections on Montale's work rather than that of either Eliot's or Valéry's fall on either side of the "Interlude" at the centre of this essay. The reason for this structure is that the cardinal expression for the most striking double aspect of ethical intuition we will come upon derives mainly from Montale's richly variegated uses of the ambiguous Italian word, "*varco*."

In Montale's high modernist poetry of an abstract personal suffering, this resonant word means both "breakthrough" and "passage." The first sense, *varco* as breakthrough, we will be understanding as referring mainly to that one aspect of ethical intuition we may call "the immediate grasping of what a specific ethical value may present of itself" – what we might refer to in one translation of Montale's final line in his great poem as "aspects darkly yellowing." And the second sense, *varco* as passage, we will be taking correspondingly as referring mainly to that further aspect of ethical intuition we may call "the continuing corrective rearticulating through reflection of just what it is that a specific ethical value actually presents of itself" – what we might refer to in a slightly varied sequence in Montale's line as "aspects yellowing darkly." That is, if the first sense of *varco* as breakthrough may reasonably be understood in a cautiously positive sense, the second sense of *varco* as passage we will find ourselves having to take finally in a more prudent, restrained, and less than positive sense. Hence the sequence of the words in the title of this essay, *Aspects Yellowing Darkly.*

PART ONE

FIRST READINGS

CHAPTER ONE

Versions of Modernity

In "Orientations," our introductory chapter, we looked at the idea of the European high modernist poetry of suffering as promising a richness of linguistic innovation and often still overlooked conceptual resources that could be of service in the eventual rearticulation of those intuitions involved in the principled moral and ethical bases for a common European social policy. Before turning to several of those modernist works themselves, in this chapter we need to elucidate in an initial way only some of the many elements to be understood today in reflective talk about modernity.

"Modernity" itself is a tendentious term that still accommodates a number of competing interpretations. One central issue is just when we might date the origins of modernity. Answering this question depends very largely on one's interests. Modernity begins for those with mainly political interests with the emergence of the nation-state in the mid to late seventeenth century. Those with mainly economic interests on the other hand see modernity beginning a century later with the onset of the industrial revolution in England. Modernity begins roughly at the same time for those who have strong sociological interests, specifically with Kant's articulation of the Enlightenment ideals of ethics and politics around the time of the French and American revolutions. For others, however, who stress the primacy of science in the modern era, the origins of modernity lie in the work of Newton. Perhaps more fundamental than the question as to just when modernity may be said to have begun then is the question of just what modernity is.

The distinguished Canadian philosopher and political scientist, Charles Taylor, believes that one of the most pressing tasks today, what he calls the modern predicament, is coming to "a renewed understanding of modernity," that is, a renewed understanding of what are the "momentous transformations of our culture and society over the last three or four centuries."[62] He also believes that one central way of shouldering this task is to describe the elements and the history of what he calls the modern identity, that is, "the ensemble of (largely unarticulated) understandings of what it is to be a human agent: the senses of inwardness, freedom, individuality, and being embedded in nature which are at home in the modern West" (ix). He first develops these important and long-standing reflections in his much discussed 1989 book, *Sources of the Self: The Making of the Modern Identity*, and then further, first in his short book, *Modern Social Imaginaries*,[63] then much more recently in his very substantial 2007 work, *A Secular Age*.[64]

Why this emphasis on understanding modernity? The short answer is that Taylor thinks such a project follows from his initial "intuition," spelled out in his just as substantial earlier work, *Sources of the Self*. Taylor's sense is that many persons today "tend in our [Western] culture to stifle the spirit," to "scale down our hopes and circumscribe our vision."[65] To recover and retrieve many of the buried "empowering goods" in our culture requires of us, he believes, a new attempt both to characterize that culture more fully and to trace its development more sharply. The long answer, and his major works are characteristically very long books, is Taylor's substantial work that stimulates fresh reflections on understanding modernity.[66]

Rilke and the High Modernist Poetry of "Subjectivation"

Whatever the fate of post-modernism, contemporary European culture has the development of modernism in the arts at its centre. Charles Taylor has characterised this development mainly as a "many-faceted movement." He calls this development of the modernist moment[67] "subjectivation."

Subjectivation[68] represents the move away from different norms and criteria seen as objective in the sense of being fundamentally independent from human beings to those that are fundamentally dependent on the choices of individual human subjects. In these senses, the subjectivation at the centre of contemporary European societies is perhaps the most influential particular form today of a quite general, radical, and thoroughly pervasive relativism.[69] Subjectivation, some might even want to claim, has become almost the air we breathe. If so, it calls today for ongoing analyses of our atmosphere lest we unwittingly suffer a spiritual climate change as well as a material one.

Subjectivation has two major elements – one concerns the content of human action and the other the manner. Such a rather loose distinction, however, often invites confusion because each element can be taken as self-referential in the same way. Thus, one can easily incline to the view that, just as the manner in which I effect any one of my actions is necessarily mine in the sense that it cannot refer to anything but my own ways of acting, so too the content of my actions cannot refer to anything but my own goals or aims or whatever.

The consequence of holding such a view comes to nothing more than the "rampant subjectivism" that, Taylor argues, characterizes much of the modernist period. And this subjectivism Taylor sees in turn as the root of both "instrumental reason and the ideologies of self-centred fulfilment" in so much contemporary reflection.

There is more than one kind of self-reference at work in this picture of modern subjectivism. While granting that the manner of one's actions indeed refers necessarily to one's own ways of performing actions, to one's own aims, desires, aspirations, or whatnot, the matter of those actions need not. For one may just as well centre the content of one's actions on matters that owe their significance to something outside or beyond or independent of one's own interests. So subjectivism represents only one of the two kinds of subjectivation. Thus, subjectivism and subjectivation however easily confused are nonetheless different.

Accordingly, Taylor has gone on to advance a second and more substantial claim, this time not about the two main features of subjectivation but about modern art in general and modernist poetry in particular. Without this distinction, Taylor thinks, one cannot understand either. "The two kinds of subjectivation have to be distinguished," he writes, "if we are to understand modern art." And to justify this claim Taylor turns, neither to any modern nor to any contemporary poet, but to one of the masters of the European high-modernist lyric, Rainer Maria Rilke (1875–1926). He takes up in particular the well-known opening of the first of Rilke's *Duino Elegies*, from the sequence of ten extraordinary poems that Rilke finally finished at the Castle Muzot in the Swiss Valais in 1922 and first published in 1923, "Who, if I cried out, would hear me among the angels' / hierarchies?"[70]

In order to understand what Rilke has in mind here in talking of "angels," one has to see that one cannot establish the meaning of this crucial word, unlike say Milton's use of the same word in *Paradise Lost*, by any reference to "certain publicly available orders of meaning" such as "a medieval treatise on the ranks of cherubim and seraphim." For the modernist period characteristically lacks such agreed-upon, entirely external, public reference points. Just as Baudelaire wrote about correspondences without almost anyone in his culture believing any more in the existence of such things, so too Rilke writes of angels without almost anyone in his culture believing any more in such things either.

Consequently, in order to understand Rilke's use of a word like "angels," reflective readers must forego any appeal to strongly external canons. Instead, they must work out the specific details of how Rilke uses this word in the changing constellations of his own poetic practices. Rilke's meaning here is most directly tied to Rilke's language, not to the cosmos. Thus, understanding Rilke's meaning entails understanding the quite individual ways in which he uses language, that is, understanding his idiolect.

We may say then that a strong contrast holds between an understanding of interpretation that derives its basic canons from outside a particular human sensibility, an "externalist" interpretation, and an "internalist" interpretation, one that does not.[71] This second kind of interpretation is requisite for understanding much high modernist poetry including Rilke's. "Rilke's 'order' can become ours only through being ratified afresh in the sensibility of each new reader. In these circumstances, the very idea that once such an order should be embraced to the exclusion of all the others – a demand that is virtually inescapable in the traditional context – ceases to have any force" (86–87).

We may connect this distinction between internalist and externalist interpretation with an earlier claim of Taylor's, namely that Rilke's poetry can be construed paradoxically as a non-subjective subjectivism. The poetry is subjective in the sense that it can exhibit a subjectivation of manner, yet not subjective in the sense that it does not entail a subjectivation of content. Indeed, as the "thing poems" in Rilke's earlier *New Poems* from 1907 to 1908 show, much of Rilke's poetry is not subjective in content at all.

The apparent paradox then in the passage from Rilke's *Nineth Elegy*, where the poet seems to exhibit at the same time both a subjectivism *tout court* and a subjectivism that after all is non-subjective – this paradox dissolves. Reflective readers may first interpret the passage internally as exhibiting a subjectivity in manner but not in content. But, while the manner of expression necessarily refers to the subjective sensibility of the poet, the content of these expressions refers, at least partly, to something external to the poet's sensibility. Correspondingly, the same reflective readers may then interpret the passage externally.

The something external we may identify as we see fit, either with the "things" the passage mentions, or "the Earth" which the passage apostrophes, or "the world" in some more elusive sense. The essential point remains that the nature of the poetic epiphany this passage celebrates is not exclusively a function of "our action," but of "a transaction between ourselves and the world" (482).[72]

More generally, Taylor thinks that the movement of subjectivation that pervades so much of contemporary Western modern society and culture is part of a major shift at the end of the eighteenth-century from representation to creation. "The change (...) here goes back to the end of the eighteenth century," Taylor writes, "and is related to the shift from an understanding of art as mimesis to one that stresses creation. (...) it concerns what one might call the languages of art, that is, the publicly available reference points that, say, poets and painters can draw on. (...) But for a couple of centuries now we have been living in a world in which these points of reference no longer hold for us" (82–83).

On this influential view, then, the movement of subjectivation is seen as flowing from a prior moment when a crucial shift takes place in the accessibility of the major points of reference for attempts to interpret poetry and works of art. More specifically, Taylor wants to interpret high modernist poetry, as here in his interpretation of Rilke's paradox of subjectivism, with the help of a general view on modern society and culture from the standpoint of what he calls subjectivation. And that movement, he argues, cannot be understood without making explicit its connection with a radical shift at the end of the eighteenth century.

We need here to elucidate some of these quite helpful suggestions about understanding one of the most important strains in contemporary society and culture. Unlike Taylor's analyses, however, we will need to situate our own related observations centrally in the backgrounds and movements of the twentieth-century's distinctive high modernist European poetry of suffering. We will be especially concerned to bring to bear on both Taylor's observations and on our own the persistently difficult matters of ethics, intuitions, and poetic representations of sufferings involved in a sustained, hermeneutic perspective as well. That perspective we will adopt later on in this essay in chapter eight. But for now we need to have more of Taylor's own suggestive account in view.

A Philosophical Story About Modernity

Taylor divides his long story in *Sources* into five unequal parts, each bearing an evocative title – identity and the good, inwardness, the affirmation of ordinary life, the voice of nature, and subtler languages. Each part is subdivided into a number of detailed and heavily annotated chapters – twenty-five in all. Each chapter is then subdivided further into sections. Readers come to understand sympathetically why Taylor opens his Preface with the sentence, "I have had a difficult time writing this book" (ix); they too have had a difficult time reading it.

The story however is less symmetrical than it may at first appear. For the main plot-line is very largely the history of how the modern identity develops from the Greek era to our own.[73] Since, however, Taylor tells his story mainly in the unusual terms of the interconnections between the identity of the self and certain moral visions of the good, he devotes the first part of his study to an extended philosophical discussion of ethics and the self. He then uses this discussion to nuance the extended historical reflections.

Taylor believes that other central matters should also be addressed, in particular the links not just between the modern identity and the self but also those between the modern identity and our understandings of philosophy of language and epistemology. Explaining some of the basic claims here, however, and providing "a full scale alternative picture" (x), he thinks, "would take another book" (521). And more than fifteen years after making this claim, he indeed published that book in 2007. Yet the story he told in told in 1989 was not just a "prelude" (x); Taylor understood his story then as a necessary one – "one has to tread this path," he wrote (499).

This story is extremely rich. Informed with a wealth of historical detail, the story is directed by a searching contemporary philosophical project, elaborated patiently over a number of years, and one that displays an extraordinarily comprehensive grasp of contemporary philosophical discussion both in Anglo-

American and continental circles. Many reflective persons are still exploring Taylor's story in a protracted way from many different perspectives and interests and in different languages.

Taylor is quick to deny that his story makes any explicit claims to pass as an historical explanation. Stressing the very many important topics he excludes, Taylor claims only to be "dwelling on certain developments in philosophical and religious outlook, with an odd glance at aspects of popular mentality" (199).

Significantly, one of the extensive developments Taylor excludes from detailed consideration is the development of Renaissance humanistic views like those he mentions in passing, *quattrocento* views on human dignity, for example, in Pico della Mirandola's *Oratio on the Dignity of Man* (1486), or those on human agency in Nicholas of Cusa where agency is a completion of the creative work of God, or the hermetic and magical background in Dee and Paracelsus for Bacon's revolutionary work, or the explorations of Alberti and Vasari in the visual arts and their expansion on the understanding of human creative powers themselves, or even Florentine neo-Platonism in Michaelangelo's and Leonardo's contrasting understandings of just what "nature" art is to imitate and from just what perspectives (cf. 199–202). Part of what he is trying to do, Taylor concedes, works against any attempt at historical comprehensiveness.[74]

Taylor thinks that his story is not to be taken as an historical explanation because he is not asking "what brought the modern identity about," a question that focuses on diachronic causation. Rather, Taylor's question is "an interpretive one," as he calls it (203). The question is: in what consists the appeal, the spiritual power, the "*idées-forces*" of the modern identity "however it was brought to be in history" (203).

The historical and interpretive questions, to be sure, are closely related; but they are also distinct questions. For each requires a related but different kind of answer, the first in terms of causal explanation and the second in those of interpretive understanding. And the interpretive question is centred on where the force of certain issues is to be found.

One consequence of raising interpretive rather than explanatory questions about the modern identity, Taylor thinks, is his being able to offer an incomplete account only. He claims however that the incompletion is unavoidable. For no interpretive investigation by its nature can do full justice to the endless complexity of understanding both the material contents and the human motivations that make up the precipitating conditions of such central Western phenomena as the emergence of the modern identity. As Taylor writes, "one has to understand people's self-interpretations and their visions of the good, if one is to explain how they arise; but the second task can't be collapsed into the first, even as the first can't be elided in favour of the second" (204).

With these precisions in place, Taylor moves quickly to formulate in interpretive rather than in explanatory terms his basic thesis about the emergence of the modern identity. "The modern identity arose," he writes, "because changes in the self-understandings connected with a wide-range of practices (...) converged and reinforced each other to produce it" (206). Consequently, Taylor's concern in articulating his story is not to address the direction of causal arrows between *idées-forces* and practices at any one moment in history. Rather, he proposes to sketch the various facets in the development of the modern identity in terms of the *idées-forces* themselves.

If these are the major lines in Taylor's own view of just what kind of story he is telling, an interpretive rather than an explanatory one, what then are the major phases in this story?

These phases comprise three overlapping historical periods. The first phase stretches from "Augustine to Descartes and Montaigne, and on to our own day." Here Taylor wants to stress the first of the three elements he conjectures as central ingredients in the modern identity, "modern inwardness, the sense of ourselves as beings with inner depths" (x). The second phase overlaps the first. It stretches from "the Reformation through the Enlightenment to its contemporary forms," with the stress falling here on "the affirmation of ordinary life." And the final phase stretches from "the late 18th century through the transformations of the 19th century, and on to its manifestations in 20th century literature." This final phase accents the third ingredient of the modern identity, "the expressivist notion of nature as an inner moral source" (x). The full story – and it is both very long and still but a "prelude" to his later works – Taylor puts under the guiding adage, "understanding modernity is an exercise in retrieval" (xi).[75]

Consider now briefly but in more detail the first phase only of this story and indeed just that part of it that deals with the emergence of the modern identity in early modern times from Descartes to Locke. We need first to sketch the trajectory Taylor follows in his account of the first phase, then to inventory the salient features in the move from Descartes to Locke, and finally to focus more sharply on just what the major claims about this movement are.

Descartes versus Plato, Montaigne versus Augustine

In discussing the first phase in the emergence of modern identity, the new focus on inwardness, Taylor ranges from Plato to Augustine, to Descartes and Locke, before coming back to Montaigne and moving to summarize this part of his story around several key points. The culmination of his very long discussion is the claim that the modern identity emerges by the end of the eighteenth century as a conjunction of three key elements of inwardness – forms of self exploration, forms of self control, and "the individualism of personal commitment" (185).

Together, these three elements make up a first sketch of the modern identity as a "three sided individualism." These three sides comprise a characteristic localisation for self exploration in the inward individual, an instrumental form of moral atomism in the understanding of self control through the protections of subjective rights, and a productive economic sense of individualism as a "new centrality of constructed orders and artefacts in mental and moral life" (197).

Although this three-sided individualism emerges at the end of a sweeping view of western intellectual history from Plato to Locke, one of the most important strands in this story concerns the Cartesian transformation of the Augustinian tradition of radical reflexivity and inwardness. This strand, moreover, is carefully intertwined with a related but different one, namely a second version of internalization or radical reflexivity that we find in Montaigne. The critical opposition here is between Cartesian disengagement of an inner subject and Montaigne's exploration of an inner self.

Each of these two strands of early modern thought suggests a fresh understanding of human agency in terms of differing accents on inwardness. The first strand suggests the Cartesian relocation of moral sources and understanding of the good in a disengaged subjectivity duly objectified for analysis, and the second a counterbalancing humanist insistence on exploring a self without insisting on its objectification. This is the opposition we need to consider more closely before taking up a strongly contrasting hermeneutic view in chapter eight.

Taylor sees Descartes as elaborating, above all by contrast with both Pagan and Christian antiquity and in the spirit of both Plato and Augustine, what he calls a "new conception of inwardness, an inwardness of self-sufficiency, of autonomous powers of ordering by reason (...)" (158). That is, Descartes both disengages the subject and proceduralizes reason. The result is that traditional moral sources are no longer located outside the subject, for example in Platonic ideas or in the will of God, but now within the subject.

With respect to Plato, Descartes substitutes a completely different understanding of self-exploration based on the new "resolutive-compositive" method of Galileo rather than on any theological inquiries informed by metaphysical theories of "logos." This change in scientific theorizing yields a corresponding change in how human beings are to be understood. Once the key to scientific exploration is seen to lie outside any appeals to a theory of ideas, the moral ground supporting these ideas also has to be located elsewhere.

Thus, just as correct scientific knowledge of things now must involve the inner representation of such things, so moral knowledge requires a similar inner representation. The point is that in both cases this inward representation is neither an imitation nor a participation but one kind of conceptual construction. Consequently, the order of things "migrates" from outside to inside and becomes an order of representation that finally generates not just knowledge but certainty as well.

Thinking becomes a gathering, a collecting, a "*cogitare*" (cf. 143–145) whose standards derive not from the world but from the thinking subject.

These standards require that the body as well as the material world be understood as entirely distinct from the subject. The main consequence is that the subject itself is no longer properly understood as disengaged from the world and its objectifications.

In sum, a different epistemology leads to a different metaphysics, and the different metaphysics leads to a different philosophical anthropology or philosophy of mind. In particular, "self mastery [now] consists in our lives being shaped by the orders that our reasoning capacity constructs according to the appropriate standards" (147).

When we turn from Plato to Augustine, we find that Descartes substitutes a new understanding of insight, one no longer dependent on a transformation of the will that finally allows insight into the good, but one grounded in the realm of independent mental substance. Unlike the Stoic doctrines that Augustine revised in large measure, Descartes's doctrines exclude the possibility of taking the cosmos as embodying a meaningful order in such a way that ethics could continue to be founded on a subjectivized physics.The world rather is a mute and meaningless mechanism to be grasped "functionally as a domain of possible ends (...) a domain of potential instrumental control" (149). Rational self mastery requires insight, a kind of intuition, but insight is directed to the realm of mind and no longer to the realm of matter.

This fresh understanding of insight in terms of the mental only leads to a new view of the passions also. Unlike the Stoics and their later baptizers who saw the passions as instances of opinion, Descartes views the passions functionally. The passions are devices that "help preserve the body-soul substantial union" (150), devices that help preserve the organism from danger by triggering certain reflexes. Accordingly, rational self mastery means keeping the passions subordinated to the instrumental control of reason. Acting efficaciously, thus, is engaging oneself through the instrumentality of the passions, but engaging oneself in a detached way from the perspective of inwardness as rational self-control.

"The new definition of the mastery of reason brings about an internalization of moral sources," Taylor writes. "When the hegemony of reason comes to be understood as rational control, the power to objectify body, world, and passions, that is, to assume a thoroughly instrumental stand towards them, then the sources of moral strength can no longer be seen outside us in the traditional mode. (...) [And] if rational control is a matter of mind dominating a disenchanted world of matter, then the sense of a good life, and the inspiration to attain it, must come from the agent's sense of his own dignity as a rational being" (151–152).

Thus, Descartes displaces temperance as the heart of the moral vision with that magnanimous generosity that arises from human dignity (cf. 154–155). And rationality itself he now takes to consist not in a vision of an external reality but in certain properties of internal thinking – “rationality is no longer defined substantively, in terms of the order of being, but rather procedurally, in terms of the standards by which we construct orders in science and life” (156). Descartes thus moves “from substance to procedure, from found to constructed orders (...)” (156).

If these are the major elements in Taylor’s view of Descartes’s role in shaping the characteristic inwardness of the modern identity, what are the somewhat different roles that Montaigne plays in this story?

Just as he had done in the case of Descartes so too in that of Montaigne, Taylor devotes an entire chapter to this second perspective on “radical reflexivity” (178), a perspective on an explorative self rather than on a disengaged subject. What Montaigne discovers in his inner explorations, far from a stable human nature, is a continuously shifting subjective terrain, what Taylor calls “a terrifying inner instability” (178). This discovery results in a different understanding of reason in terms of limits, impermanence, mutability, and contingency. And it results as well in a model of self-description no longer in terms of “the exemplary, the universal, or the edifying, but [one that] simply follows the contours of the changing reality of one being, himself” (179).

This perspective on reason and self-description also leads to a new understanding of nature. Nature becomes once again, as in antiquity but now for different reasons, the salutary guide for right action, for living well. Following the precepts of nature protects the individual, as Montaigne understands the matter, from the excesses of both philosophical abstraction and moral rigourism.

The explorations of the self in view of greater self-knowledge leads to the recognition of unsuspected limits that undermines any intellectual or moral perfectionism and reinforces the moderate demands of one’s shifting, natural self. Inner explorations of the self are to be at the service of one’s individual being and not at that of some universal human being (181). Montaigne, in short, “inaugurates a new kind of reflection which is intensely individual, self-exploration, the aim of which is to reach self-knowledge by coming to see through the screens of self-delusion which passion or spiritual pride has erected. It is entirely a first person study, receiving little help from the deliverances of third person observation, and none from ‘science’ ” (181).

Taylor draws a contrast between Descartes and Montaigne in terms of their differing aims and methods. Montaigne’s aim is sharply focused on the self as a unique individual, whereas Descartes’s aim is directed to the subject as a general substance or essence. Further, Montaigne’s method is “first-person self-interpretation,” whereas Descartes’s involves the “proof of impersonal reasoning” (182).

Moreover, Descartes insists on universalizing the standards to which any individual ought to appeal in constructing his or her subjectivity, whereas Montaigne wants to insist on the irreducible originality of that inwardness each self constructs. Montaigne characteristically tries "not to find an intellectual order by which things in general can be surveyed, but rather to find the modes of expression which will allow the particular not to be overlooked" (182). So, Taylor opposes a deeper engagement with particularity in Montaigne to a deeper disengagement in Descartes.

One striking addition to this contrast lies in the social dimension. We need to remember the deeply inter-personal motivation of Montaigne's turn inwards, the death of his friend, La Boétie. "He alone partook of my true image," writes Montaigne, "and carried if off with him. That is why I so curiously decipher myself" (cited, 183).

Thus, the context of self-explanation for Montaigne is friendship, whereas the context of the construction of the subject for Descartes is scientific community. This context clarifies just why the exploration of the self in Montaigne leads finally to no one thing such as Descartes's substantial subject. Rather, Montaigne's explorations continually arrive at questions about what an individual person most essentially is once we have acquiesced in the mutability of nature itself.

The Two Modernities

This story of the first phase in the constitution of the modern identity, with its key moment in the early modern period when the Pagan and Christian vision of reason and the moral realm was displaced through the articulation of a disengaged subject in Descartes and an engaged exploratory self in Montaigne is, however, one version only of the origins of modernity.[76] Before we can investigate, then, the connections between Taylor's moral ontology and his story of the emergence of the modern identity, we do well to consider at least one plausible alternative that like Taylor's own is situated clearly in the Anglo-American philosophical landscape.

In his book, *Cosmopolis: The Hidden Agenda of Modernity*,[77] Stephen Toulmin investigates the relations between Descartes and Montaigne from the standpoint of a preoccupation with modernity that he shares with Taylor. But, unlike Taylor, Toulmin reads the relation between these two thinkers in very different terms. For Toulmin, the modern identity emerges as the result of two turning points and not one. The first turning point comes with the humanistic discoveries of Montaigne and Bacon, and the second with the scientific discoveries of Descartes and Galileo.

These revolutions are separated by about 50 years or two generations, the 1570s and 1580s on the one hand, and the 1630s and 1640s on the other. The movement between these two moments is roughly the movement from renaissance humanism to 17th century rationalism. Moreover, the historical circumstances separating the two moments are those of a Europe convulsed in political, religious, and economic turmoil. And the result is the thorough-going turn to scientific rationalism in the interests of stabilizing the intellectual currents of the times with all the reassurances of objective standards, non-theoretical demonstrations, and natural ideals.[78]

The renaissance humanistic discoveries with their insistence on limitation, uncertainty, mutability, relativism, and contingency disappear from the centre of the crowded European stage to remain in the wings for several centuries until the use of logical rigor and moral purity are once again challenged in the work of such "masters of suspicion" as Marx and Kierkegaard, Nietzsche and Freud. In short, the need for certainty in so many fields of human activity suppresses the renaissance discoveries of utterly pervasive uncertainty – the clarities of logic triumph over the ambiguities of rhetoric, and the uses of an abstract rigor displace an always hesitant, tolerant, skeptical form of inquiry.

As Toulmin writes: "In the 1580s and '90s, skeptical acceptance of ambiguity and a readiness to live with uncertainty were still viable intellectual policies: by 1640, this was no longer the case. Intellectual options opened up by Erasmus and Rabelais, Montaigne and Bacon, were set aside (...)" (44). That is, if Montaigne's work ushered in a renaissance in the understanding of modernity, Descartes's work has to be seen as a counter-renaissance. If we are, however, to contrast it effectively with Taylor's account, we will find it useful to look in more detail at Toulmin's story.

But first, we need to notice the interesting and distinctive strategy Toulmin uses to establish a context for his later discussions. This context comprises a description of a standard account of the origins of modernity, the isolation of its controlling assumptions, the critique of these assumptions, and the proposal of a revised account.

Toulmin thinks we need to reach back to the 1630s and to the work of Galileo and Descartes that first fixed the modern understanding of scientific theories as "rational" under a certain interpretation. A generation later this interpretation was generalized to the political realm. When Toulmin talks about "the standard account of modernity," then, he is referring to the view that the origins of modernity are to be found in the 1630s and 1640s. And the basis of his claim to take this interpretation as standard is his conviction that, despite extensive disagreements over detail, this interpretation enjoys the support of an historical consensus today.

"Most scholars," Toulmin writes, "agree on the point. The 'modern' commitment to rationality in human affairs was a product of those intellectual changes in the mid-seventeenth century whose protagonists were Galileo in physics and astronomy, and René Descartes in mathematics and epistemology" (12). This consensus, however, has taken a new form today by comparison with the period before the Second World War that saw the consolidation of what Toulmin wants to call the standard view.

The standard view, as Toulmin construes it, comprises three basic assumptions which historians over the last thirty years have been busy revising. The first element of the standard view of modernity is that "the political, economic, social, and intellectual conditions of Western Europe radically improved from 1600, in ways that encouraged the development of new political institutions, and more rational methods of inquiry" (16). The idea here was that a conjunction of circumstances – trade, city growth, printing, etc. – brought about the emergence of a secular culture which flowered in a scientific and methodological revolution marked by the appearance in the 1630s of Galileo's *Dialogues Concerning the Two Principal World Systems* and Descartes's *Discourse on Method.*

The second element in the standard account was the belief that "after 1600, the yoke of religion was lighter than before" (16), "that ecclesiastical constraints and controls were relaxed in the 17th century" (18). Here the key notion was the decay of the Holy Roman Empire and the growing power of an educated laity to turn aside from the dogmatism and authoritarianism of the medieval church and to think through religious matters increasingly for themselves.

And the third element was the belief that the genuine innovations in seventeenth-century science and philosophy were both revolutionary and emancipatory. And once again the main idea here is the power of Cartesian ideas of rationality to emancipate experience from theology and to rearticulate experience in terms of a new kind of inquiry whose demonstrations from clear and distinct ideas were as accessible as the elements of Euclid's geometry.

But recent historical inquiry has challenged successfully each of these three controlling elements in the standard view of the origins of modernity. To the first belief about the radical improvement of European life in the early 1600s historians have opposed a body of materials that document recurring crises in Europe between 1605 and 1650. The second view about the presumed lightening of theological constraints in these years historians have contested on the grounds of the very great tightening of orthodoxy between 1620 and 1660 when the Protestant-Catholic conflicts envenomed the Thirty Years War from 1618–1648. Finally, historians have also challenged the third element in the standard account of the origins of modernity. Far from being the innovatory and emancipatory revolutionary movements they have seemed to be, the breakthroughs of seventeenth-century science and philosophy now seem "to look less like revolutionary advances, and more like defensive counter-revolution" (17).

Thus, Toulmin believes that more recent historical research can be seen to have effectively undermined the plausibility of the standard account of modernity's origins that still holds sway, if not among historians at least among many historians of philosophy, perhaps even with Taylor.

The third element is particularly troublesome. For, as we have seen in Taylor's discussion of Descartes, the idea that the new sciences developed a new understanding of rationality is seriously deficient. Toulmin argues that this belief is doubly mistaken.

Unlike Aristotle's concern for the rational analysis of both theory and practice, seventeenth-century thinkers narrowed the scope of rational analysis to "the theoretical arguments that achieve a quasi-geometrical certainty or necessity" (20). Further these thinkers – Newton and Boyle are examples – far from liberating rational analysis from the constraints of theological concerns, continued to frame projects with an eye fixed almost continually on theological matters. Thus, the standard account mistakenly insists on a thorough-going decontextualizing of reason which, while admittedly a goal of some seventeenth-century thinkers, was more honoured in the breech than actually sought after.

With these descriptions of modernity in mind and especially with the elements of a newly controversial standard account of the origins of modernity before us, we may now consider briefly the four major components in the revised account that Toulmin wants to argue. Each of these components, Toulmin holds, were characteristic of the earlier revolution of renaissance humanism to be found in such writers as Erasmus, Rabelais, Shakespeare, Montaigne, and Bacon. And each was shunted aside as a consequence of the scientific revolution two generations later, a revolution on view not only in Galileo, Pascal, and Descartes but also in Bunyan, Racine, Donne, and Thomas Browne. The turn was, in summary, from four kinds of practical knowledge to four kinds of theoretical knowledge – from the oral, particular, local, and timely to the written, universal, general, and timeless.

In the first shift from the oral to the written, the scientific philosophers, as Plato did with the Sophists, narrowed the broad field of argumentation to that of logic only. Rhetoric was set aside.[79] The soundness and validity of written arguments displaced the form, persuasiveness, and rational merit of oral argumentation, "the circumstantial merits and defects of persuasive utterances" (31).

The second shift affected scope. Once again, as in the celebrated *Provincial Letters* (1656–1657) of Pascal, seventeenth-century scientific philosophers effectively discredited the entire Aristotelian tradition of case studies that focused on particular circumstances. Instead, they championed against the so-called casuistry of their opponents the need for general abstract moral theory that one finds, for example, in the Cambridge Platonists. Moral philosophy was to dispense with case ethics once and for all and to devote itself to the formulation of general ethical principles only.

Similarly, the scientific philosophers successfully resisted the extraordinary explorations the humanists had undertaken into the local concerns of "ethnography, geography, and history" (32). Descartes, we remember, could congratulate himself in the *Discourse* for having gone beyond his earlier interests in history. "When modern philosophers discussed ethnography and history as irrelevant to truly 'philosophical' inquiry," Toulmin writes, they excluded from their enterprise "whole realms of questions that had previously been recognized as legitimate topics of inquiry. From then on abstract axioms were in, concrete history was out" (33).

Besides stressing the oral, particular, and local, renaissance humanists stressed as well the timely problems and issues of "legal, medical, or confessional practice" (33). Timeliness here refers to the rationality of effecting certain actions within a particular temporal framework. (One example is a mariner's previously unanticipated decision to alter course despite his actual computations.) The importance of the transient was caught in the humanist interest in jurisprudence as the ideal for a rational enterprise rather then in science. By contrast, the scientific philosophers would subordinate "the significance of local diversity, the relevance of particularity, and the rhetorical power of oral reasoning" to their formal projects for "a universal natural philosophy" (34). Such projects had no room for the transitory, only for the permanent.

In short, the scientific revolution shifted intellectual attention away from the revival of the traditional challenges of practical philosophical concerns in the work of the renaissance humanists to the new challenges of theoretical philosophical concerns with formal issues.

If this is the gist of the revised account of the origin of modernity that Toulmin would have us substitute for the standard account, then how specifically does he understand the opposition Taylor describes in detail, the contrast between Descartes and Montaigne?[80]

As for the Montaigne of the 1570s and 1580s, the Montaigne of the *Apologie* and the *Essais*, Toulmin stresses the particularities of his "personal style and ideas," the unending detail of the topics he explores, the peculiarities of his attitudes. Interestingly, Toulmin also stresses the contrast between the different roles religion plays in Augustine's *Confessions* and in Montaigne's *Essais*. In the first, religion is at the centre of the works, whereas in the second it is but one of many centres.

The tone of this work Toulmin takes as "cool and non-judgmental" (37) as befits the insistence on intellectual modesty in the face of skeptical concerns and the repeated experiences of the limitations of experience. Montaigne is also striking in his insistence on the privileged relation between soul and body whereby each must aid the other. By contrast, Descartes's separation of the soul from the body Toulmin sees as just one element in a much larger circumscription and final constriction of the mental. We have no responsibility for passions and feelings because these events merely happen to persons rather than result from persons' doings.

Further, the naturalness of Montaigne's attitudes towards embodiment, and especially towards sexuality, is lost in Descartes's apparent overriding concerns for respectability, propriety, and socially acceptable conduct. As Toulmin observes: "By the 1640s, the rationalists do not just limit rationality to the senses and the intellect (...) they also reflect the first inroads of the 'respectability' that was so influential over the next two-and-a-half centuries" (41). Rationality and logic for Descartes are to be held strictly separate from rhetoric and the emotions.

Toulmin wants to contrast especially the different kinds of individualism to be found in Montaigne and Descartes. In the latter he claims to find "a flavor of 'solipsism' " (41) in that the subject is strictly delimited from its own embodiment and consequently is construed as a mind in isolation except for its sensory inputs from the world in which it lives. By contrast, Toulmin finds in Montaigne a sense of the embodied self whose richly particular experiences are taken as representative or typical of what it means to be a human being. "For Montaigne, '(life) experience' is the practical experience that each human individual accumulates through dealing with many coequal others: for Descartes, '(mind) experience' is raw material from which each individual builds a cognitive map of the intelligible world 'in the head' " (42).

This contrast for Toulmin epitomizes the larger contrast between the decontextualized rationalism of the seventeenth-century scientific philosophers with their "theoretical ambitions and intellectual constraints" and the older "restatements of classical skepticism" in the "practical modesty and the intellectual freedom" of the late 16th-century humanist philosophers.

Rationalism with its roots in natural philosophy and humanism with its roots in classical literature are then the two revolutions at the origins of modernity. It is rationalism however with its Cartesian understandings of rationality and abstract moral value that succeeds in displacing the polyvalent skeptical exploration of late renaissance humanism in such thinkers as Montaigne. The recognition of uncertainty, ambiguity, and contingency gives way to the quest for certainty, clarity, and necessity.

Disputing the Origins of Modernity

Now, given these two pictures of the relationships between the work of Montaigne and that of Descartes, how do Toulmin's and Taylor's pictures contrast?

One important contrast is that of orientation. Whereas Taylor's discussion is largely oriented with one eye on how both Descartes and Montaigne stress different aspects of the turn towards subjectivity and selfhood, Toulmin is much more centrally concerned with how these two figures construe the relation between subjectivity and world, selfhood and embodiment. Thus if the mind-body problem can be taken as a general way of capturing Toulmin's orientation, Taylor's orientation stands rather under the sign of the problem of personal identity.

This difference in orientation has as its complement a difference in the respective attitudes towards the nature of the account that is offered. In Taylor's case, as we have seen, we are urged to view the historical discussion of the early modern origins of the modern identity as an exercise in interpretive understanding rather than as an attempt at historical explanation. By contrast, Toulmin's story continually emphasizes causal connections among the disparate events of the two tumultuous generations that separate Descartes from Montaigne. Toulmin nowhere addresses the question of just how we are expected to take his account. But the structure of that account, as well as the way the key elements are related to each other, suggest more of historical explanation than of interpretation.

A further difference emerges once we focus on several of those elements in their own right. Both Taylor and Toulmin are interested in understanding just how a certain idea of rationality gradually takes form in the work of the scientific philosophers. But, unlike Taylor, Toulmin pays great attention to the important difference within the early modern period between the shifting priorities of one kind of discourse over another. Thus, where Taylor focuses exclusively on just how radical reflexivity differs in Descartes and Montaigne, Toulmin insists on how the priority of rhetoric and argumentation over logic and argument in humanist philosophers like Montaigne and Bacon is reversed two generations later in scientific philosophers like Descartes and Galileo. Toulmin's sensitivity to differing kinds of discourse in the early modern period as well as to shifting priorities among these discourses is not characteristic of Taylor's readings.

Still another general contrast between the two accounts turns on their relative sensitivities to the problems of historical stereotyping. This is an issue that Taylor seems to pass over in silence. Toulmin by contrast is much concerned to identify just what are the cardinal elements of the standard historical account of the early modern period, to criticize these elements in the light of the most recent historiographical consensus, and finally to offer an alternative view that is designed to side step the stereotypes while continuing to narrow the gap between what happened in the early modern period and how we understand today what happened then. While both Taylor and Toulmin are responsive to the need for "thick description"[81] of any complex historical phenomenon like the emergence of the modern identity, it is Toulmin rather than Taylor who takes pains to protect his own account from any undue influences by now discredited historical stereotypes.

The most important difference between these two accounts, however, concerns neither orientation, nor historical considerations, nor thematic concerns, nor historical stereotypes, but their specific treatments of Montaigne and Descartes.

Taylor insists on juxtaposing the two thinkers whom he deals with non-chronologically, first Descartes and then Montaigne. His plan is to organize their similar reflections on radical reflexivity in complementary ways so that Descartes's disengaged subjectivity can be seen as part of an early modern pattern of inwardness that Montaigne complements with his account of the exploring self. And this non-chronological approach is consistent with Taylor's mainly interpretive rather than explanatory task. By contrast, Toulmin insists on the rigors of chronology in his discussion, carefully looking in detail at several central themes in Montaigne's works before looking in similar detail at Descartes to discover their transformations.

This final contrast leads to the most striking differences between Toulmin and Taylor. For where Taylor sees two related strands of a similar concern with kinds of inwardness in the emergence of the modern identity in Descartes and Montaigne, Toulmin sees two radically different revolutions epitomized in the work of Montaigne and Descartes where the chronologically later Cartesian revolution effectively undoes the results of the earlier humanistic revolution. Far from seeing the emergence of the modern identity in the complementary emphasis on disengaged subjectivity and on an engaged exploratory self in Descartes and Montaigne, Toulmin sees the humanistic philosophical discoveries of rationality in skeptical, contingent, and modest terms giving way to the scientific philosophical construction of rationality in terms of certainty, necessity, and metaphysical pride.

Thus the two pictures we find in these thoughtful, philosophical investigations of the origins of modernity comprise contrasting portraits of complementary figures of Montaigne and Descartes in a foreground, while in the background we find differing renderings of the understandings of history, language, body and mind, personal identity, and finally rationality itself. The question that arises then is just what effects if any the very different accounts of the origins of modernity in Toulmin and the origins of the modern identity in Taylor, centred as they are on very different ways of treating the relations between Montaigne and Descartes, should have on attempts to take the critical measure of Taylor's "given ontology of the human experience?"

If we are not to attempt that critique without situating Taylor's moral ontology in the context of his historical narrative, well enough and good. But when a situation of at least one of the three central phases of this extended narrative turns out to comprise a strongly controversial reading of the relations among rationality, moral selfhood, and knowledge in such cardinal key figures as Montaigne and Descartes, how are we to understand the link Taylor wants us to respect between his thematic inquiries into the moral sources of the self and his interpretive but apparently short-sighted historical narrative?

The main issue here – for there are several – is how to conciliate two opposed states of affairs. On the one hand, any adequate critical evaluation of

Taylor's striking proposals about articulating the moral ontologies implied in those transcendent spiritual issues that underlie our immanent moral intuitions must consider both the formal coherence of that ontology's elements as well as the historical development of that particular moral ontology itself. But the interpretive account of such an ontology's developing moral uses as opposed to an explanatory account on examination seems to conflate two quite distinct moments in the emergence of the modern identity under the guise of reading such moments as complements.

Thus the problem that comes clear is just which historical interpretation of the emergence of the modern identity is to be understood as normative in our attempts to follow the dialectic in Taylor's interpretation, the dialectic between system and history, between necessity and transcendence on the one side – what he calls givenness – and contingency and immanence on the other – what he calls emergence.

In the end we are left with the further question as to just how strongly Taylor wants us to understand the relation between his thematic and historical investigations. If one of the elements can be described reasonably well and unambiguously but not adequately criticized without reference to the other, where the other element can be suitably criticized in the light of alternative accounts but not unambiguously described (it is necessarily incomplete we remembered Taylor insisting), then just how important finally is the link between the two?

The situation is very much analogous to continuing debate today about dynamic and dialectic relations between standards and contexts when dealing with very general metaphysical and logical frameworks.[82] Here however instead of standards we have vague, brief, but stimulating talk about a "given ontology of human experience," a very different matter indeed than standards. And instead of contexts we have a sweeping, comprehensive, yet carefully argued selective juxtaposition of two major moments in the movement of European thought from the end of the sixteenth to the early part of the seventeenth century where our modern understanding of both standards and moral ontologies are forged – again a much larger matter than merely changing contexts.

It is not clear, then, how we can easily resolve this tension in Taylor's work between a shifting dialectic of metaphysics and history on the one side and the need for truly critical discussion of such a shifting dialectic on the other. And if we are not clear about how such a tension can be resolved, how would Taylor have us sympathetically but critically evaluate his extraordinarily ambitious claims to disengage the central assumptions of something so bold as "the given ontology of human experience."

Nonetheless, thanks to both Taylor and Toulmin we now have an initial view of some of the complexities involved in talk of modernity and by consequence of the backgrounds for the European high modernist poetry of suffering. With such complexity freshly in mind we may now take our inspiration from Taylor's attentiveness to R.M. Rilke as one of the European high modernist poets and turn in our next chapter to the first of three other European high modernist poets, T.S. Eliot. Nevertheless, some of the unanswered questions here that arise from confronting these two different readings of the emergence and the nature of at least European modernity will require us to return to these issues later on in this essay but from quite a different standpoint.

CHAPTER TWO

Moral Discourse and Figurative Articulations of Suffering in T.S. Eliot

We come now to the first of the three aspects of moral intuitionism that we have selected for closer inspection, the theme of moral discourse.[83] We do so with the help of a reflective first reading of figurative expressions of moral intuition and moral suffering in one of the masterpieces of European high modernist poetry, T.S. Eliot's *The Waste Land* (1922). After our first reflections here we will need to return to this work in chapter seven for second thoughts in the light of our further reflections on the high modernist poetry of Valéry and Montale.

Our interests here focus on the usefulness for comprehending moral discourse in ongoing ethical reflection in the emerging new Europe today of enlarging current philosophical discussion of the importance of the strictly literal so as to take better account of some central uses of non-literal language. We will find that the strictly literal turns out very often to be either inaccessible to much moral reflection or inadequate for its proper articulation. By contrast, the non-literal seems almost ubiquitous for much moral reflection and perhaps even essential for its proper articulation.

We may take as our general guideline here neither the kind of interpersonal suffering we will be observing in T.S. Eliot's figured discourse in *The Waste Land*, nor the kind of intensely private suffering we will be considering in the next chapter in Paul Valéry's incessant reflections in his *Cahiers* on how one might finally perceive and come to know the moral qualities of the interactions between world, body and mind. Rather, we might take as our guideline Eugenio Montale's repeated variations in the final chapter on the will to break through some mortifying moral frameworks in order to break out onto some re-vivifying ethical horizons.

Here we proceed by examining a representative instance of difficulties in understanding literal meanings in Eliot's early poetry. We first consider several instances of the unusual semantic contexts of Eliot's crucial repeated expression "nothing" in his early poetic masterpiece, *The Waste Land*. We then turn for help in elucidating the literal senses here of "nothing" to a comparison of two closely related yet rival philosophical accounts of literal meaning and interpretation. This move will allow us in concluding to formulate our first interim conclusion about moral intuitionism in terms of the importance of figurative language in moral discourse. But first some contexts.

Meaning Nothing

Several years after the First World War, in England and with his Harvard doctoral thesis in philosophy on the English idealist philosopher, F.H. Bradley (1846–1924), accepted but still not defended, T.S. Eliot was quite close to a nervous breakdown. He had suffered many personal losses.

After losing his friend, the young French medical doctor, Jean Verdenal, "*mort aux Dardanelles*," to whom he had dedicated a first collection of poems, after failing to appear for the defense of his Harvard doctorate in philosophy, after marrying abruptly in 1915 and then witnessing his wife's affair with his former philosophy tutor at Harvard, Bertrand Russell, after writing more poetry and some of his best criticism despite the anti-semitic posturings of his passing infatuations with the *L'Action Française*, after the increasing strains of his wife's worsening illnesses that friends kept referring to patronisingly as "nerves," after persistent financial problems, and after the death of his always disapproving father back home in St. Louis, Missouri, T.S. Eliot finally took his doctor's advice. He took some rest.

Eliot went to Margate. But when that change proved all too inadequate – "On Margate sands," he later wrote in "The Fire Sermon" of *The Waste Land*, "I can connect / Nothing with nothing" – he then left England for Switzerland to consult a specialist. And, while in Lausanne during November and part of December 1921, Eliot composed most of the manuscripts for what was to be one only of his several poetic masterpieces.

Parts of these manuscripts, however, still incorporated some abstruse quasi-philosophical materials dating from his Harvard years where Eliot had extensively studied not just Bradley's "absolute idealism" but Sanskrit philosophical treatises as well. And properly integrating these obscure philosophical fragments proved an essential part of the difficulty Eliot was having in bringing the poem to a satisfactory completion. Then, in late December, Eliot brought his manuscripts to Paris to show to Ezra Pound. Eliot later celebrated Pound's extraordinary help in drastically pruning the manuscript. This editorial work enabled Eliot to complete the poem.[84]

Studying the published version of this extraordinary and still partly philosophical poetic fiction, however, has made some critical readers wonder repeatedly whether Pound could not have done just a bit better. For making sense enough of some of Eliot's crucial poetic utterances there still remains problematic for thoughtful readers some three generations after the first publication of the poem and its recognition as a monument of high literary modernism.

Here is a passage from this poem that shares with much European high modernist literary work a tragic representation of the many still puzzling relations between art and life.[85] In confronting appreciative readers even today with a sense of a profoundly personal and yet more than merely individual suffering, this poetic work of verbal art continues to raise questions about whether some moral contexts, for example those that today frame ongoing discussions of an eventual common European social policy, can be understood and articulated exclusively in literal uses of language only.

> 'My nerves are bad to-night. Yes, bad. Stay with me.
> 'Speak to me. Why do you never speak. Speak.
> 'What are you thinking of? What thinking? What?
> I never know what you are thinking. Think.'
> I think we are in rats' alley
> Where the dead men lost their bones.
> 'What is that noise?'
> The wind under the door.
> 'What is that noise now? What is the wind doing'
> Nothing again nothing.
>
> 'Do
> You know nothing? Do you see nothing? Do you remember
> 'Nothing?'
>
> I remember
> Those are pearls that were his eyes.
> 'Are you alive, or not? Is there nothing in your head?'[86]

The personal suffering that this poetic and dramatic dialogue represents fictionally seems almost palpable. More, the suffering seems to lie on both sides of this tragically abortive exchange. But just what are we to take as the sense and significance in particular of the crucial talk here of nothing?

Moral Situations

The situation the poet is representing here seems to be this.[87] On the one side of this fraught exchange a woman appears to be ceaselessly badgering a stubbornly silent man in a vain attempt to goad him into saying at least something. If the man would just say something and not nothing, he might thereby respond at least minimally to the woman's explicit fears and the much more substantial although implicit anxieties they stand for.

On the other side of the exchange, the man seems to be all too resolutely silent, refusing to respond in any way, even by uttering just a single word aloud. At best, he seems to be trying to still his inner fragmented monologues with obscure mental repetitions of the word "nothing" and its elusive mental associations.

Still, the poet succeeds in representing much of the shared suffering here in the words of the man's unspoken answers to the woman's repeated imperative questions – "Speak to me. Why do you never speak? Speak." The poet does so by representing the man's unvoiced answers to the woman's insistent questions without quotation marks so as to exhibit graphically that the man's replies are completely mental.

Moreover, in the aftermath of the First World War where Eliot's Paris friend Jean Verdenal was killed in 1915 – "Men went to Catraeth as day dawned: / their fears disturbed their peace"[88] – and in the sequels to his own studies in sixteenth-century English Jacobean revenge tragedy[89] – "Those were pearls that were his eyes"[90] – these speechless replies are filled with an allusive historical, literary, and perhaps even larger despair.

The poem gradually succeeds in transposing this more than merely literary despair into an external, public sphere where some sense only of an intensely internal, private, and finally incommunicable yet shared personal suffering becomes partly available for others' reflections. The woman suffers in receiving to her repeatedly voiced appeals not even a verbal response. And the man suffers in failing to find an effective mental stratagem to fully exculpate himself morally from resolutely refusing to respond to someone's repeated and ever more urgent calls for assistance. And yet, the poet represents the man's silent replies to the woman's repeated importunings as being communicated so acutely as to give rise to still further, insistent questionings on the woman's part.

Then, suddenly, the woman breaks off entirely the already incomplete conversation with a staccato series of still more short, accusatory and this time almost epistemological and metaphysical questions – "You know nothing? Do you see nothing? Do you remember / Nothing? (...) Is there nothing in your head?"[91]

Now, such poetic representations of verbal and mental utterances exhibit both a greater verisimilitude to situations in actual life and a corresponding complexity than persons are often aware of in their own lives. Moreover, we need to note that the verisimilitude and complexity of these poetic utterances is importantly different from salient features in such notorious textbook sentences as "the cat is on the mat" and "snow is white" which figured so often a generation ago in the philosophy of language. Unlike these sentences, the poetic utterances we are concerned with here cannot be possible referents for J.L. Austin's partly humorous and famous fulminations about "etiolated uses of language."

Among the many perplexing elements in such richly imaginative poetic representations of suffering is just how we are to take the key words "literally," how we are to take them in their "literal" meanings. That is, how are we to take the words, as the dictionaries say, "in their usual or most basic sense without metaphor or exaggeration." In particular, what remains deeply puzzling here are Eliot's various, perhaps sometimes deviant uses here of the key expression, "nothing?"[92]

To see this point in the passage we are considering, which is a poetic and fictional representation only of an incomplete and aborted conversation, note several importantly different uses of the word "nothing." The man first uses the word "nothing" as nothing, that is, without quotation marks. The poet thereby represents him here as replying only mentally and not aloud to the woman's repeated questions.

Then, as if she had somehow heard aloud what the man had uttered only silently in his mind, the poet represents the woman as emphasizing the word "nothing" by repeating it aloud three times. The poet represents her as repeating the word as if by way of making some kind of reproaches to the man for his several supposed incapacities – "Do / You know nothing? /Do you see nothing? Do you remember / Nothing?"

Moreover, the poet carefully selects line lengths, punctuation, and printing conventions to highlight the word "nothing." He puts this word alone in a line of its own. He encloses the word now in citation marks (unlike the silent words of the man). And he capitalizes the word's first letter (as the poet also capitalized the same first letter in the first word in the man's three-word mental utterance earlier).

The poet goes on to represent the man once again replying only mentally to the woman's questions by citing, without quotation marks, the dramatic line – Those are pearls that were his eyes (*sic*). The line is from a Jacobean tragic play about someone who is dead and whose body has decomposed in the sea like that of one of the poet's fictional characters, Phlebas the Phoenician, in the poem, or perhaps even like that of his friend, Jean Verdenal, in life.

Finally, the poet again represents the woman questioning the man reproachfully, as if once more she had heard aloud what he had uttered only silently in his mind. "Are you alive, *or not*?" she asks (my emphasis). And the poet goes on to represent the woman bitterly breaking off her incomplete verbal exchanges with the man whose head has been full of silent musings, subtle replies, and even literary citations, most of which she somehow has almost divined, with the biting, almost metaphysical insult, "Is there nothing in your head?"

This situation, we may agree, is morally charged. That is, whether the self-preoccupied man is acting rightly with respect to the woman's insistent emotional needs has a moral and ethical valence. Reading and re-reading the poem many informed and reflective readers seem to sense that the situation represents someone who is not acting rightly.

But does the text represent the situation literally or non-literally? Moreover, what is this sense of not just a moral and ethical situation however represented, but of a particular positive or negative valence in the actions represented? Is this sense some kind of a moral insight, even a moral intuition? And if so, then can we not inadequately articulate this moral insight in literal terms only?

Literal Meanings and First Meanings

In order to focus more sharply on the language of this representative fictional and poetic piece rather than on the language of our own subsequent articulations, we need to ask now what exactly is the literal meaning of the various uses of the word "nothing." Such a question raises a number of different – and difficult – issues. Here are several examples.

Is just one of the uses of "nothing" here literal and the others non-literal?[93] If so, which uses are literal and which ones are not? Since we are always dealing with exactly the same word "nothing," how do we decide? And if we disagree in this domain, how can we settle our differences?

What is the general philosophical relevance and the particular ethical pertinence of these various uses of the same expression occurring in a literarily represented conversation?[94] Is there indeed any properly ethical relevance to the use of such expressions as "nothing," whether here or elsewhere?[95]

Is each of the two represented interlocutors using the same expression in a sentence to perform a linguistic act of a certain type with a certain content?[96]

Does each of the interlocutors use the same expression in such a way as to exhibit the same range of meaning properties?[97]

Are both interlocutors using this expression in the same ways?[98]

And what exactly is the ethical relevance, if any, of such linguistic and philosophical technical considerations for reasonably interpreting this puzzling and yet after all quite familiar failed communicative situation represented poetically in an incomplete dialogue?[99]

However diverse, questions like these invite renewed reflection on the viability of standard accounts of literal meanings for dealing with non-metaphorical expressions in moral discourse.[100] Renewed reflection is required if not yet in such complicated contexts as everyday life in the debates about inchoative European social policy, then perhaps in the fuller than merely philosophical contexts of high modernist poetry like Eliot's poetry of suffering. Just here is where some acquaintance with contemporary philosophical reflection on language and linguistics can be helpful.

If we are to appreciate better certain crucial issues about literal meaning[101] and significance in the understandings of the moral discourse that often inform the interpretation of such exemplary instances of the high modernist poetry of suffering as "The Waste Land," we do well to take up freshly several contemporary philosophical reflections on meaning. One quite important instance of such reflection can be seen in the work of the recently deceased distinguished American philosopher, Donald Davidson, and in its ongoing critical reception. Although working mainly as a philosopher of language, Davidson had an enviable knowledge of linguistics as well. As a first step then in trying to win some further clarity on our concerns here with moral intuitionism, moral discourse and meaning, consider several key elements in some of Davidson's later work.[102]

Davidson did not pay the kind of sustained, detailed attention to works of verbal art that some other contemporary philosophers have. But he was very busy with questions of sense and significance. Generally, his interests centred more on philosophical issues in linguistics and logic than on aesthetics and poetry.

In several rather late essays about metaphor, communication, and "the limits of the literal," however, Davidson looked closely at some metaphorical and stylistic peculiarities that occur widely in different uses of language and especially in literary works.[103] Behind these essays are to be found the more general questions that engaged Davidson for many years in his attempts to build on and finally move beyond the work of his teacher, Willard Quine, while notably countering the very different work of his distinguished contemporary, Michael Dummett.[104]

Davidson's central interests may be taken to comprise his twofold answer to the question, "what is it for words to mean what they do?" For Davidson, articulating what it is for words to mean what they say can be captured by describing informally[105] what someone who understands those words implicitly knows – for example, what a reasonable reader of Eliot's poetic sequence "The Waste Land" implicitly knows about the uses of expressions like "nothing." Such a knowledge, let us say, derives mainly from what he or she knows from personal experience and from occasionally consulting, say, various dictionaries.[106]

Davidson thinks that providing such a description requires a theory. The theory would acknowledge "the holistic nature of linguistic understanding"[107] in providing an "interpretation of all utterances, as actual or potential of a speaker or group of speakers." And it also would require a theory that "would be verifiable without knowledge of the detailed propositional attitudes of the speaker," i.e., a theory of saying, believing, knowing, desiring, and so on that would not turn on the very concepts it is designed to explain.[108]

In such a theory, however, the primitive notion is to be taken as truth rather than meaning. From an account of truth based on the idea of truth-conditions, an attempt is to be made to arrive at an understanding of meaning. The model for the structure of truth when truth is taken as a primitive would include, among other elements, a critical appropriation of central features in Tarski's formal semantics,[109] the relation of satisfaction between entities and expressions, "disquotational" features of truth predicates, "the pattern of assents to sentences," a maximization of the "right sort" of agreement among competing theories of interpretation (a principle of charity), and an anti-empiricist refutation of scheme-content dualisms.

Accordingly, articulating what Eliot's reflective reader implicitly knows about the uses of certain crucial expressions like "nothing" would seem to require not just reflection on one's own linguistic practices and a good dictionary. Such an articulation also seems to require constructing a descriptive and holistic theory of linguistic understanding based on truth – no small order.

Although much of the continuing work on related projects today remains rather technical, some of Davidson's later essays examine certain peculiarities of language, including a few poetic uses of language, in rather straightforward terms. An important case is the 1986 essay, "A Nice Derangement of Epitaphs."[110] Given our concerns with understanding the sense and significance of certain deliberately misused expressions in Eliot, we do well here to focus mainly on this essay.

Initially, Davidson insists in this seminal essay on distinguishing between the literal or "first meaning" of expressions and any non-literal or "second meaning" (whether we construe this second meaning as "speaker's meaning" or otherwise). Note however that literal and non-literal are not to be understood strictly as two species of meaning, since non-literal meaning is for Davidson an aspect of use and not properly of meaning.

We can see the point of calling literal meaning "first meaning," Davidson thinks, if we reflect on what we need to know in order to explain certain images in poetry. As an example of such reflection, he asks us to consider what we need to know in order to explain the controlling image in these beautifully meaningful but still puzzling lines from Shakespeare's Sonnet 53:

> Speak of the spring and foison of the year,
> The one doth shadow of your beauty show,
> The other as your bounty doth appear (...)[111]

However non-literal the meaning of these lines may be, Davidson holds that the reader cannot grasp this non-literal, second meaning unless the reader "first" understands the literal, dictionary meaning, "based on actual usage" in Shakespeare's time, of the word "foison" (glossed above in note 111 as "plentiful crop or harvest").[112]

This example, however, is not without some difficulties. Davidson seems to underestimate just how difficult it is to understand the dictionary meaning here of actual usage in Shakespeare's time. More importantly, Davidson does not seem to have taken seriously enough here the very different kinds of images that occur in poetic utterances. Grasping non-literal meanings in some instances seems to require not just something more than first understanding the appropriate dictionary meaning of the word that expresses the image. (Davidson allows for this possibility by qualifying the turn to the dictionary as "first," thereby leaving open the possibility of the interpreter making uses of other resources subsequently.) Rather, this apprehension sometimes may first require something other than grasping the dictionary meanings at all.

Perhaps we can appreciate this critical point better from some of the commentary on Eliot's famous image in his early poem, *The Love Song of J. Alfred Prufrock*. The image is of a particular evening. The poet describes the evening obscurely as "spread out against the sky / Like a patient etherised upon a table."

Here, grasping the literal meaning of the word "etherised" (that is, the colourless, volatile liquid $[Ch_3Ch_2]_2O$) in fact requires something other than "first" grasping the dictionary meaning based on actual usage in Eliot's times. Rather, one needs to recognize "first" that the use of the expression "etherised" is not observational in the literary critics' sense – we cannot properly visualize this simile – but so-called "symptomatic." The symptomatic use of the word "etherised" evokes, as the English poet and critic Stephen Spender explained many years ago, "the combination of the clinical and the romantic connotations [that suggest] the state of suspended consciousness of the 'patient' and the head of the dreamer full of the night sky and stars."[113]

So, even though his Shakespeare example may partly clarify Davidson's talk here of the literal as first meaning, his discussion of his Shakespearean example does not suffice for characterizing first meaning fully enough. For as Davidson himself goes on to point out, thereby partly undermining his own position, some readers often determine first meaning without initially taking down the dictionary at all.

That is, sometimes some readers just pick out "what the speaker was getting at" and then determine the literal meaning; other times, they "guess at the image and so puzzle out the first meaning" (435). Or, as we have just seen in the "Prufrock" case, they know how poetic images can work different effects, and they go on simply to infer first meaning. More simply, sometimes readers just use their linguistic intuitions.

Principled Linguistic Meanings and Coinciding Meanings

After exploring other approaches to distinguishing first meaning from second meaning such as appeals to speaker's intentions and hearer's ability to understand those intentions, Davidson turns to a related distinction. The distinction now is not between literal or first meaning and non-literal or second meaning, but between linguistic and non-linguistic meaning.

Davidson proposes three principles that seem to characterize the specifically linguistic meaning of signs or signals as opposed to their non-linguistic meaning (436). And he then seems to identify this principled linguistic meaning with what he previously called first meaning.

Thus, literal meaning as principled linguistic meaning is now taken to be (1) systematic ("there must be systematic relations between the meanings of utterances"), (2) shared (a method of interpreting such relations needs to be shared between a speaker and a hearer), and (3) prepared (i.e., the speaker's and hearer's knowledge of these relations "is learned in advance of occasions of interpretation and is conventional in character"). In short, literal linguistic meanings must be systematic, shared, and prepared.

This is helpful so far as it goes. But the principles of linguistic meaning that would seem to enable Davidson to characterize first meaning as principled linguistic meaning turn out to involve difficulties of their own. Here we can be very brief since it will prove more useful to detail some of these difficulties in our next section below rather than here.

If we grant that there are difficulties with these principles, then, whatever its relations to the first distinction between literal meaning as first meaning and non-literal meaning as second meaning, this further distinction between literal meaning as principled linguistic meaning and non-literal meaning as non-linguistic is problematic.

As if recognizing the need for still more work on the exact nature of literal meaning, Davidson proceeds to gloss literal meaning further by appealing to a third distinction. This distinction however is not between two kinds of meaning, whether first and second or linguistic and non-linguistic. Rather, this distinction is between two kinds of theory that Davidson believes "interpreters" (as he calls both speakers and hearers) require for effective communication.

This further distinction is between a prior theory and a passing theory. And spelling out this distinction between prior and passing theory involves adopting what Davidson then calls his "simplified and idealized proposal" about what goes on in linguistic communication.

In linguistic communication generally, Davidson believes that on one side "an interpreter [hearer, reader] has at any moment of a speech transaction" an antecedent or a "prior" theory. While his or her interlocutor is speaking, the interpreter changes that antecedent theory into a subsequent or "passing" theory. That is, while the interlocutor is speaking the interpreter is "entering hypotheses about new names, altering the interpretation of familiar predicates, and revising past interpretations of particular utterances in the light of new evidence" (441).

From the other side, "the speaker's [writer's] view of the interpreter's prior theory (...) is an important part of what he has to go on if he wants to be understood." Thus, "for the hearer, the prior theory expresses how he is prepared in advance to interpret an utterance of the speaker's," Davidson writes, "while the passing theory is how he *does* interpret the utterance. For the speaker, the prior theory is what he believes the interpreter's prior theory to be, while his passing theory is the theory he intends the interpreter to use" (442; Davidson's emphases).

The key point here is that the passing theory needs to be shared because, without such a sharing, understanding cannot be complete. Still, the shared passing theory is not to be identified with, say, linguistic competence in any general way. Yet the shared passing theory does describe the understanding of a speaker's words (on this occasion) because it includes a variety of particular items that are the result of a particular occasion only. Further, the shared passing theory is not to be identified with a theory of any individual natural language like French or English. For knowing how to interpret on a particular occasion is no guarantee that one would know how to interpret on another. Rather, the passing theory is where understanding and agreement strive to coincide in a grasp of meanings.

The understanding of these coinciding meanings as literal or first meanings is where Davidson makes his distinctions converge. "Every deviation from ordinary usage," he writes, "as long as it is agreed on for the moment (knowingly deviant, or not, on one, or both sides), is in the passing theory as a feature of what the words mean on that occasion. Such meanings, transient though they may be, are literal, they are what I have called the first meanings" (442–443).

Clearly, Davidson takes pains to qualify his discussion carefully. He says that his proposals are simplified and idealised. Still, we need to note once again, as we did with the previous comments on images, that using this discussion to elucidate the case we are dealing with – coming to understand properly the literal uses of the centrally important expression "nothing" in Eliot's poetic and dramatic representation of an incomplete conversational dialogue – brings out several interesting issues.

Talk of the hearer as an "interpreter" needs to be distinguished from talk of the critical or reflective reader as "interpreter." Moreover, the description here of what the hearer is normally doing in an ordinary conversation is not meant to capture the complex situation in the poetically represented fictional dialogue. For there the represented hearer is not so much decoding what the woman is represented as saying – changing his prior and passing theories as the "special transaction" continues – as replying silently (in his mind) to one situation with unspoken phrases and citations from a completely different situation. Finally, any talk about the sharing of a passing theory serves here to underline the radically fragmented, broken, and incomplete character of some actual and not just imagined linguistic exchanges like the ones represented in our selected passage from *The Waste Land.*

Deviant Expressions and Holistic Understanding

When we narrow our attention to such deviant uses of language as malapropisms, the (often amusing) "mistaken use of words for similar sounding ones" (*ODE*), we can immediately see further problems with this characterization of first meaning. For deviant utterances generally, and malapropisms in particular (may we add some non-standard uses of negatives as well?), "introduce expressions not covered by prior learning as familiar expressions which cannot be interpreted by any of the abilities so far discussed" (457). So, the problem now is not with the systematic and shared aspects of literal meaning. The problem is with the conjunction of these aspects with the novel nature of the meaning of these expressions, i.e., with the fact that these meanings are not "prepared" in the sense of having been learned in advance.

To solve this problem, Davidson modifies the three principles of literal, linguistic meaning which we noted briefly above in such a way that they can, when now modified, indeed accommodate malapropisms and other deviant expressions. (Note, however, that Davidson does not modify here his ambiguous distinction between prior and passing theories.) The key move, he believes, is to invoke something technical "along the lines of a Tarski truth definition"[114] as a way of accounting for just how an "interpreter" can be said to have a system for interpreting potentially unlimited utterances of novel sentences.

And what is such a definition supposed to do? The Tarski truth definition "provides a recursive characterization of the truth conditions of all possible utterances of the speaker, and it does this through an analysis of utterances in terms of sentences made up from the finite vocabulary and the finite stock of modes of compositions" (437–438).[115]

But once the various difficulties with handling malapropisms have been explored, Davidson's conclusion turns out to be very surprising. The first two principles for understanding literal, linguistic meaning – first meaning must be systematic and shared – are salvageable, he concludes, only in "rather unusual ways" (446). And the third principle – first meaning must be prepared – cannot be salvaged at all.

Consequently, the third principle must be abandoned. But abandoning this principle seems to entail also abandoning the earlier idea of literal meaning as principled linguistic meaning. And, since that idea depends strongly on the key notion of literal meaning as first meaning, abandoning the idea of literal meaning as principled linguistic meaning seems to entail also abandoning the idea of literal meaning as first meaning as well.

So the particular conclusion seems to be that we still do not have a satisfactory account here of literal meaning. And the more general conclusion seems to be that "in linguistic communication nothing corresponds to a linguistic competence" as Davidson and so many other philosophers and linguists have described it.

But such conclusions, however provisional, are a major setback to solving or dissolving Davidson's most general problem – "I want to know," he writes, "how people who already have a language (...) manage to apply their skill or knowledge to actual cases of interpretation. (...) My problem is to describe what is involved in the idea of 'having a language' " (441).

This account, we need to recall, arises out of a very general interest in articulating how competent speakers of a language succeed in interpreting one another. The particular question here is what would be a satisfactory account of what it is "for words to mean what they do." Such an account would be comprehensive enough to comprise the understanding of deviant expressions including not just malapropisms. Such deviant expressions, I take it, would also comprise non-standard uses of polyvalent problematically referential negative expressions, like Eliot's various uses of the expression "nothing" in a poem like *The Waste Land.*

The answer to this particular question is supposed to assume the form of a theory. And this theory must, among other tasks, be able to account for how "interpreters" understand previously unfamiliar utterances of "the same language." (Just why such a theory is required and just in what sense, despite the discussion of the characteristics of Tarski's definition of truth, is not spelled out.) Further, the theory must avoid begging questions and must acknowledge, as we noted earlier, "the holistic nature of linguistic understanding."[116]

The crucial element in such a theory is the double primacy of truth over meaning and literal over non-literal meaning. Davidson says little here about truth, a topic he discusses extensively elsewhere. Instead, he wants to characterize literal meaning in still more detail.

Literal meaning, we recall, is more properly to be understood as "first meaning" in the sense that understanding literal meaning is a prerequisite for understanding non-literal meaning. Thanks to the further distinction between prior and passing theory, deviations from ordinary instances of literal meaning are subsumed under literal meanings in the passing theory. But the attempt to make explicit the systematicity and sharedness of first meanings by appeal to Tarski's recursive description of truth conditions is finally unsuccessful. The result is an intriguing notion of literal meaning as "first" in some sense that still awaits a satisfactory description.

Eliot and Figurative Articulations: Initial Formulations

Roughly speaking then, these initial reflections on interpreting literal meaning with a view to expressions in poetic works of art might be formulated along some such lines as these:

(1) Understanding what it is for some words and some sentences in some literary fictional works (like some instances of the high modernist poetry of suffering) to mean what they do requires constructing a non-question begging theory of the holistic nature of linguistic understanding comprehensive enough to explain deviant as well as normal expressions.
(2) In such a theory, "truth" is to be taken as a primitive term in the light of which meaning is to be explained, and literal meaning is to be explained as epistemically prior to non-literal meaning.
(3) Further, normal literal meanings of words (and perhaps of sentences) in some expressions in literary fictional works are to be understood in terms of the prior and passing "theories" of both the writer (speaker) and the reader (interpreter); by contrast, apparently deviant meanings are to be construed in terms of literal meanings in the reader's (interpreter's) passing theory.
(4) The attention to "deviant expressions" is useful because it foregrounds one of the distinctive yet problematic elements in poetic uses of language that reflective critical interpreters have to articulate.
(5) Still, both the crucial distinction between literal and non-literal meaning and the requisite holistic theory of linguistic understanding remain problematic.

In short, whatever it may be for, say, Eliot's words in the literarily represented dialogue's question "Do / You know nothing?" to mean what they do, and for reflective readers to succeed in understanding the difficult relations here between literal and non-literal meaning in a holistic, non-question begging way while awarding the notion of truth a primacy over that of meaning is not evident.

Nevertheless, Davidson's discussions here do provide useful clarifications about the nature of literal meaning in some poetry. The stress on the holistic nature of linguistic understanding does capture some of the general ways fruitful interpretations of poetic sequences like Eliot's *The Waste Land* seem to arise in, for example, Stephen Spender's exemplary grasp of the meanings of central images. Moreover, this remains the case even if the precise ways in which the supposed literal meanings of deviant expressions are to be construed still need further discussion.

Finally, the initial distinction here between prior and passing theories is suggestive in bringing out the need for reflective readers to construct comprehensive descriptions of the idiolects, that is, "the speech habits peculiar to a particular person" (*ODE*), of individual poets. These idiolects can then serve to highlight particular uses of language within an individual poem as deviant uses with respect to the normal uses in the idiolect. Here too however we need further discussion.

Before trying to draw out the major implications here for rationally interpreting the meanings of cardinal expressions in some of the twentieth-century poetry of suffering, we will need to look more closely in the following two chapters at several other European high modernist poets of suffering. And then, before concluding our inquiries here, we will come back to Eliot's poetry for second thoughts.

CHAPTER THREE

Moral Knowledge and Perceptions of Suffering in Paul Valéry

Our objective so far has been twofold. First, we saw how both the main subject of our reflection here, moral intuitionism and suffering, as well as our three themes of moral discourse, moral knowledge, and moral motivation, may be seen to arise in both contemporary ethical reflection in Europe today as well as in the poetry of European high modernism yesterday. Second, we took up the first of three central and still problematic aspects of our main subject, the theme of moral discourse.

Our rough working hypothesis was that some fruitful linguistic and conceptual sources for specifying more fully the sources, nature, and reliability of moral intuition could be identified not just in the mainly literal descriptions of events. They could also be found in some non-literal poetic representations of human suffering in several exemplary instances of European high modernist texts.

Accordingly, we proceeded to a critical and reflective reading of several representative figurative representations of moral intuition and personal moral suffering in T.S. Eliot's *The Waste Land* (1922). We considered attentively one of the many difficult and still pertinent matters today on exhibit in that poetry, sufficiently responsive communication between men and women. We also considered how some critically reflective readers of such poetic representations might properly be said to apprehend these matters through some kinds of moral intuition. And we concluded by formulating, in a provisional way only, summary points that might serve as an initial articulation of elements of moral discourse that fresh European ethical reflection today might wish to investigate in more sustained ways than we can do so here. Even sympathetic readers, however, might object that our approach to such matters so far is exaggeratedly unconventional.

An Objection, A Reply

Perhaps what is most unconventional in these quite circumscribed attempts here to arrive at a fuller and more fruitful understanding of moral intuitionism for effective reconsiderations in the complex European ethical debates about an eventual common European social policy is the turn to poetic representations of such situations. Normally those with similar objectives in view, say renewing the articulations of the ethical bases for the progressive elaboration of a harmonized European social policy, would first appeal to the more usual empirical studies of sociological phenomena and psychological processes.[117] So, after our initial set of reflections and several of the critical reserves they may fairly be seen to generate, a brief analogy might prove somewhat helpful for better understanding the unusual approach here.

Consider then that our recourse to high modernist European poetic texts for help in further elucidating and articulating the expression, nature, kinds, and eventual sources of the as yet insufficiently specified character of moral intuitions might be compared to the use some astronomers are now making of unusual detectors for capturing the expression, nature, kinds, and eventual sources of the as yet insufficiently specified character of ultra-high-energy cosmic rays.[118] Briefly, and in admittedly metaphorical terms only, we might say that the light of some essential elements of moral intuitions fluoresce in high modernist poetic representations as the light of some elementary particles of cosmic rays fluoresces in Cherenkov detectors.

That is, just as the emerging field of particle astronomy attempting to capture more fully the properties of some cosmic rays makes use not just of direct conventional surface arrays of detectors but also of unusual and more indirect sub-surface water Cherenkov flourescence detectors, so some persons working at the emerging interfaces of moral philosophy and the philosophy of literature may attempt to capture more fully the properties of some moral intuitions. They may try to do so by making use not just of conventional philosophical analyses of the expressions of such intuitions in literal uses. They may do so also by making use of such expressions in unusual and more indirect figurative use of language. More of course could be said in defense of our approach so far, but perhaps this may suffice for now.

With these reminders and clarifications in mind, we take up in this chapter the second of the three particular themes we have identified within our general subject of moral intuitionism and suffering, the theme of moral knowledge. We again begin with a rough working hypothesis for exploring further several European high modernist poetic representations of moral intuition and suffering. Our working hypothesis here is that some attentive readings of Paul Valéry's poetic representations of varied interactions between world, body, and mind, in his very extensive *Cahiers* or critical and poetic notebooks open up further fruitful perspectives on the nature of the kinds of perception peculiar to acquiring genuine moral knowledge through moral intuitions.

Our guideline here, however, is of a different sort than previously. For by way of showing the philosophical interest for a better understanding of moral intuitionism that might be of us in ongoing discussions in the emerging Europe today by enlarging the scope of much work on moral epistemology, we try to look especially at Valéry's reflections on his own poetic practices of articulating moral intuitions rather than, as in the case of Eliot, on a poetic practice as such.[119]

To sharpen our understanding of what his literary work seems to be representing only indirectly and while looking at Valéry's work broadly rather than narrowly as in the previous case study of Eliot's poetry, we will first consider a central experience in Valéry's early work that profoundly affected both his intellectual and affective capacities for the rest of his life. This experience we will take as one of the most basic sources of a profound abstract as well as concrete suffering in his life.

We will then go on to specify how we propose to use the cardinal terms, "moral knowledge" and "perception" in the analyses of some of the most important related passages in his *Cahiers*. And we will try to sample Valéry's voluminous work synchronically under the heading of several central themes in his work rather than restrict ourselves to any strictly diachronic approach. We will then conclude this chapter with further interim formulations, this time of the variety of non-inferential perceptions apparently in view in many of the poetic representations of intuition in such distinguished literary work of European high modernism as that of Valéry.

In a later chapter we will try to draw together our preliminary results here and return to Valéry's works for second thoughts while retrieving several of the eighteenth-century Scottish philosopher Thomas Reid's (1710–1796) still often overlooked analyses of direct, non-inferential perceptions in moral situations.[120]

Unlike our initial discussions so far which were in a general sense analytic, our main task now is largely a descriptive one. Accordingly, we will be concerned to cite Valéry's[121] poetic prose in his *Cahiers* more extensively than is customary and to read some of his work more as a function of the order it exhibits than, as was the case with Eliot, in terms of any sustained critical and reflective commentary.[122]

By way of transition, then, from our previous reflections on Eliot and the relations between moral discourse and literal meanings, here are some of Valéry's meditations on language.

The Illusions of Words

Like Eliot, Valéry cross-examined the vagaries of language endlessly. He suspected the capacity of language to articulate anything satisfactorily, even his own thoughts. Many of his remarks on language might be summarized very roughly under three headings: a double danger, possible remedies, and the idea of method.[123]

"It's not the role of names," Valéry writes in the *Cahiers*, "to engender things. But we need to admit that to the degree that persons have confidence from their infancy onwards to resist learning the names things have, their minds have [already] seduced them to acknowledge that one thing must correspond to each name" (24.209).[124]

Thus, the first danger with language is construing all words as different sorts of names for things. Under this heading Valéry is particularly wary of such abstractions as "soul" or "being" or "existence." In each case the abstract word incites reflection. Yet this reflection too often proceeds only at the cost of leaving unexamined the initial assumption that words must refer to determinate things in the world. And here, just as throughout this section, when thinking about moral intuitions in terms of moral knowledge and perception we need to keep in mind Valéry's strictures on much language use.

Much earlier in the *Cahiers* Valéry touches on a related danger. For other than when we find no clear and unambiguous terms for what incites our reflection, we suppose that nothing determinate exists at all. We are inclined to believe that "what cannot be said and well said does not exist" (5.490). Although actively engaging himself repeatedly with scientists and with the sciences of his time, Valéry thought that this second danger is difficult to avoid because of a widely shared scientific world view.

The first danger is of course familiar. Since Frege, logicians, philosophers of language, and linguists have repeated their warnings. The second however is not. For the insistence on clarity, well-formedness, and perspicuity as ways of avoiding the first danger can obscure the second.

In short, the more a reflective person may be on guard against the first danger, the more he or she may fall victim to the second. In our case, that is, the more a reflective European today may be on guard against taking words for things when one talks of so-called "European moral values" versus, say, so-called "Asian moral values," perhaps the more such a person runs the risk of winding up believing that, strictly speaking, there are no moral values at all.

Valéry's own views about why each of these tendencies is a mistake are not surprising today.[125] He holds for example that many words are not names of any kind whatsoever. And so, depending on the case at issue, they may or they may not be subject to the usual conditions of reference. Further, a variety of things, states of affairs, events, and what not may exist without our as yet having words for them. Some complex mental states, for example, even though we have not yet been able to settle on their appropriate descriptions, nonetheless seem to exist. Examples are not hard to find.

Valéry's remarks about the first danger, while not very original, are still useful reminders. His remarks on the second, however, are both striking and controversial. For it is not clear just whose mental states and whose words are at issue.

It may very well be the case that I lack the words to grasp one of your peculiar moral states of mind. But that I also lack the words to grasp one of my own moral states of mind is not nearly so plausible.[126] Perhaps part of what you and I mean by "my moral mental state M" is that I cannot apprehend such a state except in words. In short, unless I can talk about my mental state M, the state in question might just as well turn out to be yours. For many would argue cogently that it could not be my mental state at all. Hence, the importance of choosing to begin our reflections in this essay with the theme of moral discourse rather than with the theme either of moral knowledge or of moral motivation.

Valéry does not pursue these matters far. Instead, he investigates how to circumvent these dangers. He proposes a double strategy. First, wherever we stumble upon abstract expressions – think of "moral values" – we are to recall the habitual company these expressions keep.[127] We are, that is, continually to reinsert such expressions into their concrete contexts. For such contexts – he means here the uses of words – will keep us, Valéry hopes, from reifying things which do not exist.

And, second, wherever we wrestle with what seems inexpressible, we are to forge novel expressions. Valéry, for example, sometimes exploits foreign language terms in order to coin neologisms. And sometimes he will express a fugitive mental state by creating instead of a word a personage, say the fictional "M. Teste."[128] Or he will appropriate a proper name which refers to an historical person, "Leonardo," and use it in a fictional way. Thus, he pursues a double strategy – but really no more than a rule of thumb – for guarding against both reifications and appeals to the ineffable.

Is there no more extensive view? The correct answer is probably a qualified "yes." For, as his views on philosophy make relatively clear, Valéry is opposed to any kind of system. Instead, he speaks of "method" where the word is to be understood with all the ironies which punctuate Valéry's readings of Descartes. "Before taking on our proper task," Valéry writes in the *Cahiers*, "we are obliged we m o d e r n s (that is, successors and both inheritors of and those inconvenienced by our possessions, or rather by the i n c o h e r e n t d i v e r s i t y of our inherited goods) first to get rid of the notions, problems, etc., that we resent the most, the debts others have contracted (...) t o r i d o u r s e l v e s c o m p l e t e l y of any credence in these questions, and, second, to re-make our vision so as to see what is to be seen and not what has already been seen (20.436).[129]

A double movement then – purge the terminology on hand of whatever unexamined residue remains from other uses; then, fashion a language as responsive as possible to the operations of one's own sensibility. The negative movement includes the entire process of scrutinizing the references of abstract terms by checking their contexts. But this scrutiny also bears on the historical baggage these terms carry. In our contexts the suggestion might be: purge much contemporary moral discourse in debates on an eventual unified European social policy within the emerging Europe today of their many vacuous expressions, and then rearticulate fresh idioms for addressing what our own European sensibilities today take to be moral and ethical priorities.

Valéry characteristically resists the language of others. He refuses to allow such uses to subvert his need to invent his own. "Language," he writes again in the *Cahiers*, "is the strongest means of the Other – [it] resides in our very selves" (15.315). And the positive movement too is an echo of a familiar theme in Valéry's work, the primacy of the physical world and its effects on what he calls the forms of sensibility.

An example of Valéry's "method" at work is the reflection in the *Cahiers* (not in the published work) on the word "love." The negative movement in this case involves a "linguistic cleansing (an exhaustion of precision) bearing on the language of sentiment."[130] What remains is a sentimental lexicon where "love" is to be distinguished from "friendship," "sympathy," etc. A positive movement follows. Valéry takes up freshly the analysis of love with an examination of its physiological and instinctive bases.

Throughout, Valéry's skepticism, his empirical interests, his scientific affinities, and his subtle varieties of materialism are at play.[131] The result is not a theory of love. Instead we have a series of telling remarks, reminders, cautions, observations, even experiments which finally yield if not a picture at least a verbal sketch of love as a "type of action completed by its facile cyclical representation, strongly recharged, manifesting clearly an exact physical and psychical excursion – finally, a return to a state of freedom and availability" (22: 318).

In many of the contemporary contexts of ongoing European Union reflection, we may think if not of the word, "love," then of the similarly overly charged and perhaps sometimes already clichéd word, "intuition." If everything is finally taken to be a matter of "intuition," then, when our basic intuitions differ, we unavoidably come to an impasse. But this cannot be right. Better then to heed Valéry's considered cautions about believing that every word stands for just one thing.

"Intuition" is one of the cardinal words in forging an eventual common European social policy. And the first step along that path must be the critical one of looking carefully at just how many different kinds of things the word "intuition" may refer to. Central to that task is reflecting on "the properties of words that depend on their having been spoken, or reacted to, in a certain way, or in certain conditions, or in the way, or conditions, they were."[132] In short, grasping less incompletely just what intuition is involves attending not just to semantics but to pragmatics as well.

Here then for initial orientations are three elements only of Valéry's general reflections on language – a caution against two persistent and mistaken assumptions, a rule of thumb, and a practice if not a method of one style of linguistic analysis. In short, we have in hand a series of sensible cautions before coming to Valéry's many non-literal representations in the *Cahiers* of mental processes and products like moral intuitions.

With these cautions in mind, then, does Valéry have something to offer us in response to our sensible concerns as to whether some intuitions may properly be said to yield certain apprehensions of what is genuinely real and not just imagined?

Insufficiencies of the Whole

In one of the more philosophical essays, "Au sujet Euréka," included in a one-volume edition he himself made from his many works and entitled *Morceaux Choisis*, Valéry settles on a word for his most general view of what there is. "What we need principally is the idea of everything we call 'the universe' and of whose origins we desire to see. (...) We make an idol of the whole and an idol of its origin, and we cannot keep ourselves from concluding to the reality of a certain body of nature whose unity corresponds to that unity of our own of which we feel certain."[133]

Valéry is immediately at work here on trying to retrieve some context for misleading abstractions. The words "whole" and "universe," we will see, finally give way to a trinity which Valéry returns to continually.[134] "Note," Valéry summarizes in the 1939 Zaharoff lecture at Oxford at the end of his life, "that everything I have said or believed to have said passes between what we call t h e e x t e r n a l w o r l d, what we call o u r b o d y, and what we call o u r s p i r i t – and requires a certain confused collaboration among these three great powers."[135] His intellectual ambitions were always very large indeed.

This constellation is at the centre of Valéry's work. When put summarily as here, these matters of course remain abstract. Moreover other elements also require some consideration. The notion of "the Other" for example is important in connection with Valéry's extensive reflections on language in relation not just to his speculations about readers' roles in the performances of literary artworks but especially in connection with his suffering through many deeply affective engagements with other persons in his long life.[136] But these other elements remain secondary here. And the central terms themselves, while indeed abstract, take on a concrete fullness in their uses thanks to Valéry's repeated attempts at fresh description.

Before recalling these descriptions, we must note the context here that many believe provides the key to Valéry's unresolved struggles with his own intense personal sufferings, both intellectual and emotional. That context Valéry himself situated in the early years of his poetic work, roughly between 1892 and 1895. With the sole exception of some psychoanalytic critics, virtually all of Valéry's readers agree about the fundamental importance of this context. More specifically, the key events are crystallized in the expression *la nuit de Gênes*, "the night in Genoa."[137]

Valéry's daughter, Agathe Rouart-Valéry, in her long and revealing biographical chronology at the beginning of the Pléiade edition puts the matter with admirable discretion. On September 14, 1892 after finishing his law studies at Montpellier Valéry left with his family for a vacation at his maternal grandmother's home in Genoa, the city of Eugenio Montale. "He left Montpellier after having gone through an acute sentimental crisis, and he found himself a prey to doubt and to great discouragement. He was ready to renounce any pursuit of a literary career."[138]

This passage alludes to two separate matters. The first was Valéry's experience of no longer being the undisputed master of his own affectivity. A woman whom he first chanced to see several times in Montpellier but only from afar, seems to have deeply troubled him in the sense of having deeply upset him emotionally. Despite all his efforts, he could not rid himself of her disturbing effects on him.[139] The second matter was his realization on reading the poetry of Mallarmé that he was no longer the undisputed master of his own intellect either. For despite Valéry's precocious intellectual successes, the quality of Mallarmé's work seemed so superior to his own intellectual capacities that Valéry thought working any more at literature simply futile.

Thus, as a young man with many achievements already behind him, Valéry was caught up short by an intense experience of his own limits. What he was later to call "the whole," had, so to speak, broken in on him, emotion overwhelming him with passionate immensities, and Mallarmé's superb artistic achievements subverting the previously unqualified confidence in his own artistic capacities (the twenty year incapacity to write poetry again).

Finding limits forced irresistibly upon him, Valéry doubted his control over both his sensibility and his intellect. From this time on a radical self-doubt, reinforced by his predilection for Descartes, marks Valéry's work indelibly. And this extraordinarily personal two-fold and protracted experience of incapacity is what marks the finally ineradicable place of suffering in Valéry's life and works.

Deeply rooted in the normative events of Valéry's growth as a mind, the double experience of radical limitation will eventually lead to the sense of "the whole" as a conjunction of world, body, and mind. The experience is that of M. Teste.[140]

The Real and the World

Valéry is anxious to separate the notion of the world from that of the real. The first he attaches to that irreducible fullness of experience which he often evokes in some of his most celebrated poems and in many of the descriptive passages in his prose. Good examples can be found, in say, the speeches of Socrates in several of Plato's most artful philosophical dialogues which often served Valéry for inspiration. The second notion, however, is spurious in the sense that the word refers to nothing concrete at all. The word "real" is not superfluous; but it must not be understood as referring to anything that actually exists in the spatio-temporal world. In short, "the real" for Valéry is a fiction.

But we must not overlook a nuance here. Thus, in his 1937 "Discours sur l'esthétique," Valéry writes: "The real refuses the order and the unity that thinking wants to inflict on it. The unity of nature appears only in the system of signs that is expressly designed with that end in mind. And the univese is nothing more than a more or less convenient invention."[141] Hence, whatever difficulties the word "real" may have when used abstractly, the word nonetheless can be given a particular context that confers on it a sense and a reference. Here Valéry uses the word "world" to refer to that residue that continues to escape the calculations of many mathematical physicists. For besides supporting our attempts at understanding, the world continues to frustrate these attempts as well. Talk of "the real" makes sense for Valéry then only so long as we insist in speaking also of those irregularities that have yet to find their fixed places in scientific laws.

The world accordingly is a mixture of regularities and irregularities. Valéry puts this matter concretely in the 1895 introduction to his "Leonardo:" "The world is irregularly sown with regular dispositions. Crystals are an example: flowers, leaves; some streaked ornamentations, stains on sands and in water, and so on. Sometimes these effects depend on a kind of perspective and on non-stable groupings. Distance produces or changes them. Time shows them or veils them."[142] Valéry observes how, once we adopt a larger scale of reference, the most striking asymmetries appear to have an order. Whatever symmetries the sciences finally settle on are not for Valéry the whole story; other elements still await consideration – something is always and necessarily left for still other sciences to wrestle with.

Valéry then does not understand the world's "reality" as a thing but as a persistent state of affairs, a feature of the universe that in principle can never be regularized, a randomness, an arbitrariness, an absence of sorts that necessarily resists any final scientific formulation. "We come to represent for ourselves the world as it allows itself to be reduced here and there to intelligible elements. Sometimes our senses suffice; other times we make use of the most ingenious methods but gaps remain. Our attempts remain full of deficiencies."[143] And this emptiness in all its dark resistance to our understanding is part of the domain that encroaches on the body.

The suggestion for our purposes is that some intuitions may be said to apprehend aspects of the world rather than aspects of the real. That is, what one may be said to grasp when one intuitively apprehends a particular moral or ethical value that might be part of the principled bases for an eventual common European social policy is not so much to be described in terms of the evanescence of a metaphysical real but in those concrete largely but not exclusively empirical terms of the world. But what then of "the world?"

Orders and Disorders

The world that is the object of so many of our intuitions needs to be understood partly in terms of the body. For Valéry, the continuities between body and world have more than one dimension. The physical body shows many of the rule-governed features and traits of the physical world. But Valéry claims that the body participates also in a kind of worldly chaos.

The body, Valéry would say, is contiguous with the disorders of the real and not just with the order of nature. Just as the lucidities of mind cloud over with the fusions of the body's tempestuous moments, so the body's coded regularities occasionally break open onto an ambiguous world. Here, continuities echo the measures of the body's movements, and yet vast areas of incomprehensible chaos continue their haphazard and endless play.

For Valéry then, order and disorder, and especially descending levels of disorder, are what lie at the origins of those surges in consciousness where a spontaneous power eddies suddenly into the mind and ripples into manifold emotional states. And from the harmony of those states arise those mental acts that in turn lead to the making of poetry.

Speaking of Mallarmé in 1926 Valéry wrote: "With all his soul he thought that the universe could have no other object that finally to produce a complete expression of itself. (...) The world," he used to say, "is made for resulting in a beautiful book. (...) He found in the world no other meaning, and he thought that everything had to end up by being expressed (...)."[144] This dark moment of the world Valéry thinks invisible in the clear light of mathematics, physics, and every species of literal discourse; it can be glimpsed, however, in the infrared and ultraviolet figures of metaphor. The world for Valéry comes to expression not in books but in metaphor. What then is the stuff of metaphor that can compass such dark sayings?

The title of Valéry's essay, "Poésie et pensée abstraite," is an articulation of a basic tension that Valéry investigates. Abstract thought at best is misleading; often, it is simply illusory. Valéry's task was to avoid the illusions of abstract thought without thereby losing himself in the endless detail of formless spontaneity. As he wrote in a revealing preface to a book on his thought published in 1943: "My one constant concern, my sole permanent instinct was doubtless to represent to myself more and more sharply my mental 'functioning,' and to preserve or to recover as often as possible my freedom from those illusions and 'parasites' that the inevitable uses of language impose."

Reaching this goal involved exploiting the figurative resources of language, especially metaphor. Metaphor thus is one way of developing different perspectives on ideas without courting the dangers of empty abstractions, a way of achieving a certain kind of distance from the world.[145] For Valéry believes that the world the artist evokes in metaphor, a fictional world, is completely independent of the world of everyday experience. A fictional world has both its sources and especially its uses in the real world.

As for the sources of metaphor, Valéry holds that the close connection between the mental and the real enhances our capacities for expression. In the 1920 marginalia to the "Introduction à la méthode de Léonardo di Vinci," Valéry writes: "I would say that what is most real in thinking is whatever does not derive from naive images of sensible reality but from observation (...) of what comes to pass within us, of what leads us to believe that the variations of the two worlds are comparable, of what allows us to experience largely speaking the psyche by means of metaphors borrowed from the sensible world and in particular from those actions and operations that we are able physically to bring about."[146] Figurative uses of language may be as misleading as abstractions. But unlike the case of abstractions a relation exists between the figure and the real, Valéry thinks, which serves as a solid basis for metaphorical uses of language.

Metaphor however not only has its sources in the world; it has its uses there as well. Valéry thinks that these uses are more complex than those of expression only. What governs poetry is the rule of metaphor. And poetry itself produces what he calls "fiction."

In his 1937 text, "Necessité de la prose," he writes: poetry "is productive of fiction." And he then goes on to spell out the place and the roles of these fictions. "And note that fiction is our life. We live continually in producing fictions. (...) We live only by those fictions that are our projects, our hopes, our memories, our regrets, and so on; we are a perpetual invention."[147]

The fictional world that metaphor establishes however is not left completely undetermined. Valéry insists on defining this world basically in terms of the distinction between what exists and what does not. In the same place, for example, he writes: "Note especially (...) that all these fictions necessarily connect with what is not and oppose themselves no less necessarily to what is; further – and this is a curious matter – it is this what is that engenders what is not, and it is this what is not that responds constantly to what is."[148]

Whatever the refinements this distinction calls for – and we need only think of Valéry's work on the concept of time in the late 1890s, and especially his *Memoire* on attention, to recall how nuanced an account he was capable of – the point here is clear. Metaphor both arises within the movements between world and mind and is deployed in these spaces as well. Unlike abstractions which lack context, metaphors are necessarily contextual in the sense that they cannot avoid reference to the spatio-temporal world.

The bases of metaphor however are even more specific. For Valéry holds that metaphor is rooted in the body, particularly in the visual processes, a point to which we will return shortly. An indication of Valéry's thought can be found in his 1932 essay, "Discours en l'honneur de Goethe," a text, one should note, with which Valéry was not completely satisfied as he indicated in his letter to Gide of 7 June 1932. For Valéry, Goethe lives "voluptuously in the visual; he lives by his eyes, and his large eyes are never tired of letting themselves be impregnated with shapes and colours."

This remarkable exteriorisation that Valéry finds in Goethe is the key to his poetic vocation. "This genius for transformation," Valéry writes in the same place, "is essentially poetic. For it presides both at the formation of metaphors and figures thanks to which the poet makes play of the multiplicity of expressions as well as at the creation of dramatic characters and situations. But in the poet and in the plant the same natural principle is at work. Every being has a capacity for adaptation, and it is this variable capacity that mesures their capacity for life, that is, for remaining what they are while having more than one way of being what they are."[149] Goethe's protean capacity flows from his genius for metaphor. And this genius itself is firmly embodied in a multifaceted sensibility that crystallizes in Goethe's visual powers.

Goethe's case well illustrates Valéry's conception of poetic experience as the "infinite aesthetic," a theme that Valéry developed in a 1934 article of the same title (II.1342). The sense of Valéry's expression might be glossed as "the sensual pleasures for themselves of sensations and perceptions that normally diminish and disappear very quickly once they undergo the 'classifying operations' of the intellect."

Valéry himself writes in the *Cahiers* (20.231) of this infinite aesthetic as follows: "The eye appreciates colour and proportion and enters on the aesthetic path – that is on the desired recovery of what it is perceiving – by a derivation of the perception of its own recognition." And in another place in the *Cahiers* he writes that the aesthetic infinite sets up "an oscillating system, an alternating equilibrium (...) between the value of the sign and the substantial (or actual) value, a stable exchange – seeing and knowing (or understanding) replying to one another mutually regenerating one another" (19: 440). Metaphor for Valéry, then, is this play of sensibility through the mind's embodiment in the metaphorical expression as necessarily dynamic.

In one of his many discussions of Valéry's poems, the widely influential French philosopher Alain[150] called attention to this dynamic feature of metaphor. Thus in commenting on *Charmes* in 1929 (see BN 164 ff) he writes: "If we take the metaphor at the level of thought we can understand nothing. The metaphor cannot be compared at all with what enlightens but only with what measures something. (...) The metaphor is not image but movement; or, better, the image is nothing but a kind of painting without consistency, only a human bodily movement that expresses more a presence than a form."[151] Metaphor thus is movement but a movement in language directed towards an object. In the movement of metaphor the embodied mind is both elated and composed.

Thus the literary artwork to the degree that it centres on the proliferation of such metaphorical movements, reconstitutes a unity of the whole – world, body, and mind – which is repeatedly broken in the activities of explanation and understanding. This complex sense of the whole is the burden of Valéry's poetics of desire, a poetics that in different degrees makes up so much of the necessary intellectual backgrounds for understanding the twentieth century's distinctively high modernist poetry of suffering. And it is to some of these metaphorical movements reconstituting such a unity of world, body, and mind that many of our most basic moral and ethical intuitions may well award us privileged cognitive access.

Before examining further how Valéry goes on to represent poetically in his *Cahiers* each of the three constituent elements of "the whole," we need to specify more fully how we are understanding our own key terms of analysis.

Moral Knowledge and Perception

Like the expression "moral discourse" in the previous chapter, the expressions, "moral knowledge" and "perception" here are ambiguous, for each can mean either a process or a product.[152] Accordingly, for our purposes here which centre on philosophical ethics and the distinctive European high modernist poetry of suffering rather than on moral epistemological issues as such, we will need to pin down the meanings of these ambiguous cardinal terms. Just what then are the relevant senses here of the expressions, "moral knowledge" and "perception," as we will go on to use them in reflecting on Valéry's poetic representations in some of his *Cahiers*?

Standardly,[153] we may understand our first crucial term, "perception," to refer here mainly to the operations of our internal senses ("proprioception") and to those of our external ones ("exteroception") that provide us with information about things (including objects, events, persons, and so forth) and facts in our environments.[154] Perceiving facts such as the fact that the cat is on the sofa is epistemic in the sense that it is required for genuine knowledge. "[O]ne cannot see that there is a cat on the sofa without, thereby, coming to know that there is a cat on the sofa. Seeing a fact is coming to know (that there is a fact) in some visual way."[155] By contrast, perceiving things such as objects or events is non-epistemic in the sense that it need not issue in genuine knowledge. "One can see a cat on the sofa and mistake it for a rumpled sweater."[156]

We are especially interested here in there being basic kinds of perceiving things and facts, direct and indirect. We directly perceive, for example, that the reddish stove top in the store is hot by immediately experiencing physical pain when we touch it. We indirectly perceive that the stove top is hot by mediately recognizing, say, from its reddish image on the in-store camera, that if we touch the reddish stove top then we will experience the same physical pain.

As further reflection on examples like these suggest, however, it is not clear that we are perceiving the same thing when we perceive that thing both directly and indirectly. Are we to understand that when we directly perceive some thing, then exactly what we are perceiving is an object, whereas when we indirectly perceive apparently the same thing, then exactly what we are perceiving is actually an image and not an object at all? Besides, what could it mean to say that in some cases what we perceive are actually facts and not things at all? Many objects we may assume are directly perceptible. We directly perceive the cat on the sofa. But is the fact that the cat is on the sofa directly perceptible? Probably not.

Most moral realists who are intuitionists need not hold that there is some distinctive species of perception whether direct or indirect that is peculiar to morality alone, say moral perception. They need only hold, and be able to defend, a weak direct realist view that for some perception-like moral intuitions at least some kinds of objects (perhaps abstract objects and not physical ones) and some facts about these objects (perhaps the fact that this abstract object is a moral truth) can be perceived or intuited in some direct, unmediated fashion.

We need to say here, rather barbarously, "perception-like moral intuitions" because the meaning of the word "perception" in the senses in which we are now using the word here, although often very closely related, is not identical to the meaning of the word "intuition." Philosophers today standardly understand intuition as "an alleged direct relation, analogous to visual seeing, between the mind and something abstract and so not accessible to the senses. What are intuited (...) may be abstract objects, like numbers or properties, or certain truths [e.g., moral truths] regarded as not accessible to investigation through the senses or calculation. "[157]

By contrast, as we have just recalled, philosophers today standardly understand perception as internal or external sense operations that provide us with information about things and facts in our environments. In both cases we are talking about processes and not products. But in the case of intuition we are talking mainly about one kind of direct relation between the mind, things, and facts, whereas in the case of perception we are talking mainly about different kinds of direct and indirect relations between internal and external senses and things and facts. And of course this makes intuitive processes non-identical with perceptual processes.[158]

On this version of a direct realist view the primary objects of perception are things themselves, and perception delivers the basic facts about these things. By contrast, a representative realist view holds that the primary objects of perception are not the things themselves but sense data, and that perception delivers the basic facts not about these things but about the sense data. Philosophers today continue to investigate such controversial views.[159]

As for our second crucial term, "moral knowledge," we may take "moral knowledge" here to refer mainly to knowledge of the moral world as a domain of moral truths. This is the view of a moral realism where what moral knowledge knows as morally true or morally false is to be found in the nature of things.[160] We recall Kant famously talking about "the starry sky above and the moral world within." And we will see that the notion of "the world" will turn out to be central for Valéry.

The view that either there is no moral world as such, or, if there is a moral world, then "we are not adapted for knowing about it,"[161] is the opposite of moral knowledge. This is the view of a moral skepticism where "nobody ever knows that any substantive moral claim is true."[162] Note that, unlike moral scepticism and moral realism which are both philosophical views, moral knowledge itself is not to be understood as a philosophical view.

Moral knowledge is not the same thing as moral epistemology.[163] Moral epistemology may be taken as focusing on the rational justification not just of beliefs but also of actions. By contrast, moral knowledge may be taken as focusing mainly on the nature, kinds, and contents of normative judgments of and normative principles for actions. These are principles for and judgments as to determining whether particular actions are morally good and morally permissible or morally bad and morally impermissible.

With regard especially to judgments, recall that not all normative judgments need to be reflective judgments in the sense of judgments that follow upon some explicit moral theory; some may be common sense judgments and not theoretical at all, and others may even be pre-reflective judgments. More succinctly, we may say here that moral knowledge turns on whether the normative claims that constitute normative moral and ethical judgments are to be understood as true or false.

If we may fairly characterize moral epistemology today as "the discipline at the intersection of ethics and epistemology that studies the epistemic status and relations of moral judgments and principles,"[164] then perhaps we may characterize moral knowledge here as knowledge of the truth or falsity of such moral judgments and principles. Thus, moral knowledge is neither a sub-discipline of philosophy nor a particular philosophical view. Rather, moral knowledge is a capacity some persons have to guide their attempts to act rightly in realising the morally and the ethically good on the bases of justified true beliefs that are not justified just by accident.[165]

Such an understanding of moral knowledge assumes that there are moral truths and ethical truths just as there are empirical truths and mathematical truths. Moreover, just as some persons are capable of knowing empirical and mathematical truths, the further assumption here is that some persons are also capable of knowing moral truths and ethical truths. Exactly what specifies the separate category of moral truths and ethical truths from empirical and mathematical truths, however, remains a matter of continuing philosophical controversy. For example, many naturalistically inclined moral philosophers would reject the claim that moral truths are specifically different from empirical truths. And much contemporary moral philosophy is busy exploring empirical aspects of current moral issues.[166]

But just who are these morally capable persons? And how could we ever identify someone like Paul Valéry as such a morally capable person?

Some would propose that such persons are to be characterised pre-eminently as "competent moral observers." What makes such moral observers "competent" is said to be their ability to acquire and to apply "clear and distinct perceptions of wrong-doing features in actions." But when we examine much of what someone like Valéry writes, we can quickly see his capacities for applying such Cartesian categories as clearness and distinctness to many things. So, just how is such a criterion supposed to work specifically with respect to moral matters?

Here is how this criterion for a competent moral observer is supposed to work. "Thus I might be supposed to know that torturing cats is morally wrong on the grounds that when I observe or merely think about the action of torturing cats I perceive immediately its wrongness. However, my claim to be a competent observer is established by my delivering judgments taken by others to be correct."[167] So, are we then justified in taking Valéry to be a competent moral observer just on the grounds that on the evidence of his works he indeed does deliver judgments and on the evidence of his correspondence many of his judgments are taken by others as correct? Perhaps not. For at least two serious difficulties confront such a view of what makes a person a morally competent observer.

First, let us imagine that, when the former vice-president of the United States observes or merely thinks about the action of torturing Taliban prisoners, he may perceive immediately its rightness. He delivers his judgments that such actions are permissible. And others (such as some then high-ranking Ministry of Justice lawyers) take these judgments as correct (and even contrive to invent legal justifications for such judgments). By contrast, when the actual president of the United States merely thinks about torturing Taliban prisoners, he may immediately perceive its wrongness. He too delivers his judgment that such actions are not permissible. And others take his judgments as correct. Are we then to understand that the former vice-president and the actual president are both competent moral observers?

But how could they be if they contradict one another, as they unmistakeably do, on the moral permissiveness of torture? That torture is at the same time and in the same respects both morally acceptable and morally unacceptable cannot ever be the case. So, presumably being capable of immediately perceiving the moral rightness or moral wrongness of certain actions, of delivering one's judgment, and of having one's consequent judgments taken by others as correct cannot stand up alone as a criterion for identifying just who is a competent moral observer.

A second difficulty for this alleged criterion now arises from the counter example we are considering. For the reason why these contrasted "immediate perceptions" of the moral valence of torture undermine the satisfactoriness of the alleged criterion for competent moral observation is an important basic assumption. The assumption is that immediate moral perception is basically like immediate colour perception in being common across actual human species.

But this basic assumption is highly questionable.[168] For while the former vice-president and the present president belong to the same biological species, *homo sapiens sapiens*, it is clear, on the bases of their considered and repeated experiences with reflection on torture and from both their words and their actions, that they do not in fact share the same immediate moral perceptions. And since they do not, then relying mainly on the assumption that immediate moral perception is uniform cannot suffice to establish immediate moral perception as a satisfactory criterion.

Now, with at least this much as background to these complicated issues, perhaps it suffices here merely to indicate another criterion without arguing the matter here any more in detail. Let us say then that those persons holding true beliefs that are appropriately justifiable with adequate evidence properly related to their truth and who use valid arguments incorporating such true beliefs justified in these ways can gain reliable access to some moral knowledge of some moral truths. Such persons may properly be taken to be morally competent observers.

So, not all morally concerned persons need be moral sceptics. For at least some morally concerned persons such as the ones we just described do have some moral knowledge properly speaking. We need not then be agnostic about the possibility of moral knowledge. Perhaps, however, as we will go on to investigate later when we return to Valéry, the distinguished high modernist European poet Paul Valéry was.

Valéry and Moral Knowledge: Initial Formulations

After this initial inquiry into Valéry's poetic prose in his *Cahiers* perhaps we may not unfairly formulate in a provisional way only several of the promising insights so far about moral intuition and the sources of moral knowledge.

(1) Some attentive readings of Paul Valéry's poetic representations of varied interactions between world, body, and mind would appear to open up further fruitful perspectives on the nature and kinds of perception peculiar to acquiring genuine moral knowledge through moral intuitions.
(2) One such perspective is the variety of non-inferential perceptions apparently on view in many of Valéry's poetic representations of different kinds of intuition both in his own life and in art.
(3) Many of these cognitive perceptions are connected with Valéry's personal experience as a man of his times, as a truly distinguished poet and critic, and as a professor at the Collège de France, still the pinnacle of France's academic hierarchy.
(4) Others however appear to be of a moral nature and focus on his own personal sufferings of both affective and cognitive limitations in the absolute sovereignty he hoped to hold over his extraordinary but not unique poetic talent and especially over his own troubled affectivity.
(5) What especially appears to call for further reflection are the implications of the richly figurative language Valéry characteristically fashions for representing these moral perceptions of both a concrete and an abstract suffering in his journals even more so than in his poetry.

We need now, however, temporally to suspend further inquiries here about Valéry's poetically rendered perceptions of suffering before returning for second thoughts in a later chapter, and move on to our first readings of another instance of the European high modernist poetry of suffering, Eugenio Montale's.

CHAPTER FOUR

Moral Motivations and Suffering in Eugenio Montale

The objective of our previous chapter was informally to confirm a second rough working hypothesis about another aspect of moral intuition. According to that hypothesis, some critical and reflective readings of Paul Valéry's European high modernist poetic representations of varied interactions between world, body, and mind in his very extensive *Cahiers* open up fruitful perspectives on the nature of the kinds of perception peculiar to acquiring genuine moral knowledge through moral intuitions.

By way of showing the philosophical interest for a better understanding of moral intuitionism and suffering for perhaps enlarging the scope of much work on moral epistemology today in view of putting more of that work at the disposal of ongoing reflections in the European Union on an eventual common social policy, our focus was Valéry's reflection on his own poetic practices of articulating his artistic intuitions.

Before turning to that work in detail, however, we considered one general objection to our somewhat unconventional appeal in these chapters to poetic representations of moral situations rather than to psychological or philosophical analyses only of moral intuitions. And we tried to respond to that objection generally by developing an analogy from contemporary procedures in the emerging field of particle astronomy.

We then looked at Valéry's voluminous work broadly in order to sharpen our understanding of what his literary work seemed to be representing only indirectly. And we considered a central experience in Valéry's early work that profoundly affected both his previously undoubted self-confidence in his intellectual and affective capacities for the rest of his life. This experience we took as one of the most basic sources of the persistence of a profound abstract suffering in his life.

We then specified how we proposed to use the terms, "moral knowledge" and "perception" in the analyses of some of the most important pertinent passages in his *Cahiers.* We investigated Valéry's work, however, only synchronically under the heading of several central themes in his work rather than limiting ourselves to any strictly diachronic approach. We concluded as earlier in the case of T.S. Eliot, with several interim formulations about non-inferential perceptions apparently on view in many of Valéry's poetic representations of intuition in his *Cahiers.*

In this chapter our objective is to state and then confirm as best we can another rough working hypothesis about the third of the themes we identified within our general subject of moral intuitionism and suffering, namely moral motivation and ethical liberation.

Perhaps we might put this further working hypothesis as follows. Some attentive readings of Eugenio Montale's poetic representations of various moral situations and states of affairs in his early European high modernist poetry of an abstract suffering open up a novel standpoint on the nature of both moral motivation and ethical emancipation. This standpoint sometimes may yield moral intuitions of external objective moral values; it may also sometimes result in certain kinds of ethical liberation from distorting moral frameworks. We will look at the notion of moral motivations in this chapter while reserving the idea of ethical liberation for second thoughts in chapter five.

We may take as our guideline here neither the kind of interpersonal concrete suffering we observed in T.S. Eliot's figured discourse in *The Waste Land*, nor the kind of intensely private general suffering we observed in Paul Valéry's incessant reflections in his *Cahiers* on how one might finally perceive and come to know the moral qualities of the interactions between world, body and mind. Rather, we will find it fruitful to follow Montale's repeated variations on the will to break through one kind of spiritual suffering some mortifying moral frameworks comprise in order to break out onto some re-vivifying ethical horizons. And once again as with Eliot but not with Valéry, we will focus here on Montale's poetry rather than his poetic prose.

Another Objection, Another Reply

Before turning to the linguistic richness of that further instance of the European high modernist poetry of suffering and its extraordinary exhibits of morally and ethically charged intuitions, we may find it helpful once again to consider very briefly another general objection. The objection this time arises from our dealings in our previous chapter with Valéry's work and the supposedly direct perceiving of some moral qualities or properties.

We tentatively concluded there that basic qualities of some moral states of affairs such as personal suffering may present themselves indirectly in such ways as to raise fresh issues about how persons perceive them, how, as many like to say, they "see" them. In particular, perceiving or seeing the primary qualities of such situations is said to include both sensations and their related beliefs. And these beliefs themselves are said to comprise true and false moral judgments about external and objective moral values. In short, we seemed to be concluding in our previous chapter that reflection on such rich descriptions as Valéry's may bring some persons to "see" some external and objective moral values that are the proper objects of true and false moral judgments.

Someone might well object, however, that such an account appears to depend too heavily on what is finally an unsatisfactory analogy for perceiving moral matters, the analogy of vision or seeing. We are said to perceive moral matters as if we were seeing them. Yet here we seem to be talking not just about seeing moral matters generally, but in particular about seeing moral things and moral facts. That is, we seem to be talking at once about seeing primary moral qualities, seeing moral sensations, seeing moral beliefs, seeing moral judgments, seeing moral truths, seeing moral falsehoods, and seeing moral values.

But if we are finally trying to get some fresh conceptual grasp of moral intuitionism and its possible uses in ongoing debates about the eventual contents of a harmonized European social policy, all this surely seems to be just too much "seeing." After all, as we will consider when we come to second thoughts about Montale in the next chapter, even Reid himself had to make an exception to his theory of perception in order to account for what he understood as our sensation-free direct perception of "a real figure projected onto the retina (...) representing the spatial relations of the parts of an external object."[169]

We cannot take up here all these particulars in the requisite detail. But once again a recent physical phenomenon might prove helpful in dissipating some of the unease that can arise from this general kind of objection.

Consider then that resolving difficulties with supposedly proper analogies for perceiving, which not only Reid but Molyneux (1656–1698),[170] Locke, Berkeley and so many others even today continue to wrestle with, requires a fair amount of continually expanding empirical input. If we are to construe the perceiving of moral values on some analogy with visual perception, then to obviate at least some general objections we had better be sure to review carefully at least some recent physiology.

Now at least some moral perceivings of the salient properties of certain moral situations and states of affairs might not misleadingly be compared with at least some visual perceivings of the salient physical properties of certain physical situations and states of affairs. Briefly, the light of some essential elements of moral intuitions might be said figuratively to impinge on our perceivings of some moral situations as the light of some essential elements of some physical states of affairs can be said non-figuratively to impinge on certain intrinsically photosensitive retinal ganglion cells.

That is, just as some physiologists have recently developed quantitative studies of the light response properties of a newly discovered class of retinal photoreceptors that are not only specifically different from the retinal photoreceptors of the rods and cones in the human eye but also both more powerful (by three times and hundred times respectfully) and utterly distinctive in providing "non-image forming aspects of visions," so some persons working at the emerging interfaces of moral philosophy and the philosophy of literature may develop new visual analogies for better grasping how non-representative aspects of morally salient value qualities of some moral situations may arise.[171] But, as previously in our imagining a plausible defense strategy for replying to a general objection to the interim results at the end of our second chapter, so too here: more would need to be said, but perhaps this much may suffice for now. We turn now to Montale's poetry.

The Suffering of Stones

Recall one of the most resonant voices of twentieth-century European high literary modernism. With its many echoes of Mallarmé and Baudelaire, of Rilke, Eliot, and Valéry, and its enduring concerns with the twentieth-century poetry of both a concrete and an abstract suffering, the voice is from Eugenio Montale's first collection of poetry published in 1925 at the age of 29, *Ossi di seppia* (*Bones of the Cuttlefish*).[172] The untitled poem is called after its first words, "Qualche scendendo (...)" One of its English translations reads as follows:

> Sometimes descending
> the dry slopes already
> abandoned to the fragrant
> autumn that inflated them,
> I no longer felt in the heart the wheel
> of the seasons and the dripping
> of inexorable time;
> but completely, the presentiment of you
> would fill my soul,
> surprised by the gasping
> of the air, motionless at first,
> upon the stone that hemmed the path.
> Then, I would notice it, the rocks
> wanting to break off, stretching out
> towards an invisible embrace;
> the hard matter could hear
> the nearby whirlpool, and throbbed;
> and the clumps of greedy reeds
> were conversing with the hidden

> waters, nodding in assent.
> You, vastness, redeemed
> even the suffering of the stones:
> in your jubilation the fixity
> of finite things was justified.
> (...)[173]

This moving and at times beautiful voice can be annoying. And it can still unsettle many readers even today – it irritates us, it upsets us. For in a post-modern era we are no longer intellectually comfortable with what seem to be its merely literary seriousness, the confusions of its deceptive transparencies, the figured earnestness of its invocations, the now suspect surmise of something more than material at the heart of the expanding universe, the misplaced righteousness in its attentiveness to a merely fanciful suffering, and the belle-lettristic grandeurs of its hyperbolic apostrophe – "tu vastita"!

These posturings are after all fictional – they can be no more than the early Ligurian strains of Montale's singing words. How could these poetic words ever be reasonably taken as yours, how could they ever be taken reasonably as mine? And, in times like these, after the bloodiest of centuries, why should anyone ever take the time to investigate such matters anyway?

After considering some of the literary backgrounds to Montale's poetry, we will try to understand more fully what could properly count as rationally interpreting this distinctive twentieth-century European high modernist poetry of suffering.[174] In particular, we will try to attend thoughtfully to Montale's poetry of *varco*, to his poetry of passage and breakthrough, of hesitation and ambivalence about the possibilities of personal transcendence when the primacy of the intensest immanence is deliberately qualified by a poetics of impoverishment, emptiness, and the contemplation of self-extinction. Trying to read not uncritically such a poetry of abstract suffering in sufficient detail, however, will require us first to pursue some of the most salient tensions between mainly epistemological and mainly metaphysical construals of reason in any reasonable interpretation of the lexical and syntactic complexities of lyric poetry generally.[175]

Retrieving the Philosophical

Recall another of Montale's early poems, "Forse un mattino (...)."

> Perhaps one morning while going along in the air of glass,
> and, looking back, I should see, with the terror
> of a drunken man, the making of a miracle:
> nothingness at my shoulders, the void behind me.

> Then as on the screen, suddenly, trees houses hills
> will assemble themselves for the usual deception.
> But it will be too late; and I shall go on, quiet,
> with my secret among the men who do not turn.

In 1976, when many distinguished friends celebrated Montale's eightieth birthday, the postmodernist Italian novelist, Italo Calvino, presented a memorable and markedly philosophical interpretation of this poem.[176] Much of the interest of Calvino's interpretation, however, has centred on his careful and illuminating description of how, over the years, a poem memorized early in life gave rise to significant distortions that, in turn, came to shape the extraordinary imaginative power of Calvino himself. But Calvino's interpretation is also interesting for both its philosophical details and especially for the difficult problems these details imply for any reasonable elucidation of Montale's poem.

Besides highlighting the influence on his own work then, Calvino's interpretation touches on a number of philosophical aspects the poem suggests. For example, Calvino discusses questions about the subjective character of our experiences of space. And he draws on materials from Merleau-Ponty's *Phenomenology of Perception* (1945) to show how some experiences, such as dreams or drug-induced states or drunkenness, can alter the individual's sense of the objective and empirical elements of spatial perception.

Calvino considers as well several temporal features of visual perception and their pertinence to Montale's use of the movie-screen image. He touches on the difficult matter of the existence of other minds in speculating on whether changes in the objects of visual perception as represented in the poem entail changes as well in the putative existence of the other persons represented in the poem.

But however pertinent and fruitful any one of these philosophical themes might prove after closer inspection in connection with the actual working, sounds, and rhythms of this poem, one major theme only anchors Calvino's interpretation. For Calvino, Montale's poem is about "the disappearance of the world."

Uncharacteristically with respect to much of Montale's other poetry, this poem presents details of no specific landscapes. The scene is urban rather than natural. And the persons are represented in groups rather than as individuals. The poem in short "is one of the few occasions when the other truth presented by the poet beyond the continuing wall of the world is revealed (...) This truth is neither more nor less than the world's unreality" (216). Accordingly, Calvino takes the crucial expressions of the poem to be "nothingness at my shoulders, the void behind me." And, in his own quite striking language, Calvino goes on to offer a particular interpretation of these lines. We need to consider this interpretation in more detail and ask just how it may be understood as a reasonable interpretation.

"The 'void' and the 'nothingness' are 'at my shoulders,' 'behind me,' " Calvino writes. "This is the essential point of the poem. Not an undefined feeling of dissolution, but rather the building of a cognitive model which is not easily refuted, and which can co-exist in us with more or less empirical models" (217).

Construing the poem as the presentation of a "cognitive model" and suggesting that such models are neither exclusive nor uncontroversial – their structures and significance allow of argument and refutation – Calvino formulates his specific interpretation in the form of a hypothesis. "The hypothesis can be stated in very simple and rigorous terms: given the dual nature of the space surrounding us – a visible field before our eyes, an invisible field behind us–we define the first as a scrim of illusions; the second as a void which is the world's real substance. (...) The model of dual or bipartite space is never denied by the text; indeed, it is affirmed by the redundancy of the third line – 'nothingness at my shoulders,' 'the void / behind me' " (217). But however simple and rigorous Calvino finds his hypothesis, we still need more detail.[177]

Calvino goes on to discuss, in biological, evolutionary, and genetic terms, how space is initially discriminated into interior and posterior fields; how the anterior field comes to define the world as opposed to the non-world of the posterior field, and how, despite the mobility of the human head, the visual field is inseparable from the anterior spatial field. Consequently, Calvino proposes that Montale's protagonist can be understood as someone who (miraculously) turns round so quickly that he is able "to look at a space still unoccupied by his own visual field. (...) What he sees is nothingness, the void" (218).

What makes this miracle possible? Calvino thinks that the peculiar aspects of the winter air (presumably in Italy) – "the concreteness of this invisible air, which seems precisely glass, and its self-sufficient solidity" – is what makes the miracle possible – "the precise specifying of the medium that expresses the sense of nothingness."

More specifically, Calvino describes what "triggers" the miracle as "the natural, i.e., atmospheric element – the dry, crystalline transparency of the winter air, which renders objects with such clarity that it creates an effect of unreality, as though the halo of mist usually hazing the landscape (...) were identified with the thickness of existence" (215). Once again, however, just as in the formulation of his interpretive hypothesis, the explanation Calvino offers here, while richly suggestive, is difficult to formulate very clearly.

If nonetheless the crystalline transparency of the winter air is what makes the miracle possible, the consequences of the miraculous vision for the protagonist are then taken to be, in Montale's evocative word, the "reassembling" ("*accamparsi*") of the world. The things of the world moreover are reassembled just as in a movie theatre the images of things continually scroll by one another on a white screen. In particular, the suddenness of the turn round (the "*rivolgendomi*") that occasions the miracle gives rise to a gnosis, a secret and special knowledge of things as they actually are, whereas the ordering perception of things in a visual field gives rise to apparent knowledge only.

The usual kind of knowledge then is clear, stable, corrigible, testable. But the knowledge of things as they actually are is unclear, dizzying, intuitive, non-testable. And above all, this unusual kind of knowledge is terror-stricken. Moreover, what one ordinarily "knows," the everyday empirical world, is to be taken as "the usual succession of images on the screen, an optical illusion like that of the movies, in which the speed of the shots persuades you of their continuity" (220). This illusory empirical world is the world of "real" things. The world of actual things however, the world of things as they actually are, this world disappears.

With the disappearance of the actual world, "trees houses hills" disappear as well. Whether other persons disappear too is left in suspense – the poet's "I" certainly remains. The disappearance of the world is a disappearance pre-eminently of nature. In short, the protagonist is presented as some day coming to a knowledge of the truth of things and the truth of the world, this unreality.

In the light of these considerations we can understand why Calvino calls Montale's "Forse un mattino" a poem, in short, "of abstract imagination and insight." (214). And, on the evidence of this richly suggestive philosophical interpretation, we can also understand why Calvino's reading is justly celebrated.

But, perhaps ungratefully, we may also ask, has Calvino gotten Montale's poem right? In particular, just what is the understanding of reason and rationality implied in Calvino's specific interpretation of what he calls "the essence of the poem" as "the disappearance of the world," the "truth (...) of the world's unreality" (216)? More simply, what could ever count as getting the poem right? To deal with this question not inadequately, however, requires our detailing some concerns about epistemological construals of reason and rationality. Only then can we return to Montale's perplexing lines in "Forse un mattino" of "nothingness at my shoulders, the void behind me" in better founded hopes of disengaging from that poetry some insight into moral motivations.

Epistemically Rational Interpretation

Although Montale was not to leave Genoa and the sun-bleached summer seascapes of Monterosso for the cityscapes of Firenze till 1927, already ten years earlier he had come to know the very different landscapes of northern Italy. Assigned in the closing months of the First World War to the Trentino as an officer in the Italian infantry deployed against the Austrians in the Alpine hills above the Leno river, Montale later celebrated in memory the capture of an Austrian soldier who had carried Rilke's poems in his fieldkit.[178]

He also celebrated the phantasmagoric night combats near the village of Valmorbia, in the "gentle valleys" ("*valle morbida*") below.[179] Included in *Ossi di seppia*, the second of these poems, with its evocations of the elusive yet central notion of "world," can help bring our discussion of epistemically rational interpretation into sharper focus.

> Valmorbia, across your glens cloud-blossoms
> scurried, wildflowers in the breezes.
> In us, whirled by blind chance, oblivion
> of the world was born.
> The barrage stopped, in the lonely
> vale no sound but the husky Leno.
> A rocket sprouted on its stem, wailed
> faintly through the air.
> The bright nights, all one dawn,
> led foxes to my cave.
> Valmorbia, a name – and now, in my dim
> memory, land that lightens.[180]

This poem exhibits a very thickly worked texture of sound and sense. The poem's many features – among others, its heavily stylized description of an unfamiliar landscape, its mythic echoes and strongly accented literary allusions, its extraordinary use of the suggestive power of both the sounds and etymologies of proper nouns, its use of repetition, its Arcadian transformations of a shell-pocked, war-torn, almost lunar landscape – all would require sustained critical attention. Our concerns however are narrower.

Suppose then we try to propose a reasonable interpretation of the poem, and see whether an epistemic understanding of rationality could account for that reasonableness.[181] We may adopt initially something like Calvino's perspective on such a poem, and then go on to entertain as a working hypothesis the idea that "Valmorbia," although unlike "Forse un mattino" in its situation of material objects and emblems in a specific landscape, strongly resembles that poem in its theme. "Valmorbia" too is about what Calvino calls "the other truth," the truth of "the world's unreality."

Calvino's own hypothesis about "Forse un mattino" might then be applied to "Valmorbia": "given the dual nature of the space surrounding us – a visible field before our eyes, an invisible field behind us – we define the first as a scrim of illusions [that is, the hills, the valley, the sound of the river, the airy bronze, the barrage, the rockets, the shell-lit night, the foxes], the second a void which is the world's real substance [that is, the glens, the cloud blossoms, the flower exploding on its stem, the cave-trench, the all-one-dawn, 'the land where night never comes']."

This reading, however, seems to oppose the real world as the empirical to the actual world as the imaginary. But this impression holds only so long as we fail to pay sufficient attention to the crucial supposition earlier in the poem – "In us (...) was born / oblivion of the world" – and to the crucial repetition at the very end of the poem – "Valmorbia, a name." For once these expressions are given their due, then we may reasonably construe the oppositions here as holding not between the empirical and the imaginary, but between the real world as the set of illusions arising from the empirical appearances of things and the actual world as the non-empirical void that the illusory always conceals.

"Valmorbia" like "Forse un mattino," we might say then, is about the disappearance or oblivion of the so-called real world ("*oblio del mundo*") in the nascent ("*nasciva*") realisation and dawning ("*tutte un'alba*") of the actual world as a void.

When contrasted with Calvino's own masterly interpretation of "Forse un mattino," we need to concede, our Calvino-like interpretation of "Valmorbia" is evidently strained. I would want to suggest nonetheless that this interpretation is rational; it is not however reasonable enough. That is, an interpretation may well satisfy the descriptions of even a sophisticated epistemic rationality without accounting sufficiently for the appropriately metaphysical aspects of reason itself. In short, reasonably interpreting some instances of the poetry of suffering such as the highly abstract war poems of Montale requires more than even a sophisticated epistemic understanding of rationality. To see how this is the case, consider briefly just what an epistemically rational interpretation is.

An epistemically rational interpretation is one where it is reasonable to believe the propositions that comprise the interpretation so long as "Those propositions are uncontroversial for you, given what else you believe and given your own deepest epistemic standards."[182] The standards themselves are to be understood as "a matter of what you would believe about the truth-preservingness of various arguments were you to reflect to the point of stability, if there is one" (179). And the point of stability is to be taken as "the point at which further reflection would not alter your opinion of the argument." Such a point is said to be reached "when you yourself, no matter how much more you reflect on the matter, would not regard your opinion as mistaken" (180).

In other words, you may take the interpretation of the Montale poem as epistemically rational if, among the many beliefs it comprises, no one of these commits you to believing "anything you yourself would not be satisfied with were you to be appropriately reflective" (170). This is the fallibilist mark of an epistemically rational interpretation; we cannot exclude the possibility here of error, of our being mistaken.[183] More generally, you can take an interpretation as epistemically rational if the set of beliefs that comprise the interpretation can be judged from some perspective as satisfying your goals as the interpreter.

While fallibilist, such an epistemically rational view of interpretation is nonetheless sufficiently detailed enough to be clearly opposed to other views. In particular, when the beliefs about the poem are viewed as uncontroversial for you given your own "deepest standards," these standards are not taken as "objective" in either of two current senses. That is, the standards at issue in this epistemic version of rational interpretation are neither those that govern rational belief as a function of their objective probability on the evidence available, nor those that govern rational beliefs that arise from a reliable source only. They are simply the interpreter's own most fundamental and most foundational standards.

Despite the questions, however, that may arise here about whether such a notion of the rationality of interpretation can be "objective" at all, this epistemic version of rationality seems superior to both a traditional foundationalist account (roughly, a body of propositions may be known properly speaking only if based upon certain foundations) and a traditional coherentist account (roughly, a body of propositions without certain foundations may be known by reason of their interconnected strengths). For, unlike the present view, neither of these accommodates fallibilism (no guarantee of knowledge or truth). That is, only the epistemic version tries to provide a notion of rationality, not in terms of the successful pursuit of a goal like truth, but in terms of "understandable failure" (177).

We may say that, traditionally, it is foundationally rational for an interpreter to believe those propositions that "are adequately supported by propositions to whose truth you [the interpreter] have some kind of special, infallible access" (169). Fallibilism is excluded. And we may say that, again traditionally, it is coherently rational for an interpreter to believe those propositions the truth of whose total set is consistent. Otherwise, should even a single proposition of the interpretation be false, then, because the total set would be inconsistent, believing any other proposition of that set would also be inconsistent. Since this view leaves little that can be believed, fallibilism is again excluded.

Nonetheless, all three views under consideration here – the epistemic, a traditional foundationalist, and a traditional coherentist view – do address the same question. For the interpreter that question comes to just which attitude is rational for the interpreter to adopt with respect to any particular proposition the interpreter considers incorporating into the interpretation – belief, disbelief, or the withholding of belief. Importantly, none of these three views centres on issues about the degrees of belief.

By contrast, were Montale's interpreter to adopt some version of a probabilist approach (in the interpretation of literary works of art, reasonable degrees of probability about critical hypotheses are attainable), then the question to be considered about any proposition that might finally figure in the interpretation would be just what degree of belief in the truth of the proposition would it be rational for the interpreter to accept. Similarly, were Montale's interpreter to adopt still another approach, say a reliabilist one (a literary critical hypothesis may be known to be true if it follows from a "reliable process of belief formation"), then the issue would be just what would be needed to add to a particular true belief "in order to get knowledge or at least a good candidate for knowledge" (170).

With these considerations in place, and taking account of several subsequent revisions that have been argued and adopted, we can now state more precisely just what is the epistemic rationality of an interpretation. Let us say then somewhat formally that it is epistemically rational for an interpreter I at t to believe $p =_{df}$ There is a doxastic system D and a set of epistemic standards E such that (i) D is I's doxastic system at t; (ii) E is the set of I's deepest epistemic standards at t; and (iii) E licences believing p in D.[184]

In other words, my interpretive belief that Montale's poem, "Valmorbia," is about the disappearance of the world is rational to the degree that I have a set of interpretive beliefs, a set of my most profound epistemic standards, and that these standards license me to believe, as a part of my set of interpretive beliefs, that "Valmorbia" is about the disappearance of the world.

Moral Motivations

With these elucidations of how interpreting a poem can be epistemically rational in hand and before examining these poems more closely we need now to specify just how we are to understand our cardinal term here, "moral motivation."

In everyday common English parlance, native English-language speakers use the word "motivation" to refer either to "an act of motivating something or someone," or to "the state or condition of being motivated." More fully, motivation is "the (conscious or unconscious) stimulus, incentive, motives, etc., for action towards a goal, esp. as resulting from psychological or social factors; the factors giving purpose or direction to behaviour."[185]

In particular, many English-language philosophers today, while keeping in mind the basic ambiguity here between motivation as most often an act (providing a motive) and motivation as most often a mental state (a motive), focus critical attention on something else.[186] They regularly inquire into what rational grounds there may be for believing persons when such persons adduce the specific reasons, intentions, desires, volitions, sentiments, feelings, emotions, purposes, goals, and so on for acting in the specific ways they do.[187] Knowing what we already do about our complicated selves, how can belief in others' self-interpretation be rational and reasonable?

More specifically, many philosophers investigate the relations between reasons and causes in satisfactorily explaining actions. Although sometimes reasons and causes for some actions overlap, nonetheless we can usually distinguish between what elements of an action directly result from a cause and what elements merely follow from a reason. A swimmer waves to you from the ocean with a reason, but shivers from a cause. Experiment on the part of behavioural scientists is sufficient for determining whether some particular action, say the swimmer's shivering, is the result of a cause, whereas a person's intention is sufficient for determining whether some other particular action, a swimmer's wave, follows from a reason.

In contrast with appeal to causes or to reasons, motivation as a mental state or motive "is often invoked precisely when there is a departure from normal reasons."[188] Your swimmer friend later tells you with apparent sincerity that she waved to say hello. But you wonder whether her actual reason was different from her declared reason, however sincere. That is, you wonder about her motive – perhaps, whether she consciously was so aware or not, she really wanted you to join her?

Thus, some explanations of behaviours may appeal to causes, others to reasons, others to motives, and still others to various combinations of causes, reasons, and motives.

When some philosophers focus more sharply on the moral domain, characteristically they most often focus on whether there are distinctive kinds of motivation to be found in the moral domain, or whether moral motivations there are only apparently distinctive.[189] Doubts about distinctive moral motivations are similar to doubts about distinctive moral perceptions we considered in our reflections on Valéry's poetic representations of the perceived whole of world, body, and mind. One way to put such doubts about the existence of distinctive moral motivations is as follows. "If we understand morality as a distinctive domain of normative reasons," one philosopher writes standardly, "then it begins to seem that the motivations that render moral conduct possible might simply be those general capacities (...) that enable agents to understand what they have reason to do and to act accordingly."[190]

We need, however, to distinguish between whether there are distinctive motivations in the moral domain on the one hand, and, on the other, whether there are distinctive patterns in the beliefs, desires, and intentions that often constitute such motivations. And even though much debate about such matters continues, with a distinction like this one on hand we can understand why many philosophers are inclined to hold for something being genuinely distinctive about moral motivation.

For example, the same philosopher writes: "If human agency involves essentially a responsiveness to normative [i.e., rule-like or principle-like] requirements, then the motivations of moral agents will reflect their distinctive responsiveness to the norms at the heart of morality (...) our access to what is distinctive about moral motivation will be by way of understanding what is distinctive about the values that structure morality as a unified domain of normative considerations. This is in keeping with the general interpenetration of the normative and the psychological [i.e., roughly, between the non-empirical and the empirical] that is characteristic of the whole subject of moral psychology."[191]

In our investigations, then, of Montale's poetic representations of moral motivations, we may take our further discussion of moral motivation as mainly discussion of what actually structures or patterns our distinctive responses to the varied ways in which moral values present themselves. Some of those responses we will surmise with the help of Montale's work would seem to result in something like what we may call with help from our second key expression here, "ethical emancipations."

But return now to the poetic representations of some moral situations in the early high modernist lyric poetry of Eugenio Montale.

A Strict Immanence?

Here are several stanzas then from the second half of another Montale poem, his much celebrated high modernist lyric, *Casa sul mare* (1925). Among many other things, perhaps this piece may present us with a poetic representation of both a moral motivation that we are reflecting on here and of an ethical emancipation that we will reflect on in chapter five.

> You ask: Is this how everything vanishes,
> in this thin haze of memories?
> Is every destiny fulfilled
> In the torpid hour or the breaker's sigh?
> I would like to tell you: No. For you
> the moment of your passage out of time is near:
> transcendence may perhaps be theirs who want it,
> and you, who knows, could be one of those. Not I.
> There is no salvation, I think, for most,
> but every system is subverted by someone, someone
> breaks through, becomes what he wanted to be.
> Before I yield, let me help you find
> such a passage, a path
> fragile as ridge or foam
> in the furrowed sea.
> And I leave you my hope, too meagre
> for you my failing strength to foster
> in days to come. I offer it
> to you, my pledge to your fate, that you
> break free.
>
> My journey ends on these shores
> eroded by the to-and-fro of the tides.
> Your heedless heart, so near, may even now
> be lifting sail for the eternities.[192]

Independently of our particular interests, literary critics have taken this poem as a "dividing point" between the poetry of *Ossi di seppia* (1925) and that of *Le occasioni* (1939). The poem "looks forward to the menacing interiors of Montale's late poetry," one critic writes, "as well as back to the seashore of his autobiography. The decisive and peremptory opening ('Here the journey ends') is followed by the matching opening of the other three strophes in the poem, all suggesting that a season and a whole experience have come to an end."[193]

Thus, *Casa sul mare* would seem to have an unusual importance both in *Ossi di seppia* and in Montale's work as a whole. But what, specifically, is at least the second half of the poem about?

In addressing such a question, several of Montale's most distinguished interpreters write: "Before the spectacle of the sea man is faced by the same alternative as in '*Falsetto*' [a 1924 poem famous for its dramatic meditation on life and the "momentary apotheosis" of a young woman, Esteria, surfacing after her dive into the glittering sea]. (...) To the finite itinerary of a human destiny consummated in passing whiffs of memory, the poet contrasts the wildly improbable salvation of the wilful companion."[194]

And, looking back to the lines about transcendence just cited, the interpreters conclude: "In this passage the difficult [passage or] *varco* ['*passi il varco*,' 'someone breaks through'] (...) is being crossed by a privileged human being, even if it is qualified by the heavy weight of a 'perhaps.' Yet the passage is an arduous one. (...) Once again – we think back to Esteria in '*Falsetto*' – the marine adventure may possibly represent a salvation, but it is fraught with danger, with this fragile escape route in the midst of a rough sea. The companion may take the risky ticket for an unlikely eternity, while the poet accepts the lulling quietness of a finite death."[195]

Suppose we were to narrow the scope of this extended interpretation and, for our other than exclusively literary critical purposes, centre our attention on just what the interpretation takes the passage on transcendence to be about. And having already cited the passages extensively, suppose we were to agree that "the interpretation" at issue here comes to something very close to the following free paraphrase.

Montale's *Casa sul mare*, we might then say, is about one way of responding to a deep question concerning fate and destiny. This way is one of offering, against his strongly considered convictions, to explore what the poet's *persona* presents as a weak possibility only, and this only for a small minority. The offer is to find a passage between life's basic polarities and thereby create the possibility of a *varco*, both a break-through and a passage through the fundamentally polarised situation every human being must suffer.

This basic polarity is the lived tension between the temporal, the finite, and the richly coloured but finally mortal silence of a strict immanence. The figure of this strict immanence is the land and the timeless, the infinite, and the terrible unlikelihood of a transcendent speaking response to a perpetual aspiration figured in the sea. (For the poet-*persona* the quiet land is to be cultivated, but creatively, whereas for his interlocutor the terrible sea may perhaps be dared, but if so, then once only.) Most generally, then, the poem is not just about polarities but about overcoming by breaking through and passing through the suffering these profound polarities continually cause, the suffering of the deep pathos of things.

But, we may well ask, is such a general interpretation still faithful enough to Montale's very particular poetry?

"The poet straddles two worlds," one of Montale's English translators, William Arrowsmith, writes in connection with later poems such as "The Eel" in *La Bufera e altro* (1956), "body and soul, matter and spirit, immanence and transcendence."[196] And the task for the translator, the reader, and for the interpreter is "to locate the hidden transitional pivot beneath the seemingly unpredictable thematic swerve, prosodic jump, or even pointedly abrupt silence or aposiopesis [i.e., the rhetorical device of "breaking off in speech"]. When we find that pivot we are in touch with what Montale elsewhere, in a metaphysical connection, calls 'the brief cycle where everything is changed,' the 'ditch of memory,' or that void of suffering that precedes all transformation, all individual becoming" (15). Accordingly, we might say that the formulations here of the interpretation of *Casa sul mare* in the very general terms of immanence or transcendence and especially of an abstract suffering is not unfaithful to Montale's central concerns.

But, if not unfaithful, is the interpretation rational? More specifically, in what sense if any can we properly say that such an interpretation is not just "epistemically rational but metaphysically reasonable?" Before we can understand and then pursue such a general question, however, we need to see how such a question can arise from certain elements in the poem that generate the interpretation.

Recall Montale's abiding concern with what he himself called "the transcendental 'I.' " "The man who communicates," Montale has written, "is the transcendental 'I' who is hidden within us and recognizes himself in others" (17)

This concern arose out of Montale's preoccupations, like those of Eliot and Valéry, with degrees of solitude and solipsism. His strategy to counter these ineluctable threats was to emphasize the indispensability of openness to others, pre-eminently through sympathetic and imaginative poetic communication. Montale possessed "the human, and humanizing, imagination, the capacity for otherness and the sympathetic openness towards those feelings that are not our own but from which we cannot divide ourselves except by becoming human, even inhuman" (17).

In *Casa sul mare*, what calls for interpretation is precisely the communicative situation whose subject is doubly obscure. For not only the subject of the exchanges between the two poetic *personae* is unclear; the identity of the speaking subject is also unclear. If after repeated re-readings and judicious study of the available commentary, the poem strongly suggests something like what we have formulated above in terms of *varco*, just what more should a reasonable interpretation be required to include?

When we return to the poem in search of more detail to deal with such a question and after surveying carefully the first half of the poem not cited here, we come to focus sharply on the situation in the poem's second half. The poem represents the speaker as responding to a question about what the speaker has already averred in the preceding two strophes. There the speaker spoke about where "the journey ends "– "Here (...) in these petty cares dividing / a soul no longer able to protest," "Here (...) on this shore / robed by slow, assiduous tides." In short, things and their memories inevitably pass away.

The speaker, however, is represented as trying to reply to a specific question. "You ask: Is this how everything vanishes, in this haze of memories?" And the question assumes that what the speaker had previously said comes to a description of everything not only passing away, but passing away finally in the dissipation and dissolution of memory itself. The strong suggestion is that things themselves pass away finally only after the individual and collective memory of their being has already passed away first.

But this question is difficult to understand. And the question that immediately follows, presumably representing a reformulation of the same question but this time with still further nuance, complicates the matter very greatly – "Is every destiny fulfilled / in the torpid hour or the breaker's sigh?"

Whatever the sense may be of the relation between these two questions that we finally might be able to win consensus on, the poem continues by immediately providing representations of the speaker's protracted reply. The substance of this reply is what the interpretation has already tried to articulate. What the interpretation has left out, however, is the striking and deliberate because repetitive suggestiveness of who the speaker is and to exactly what the speaker is referring in his insistence on *varco*. Each remains indefinite, indeterminate.

"I would like to tell you," we first read. Then a distinction: maybe you but "Not I." Immediately afterwards comes the explicitation, "I think." Then the specification of the speaker's standpoint – "Before I yield" – followed by the extraordinary gesture of encouragement in what the speaker understands to be a most probably hopeless venture – "And I leave you my hope (...) I offer it. (...)"

But whose voice is this, who is this speaker? Is this speaker Montale, or his poet-*persona*, or a character whose views Montale represents but does not endorse? Or is the speaker Montale's metaphysical ideal, the "communicative man?" The "I" remains indeterminate.

Similarly indeterminate is the nature of the *varco*. For this word "*varco*" is strongly ambiguous, referring as we have already noted either to a passage or to a breakthrough. While related, these two things of course are not the same. So is the *varco* to which the speaker repeatedly refers, a "passage" between transcendence and immanence, between the finite and the infinite, the temporal and the eternal? Or is the *varco* a "breakthrough?" If the latter, then are we to understand the *varco* as a breakthrough from the temporal, finite, and immanent to the eternal, infinite, and transcendent? Or is the breakthrough to a "salvation" to be found in some identification with the transcendent?

Still further, is the breakthrough to be taken finally as a liberation from mortality and death to life and immortality? Finally, is the *varco* in some senses to be taken as both a passage and a breakthrough? But just as in the case of the previous questions about the identity of the speaker, so too here as to exactly what the speaker is talking about, the poem does not say in any determinate way.

Now the interpretation of the poem we have worked out above can be shown to be rational. For, among many other things, the interpretation does capture the subject of Montale's poem, its theme. But the interpretation cannot articulate the other subject of the poem, that is, the nature of its speaking subject and the determinate subject of the speakers' reference, without being more than rational. How is the interpretation to account for, let us say, Montale's ideal communicative person and his ideal poetic value of *varco* and the objects it constitutes?

Such an interpretation needs to aim then not just at an epistemic rationality but at something more, at what we mentioned tentatively above as "a metaphysical reasonableness." By way of anticipation of developing second thoughts about Montale's work in our next chapter on ethical emancipation, we may say that interpretation of such work as Montale's *Casa sul mare* turns out to be metaphysically reasonable when it succeeds in incorporating a substantive and creative idea of reason as productive rather than just an instrumental and functional idea of reason as procedural. Before we try to elaborate such second thoughts, however, we need now to pull together several initial results from our first readings of Montale's high modernist poetry of suffering.

Montale and Moral Motivations: Initial Formulations

Perhaps we might not unfairly summarize in a provisional way only several apparent results from our first readings here of Montale's poetry.

(1) Some attentive readings of Eugenio Montale's poetic representations of various moral situations in his early European high modernist poetry of an abstract suffering appear to open up a novel perspective on the nature of both moral motivation and ethical emancipation.

(2) This perspective sometimes would seem to yield moral intuitions of external objective moral values that appear to underlie much moral motivation.

The epistemic reliability of such intuitions, however, is vulnerable to the charge of being arbitrary in the sense of being unwarrantedly subjective.

(3) A particular interpretive belief about a high modernist poem like Montale's "Valmorbia," nonetheless, may be said to be rational and not arbitrary to the degree that it is a coherent part of an interpreter's set of interpretive beliefs. This set of beliefs must also include the interpreter's most profound epistemic standards that basically license the interpreter to hold the belief about the poem that he or she actually does.

(4) Supported with such epistemic reassurance, further discussion of Montale's poetic representations of moral motivation may properly be taken as discussion of what patterns a competent interpreter's intuitive responses to the varied ways in which moral values present themselves in Montale's high modernist poetry of suffering.

(5) A not inadequate interpretation of such poetry, however, needs to incorporate not just an epistemic rationality but "a metaphysical reasonableness." That is, critically reflective interpretation of such work as Montale's "Casa sul mare" must also incorporate a substantive and creative idea of reason as productive rather than just an instrumental and functional idea of reason as procedural.

With these initial formulations in hand and before returning to Montale's work for further reflection on not just moral motivation but on ethical emancipation as well, we do well to look back briefly now in the following "Interlude" on some of what our three first readings on moral discourse, moral knowledge, and moral motivation have suggested so far with respect to our main theme of moral intuition and suffering.

INTERLUDE

Just as in our introductory chapter, "Orientations," and at the end of this essay in our concluding chapter, "Envoi," so too now we need to return with some of our initial, tentative findings from our first readings of the European high modernist poetry of suffering to the basic and quite general problem that any eventual common and harmonized European social policy must finally address satisfactorily. That problem is how we might come to know the just principled bases of any such common social policy and thereby be able to achieve consensus among the current 27 members of the European Union. Central to resolving that general problem is understanding the nature and the kinds of moral intuitions that most often ground our most considered opinions.

One of the fundamental problems such a common European social policy will have to deal with is the currently much disputed and particular issue of general access for all children to health services in any one of the EU countries. We should first look at some of the details of this problem and then consider in the light of these details some of the suggestions of our interim findings so far. The gaps in those findings may help point us to those areas that will require second thoughts in the second part of this essay.

Sick Children in Europe

Besides the particular problem of elaborating a common immigration policy for all present and future members of the EU which we looked at in some detail in "Orientations," another quite basic European problem that still awaits its satisfactory solution is a common health policy governing access to health care, especially for poor children. Towards the end of November 2009 two important events converged to underline the seriousness of this problem. The first was the rapidly increasing evidence of the spread of the newly emergent A(H1N1) human virus, and the second was the 20th anniversary of the International Convention on the Rights of Children.

In Europe, both events came together with the rather sudden realisation that one of the basic rights of children in Europe and elsewhere was continuing to be infringed.[197] For in the case of the surprisingly many indigent as well as unaccompanied migrant children in the EU, common access to proper health care was for the most part not possible. The underlying difficulty was the insecure situation of many very poor children in EU member states, the continuing uncertain legal status of unaccompanied migrant children, and the greatly varying measures that EU countries were taking to protect their citizens against the increasingly dangerous virus.

With respect to children's human rights and access to health care, EU leaders meeting at Laeken in Belgium in 2001 had elaborated a first set of eighteen indicators of social performance. They designed these indicators to serve the EU member countries in their new attempts to develop so-called "multi-faceted approaches" to resolving deeply entrenched and quite serious persistent social problems. This initial work drew on a substantial body of social science research over the previous generation of scholarship. Among other topics, this work also included specific concerns about children's health. Subsequently, various expert commissions carefully reconsidered and redefined the nature of the initial indicators. And these commissions have successively reformulated, multiplied, and substantially improved the indicators in many ways.

European Council meetings, especially in 2005 and 2006, confirmed the basic importance of the "Laeken indicators" for constructing an effective EU social inclusion policy.[198] These concerns for basing eventual common policies on reliable indicators became more urgent with the complications affecting European social policies that derived from the rapid expansion of the EU in subsequent years as well as with the worldwide financial and economic crisis beginning in September, 2008. A general concern emerged for developing child-focused indicators including those for access to health.

Further meetings of the European Council from 2006 on have continued to include protracted discussion of the role of children's health.[199] The evolving contexts for these meetings have included the effects of globalization on the growing awareness for the necessity of concerted action among countries to solve certain transnational problems, the United Nations increasing difficulties to realize its September, 2000 Millennium Development Goals, and the necessities for the EU to review the role of the social dimension in the course of preparing its revised Lisbon Strategy which heads of government and the European Council of the EU had first adopted in Lisbon in March, 2000.

In 2005, for instance, the European Commission as part of its review of the Lisbon Strategy elaborated a "Social Agenda 2005–2010" that included measures about common health policies. And in 2006 the European Council called on all EU member states "to take necessary measures to rapidly and significantly reduce child poverty, giving all children equal opportunities, regardless of their social background."[200] Among these equal opportunities were equal chances to have regular access to proper health care understood as a basic human right of children in full compliance with the UN Convention on the Rights of the Child to which all member states of the EU are signatories.

On November 20, 1989, the United Nations adopted the Convention on the Rights of the Child in the General Assembly Resolution 44/25.[201] (The Convention defines "children" as, generally, all persons from their ages of birth up to their 18th birthday but not above.) The Convention included no fewer than fifty-four Articles. Despite persisting differences in the judicial treatment of children, the Convention nonetheless reinforced the widespread conviction in Europe and elsewhere that proper protection and promotion of children's freedoms and rights require regular external intervention. Such protection and promotion cannot be left entirely to the quite limited autonomy, if any, of the children themselves. Twenty years later, although much progress has been accomplished, very much remains to be done, including notably providing regular access for children to proper health care.[202]

The Convention covers both the material and the non-material well-being of children. It calls upon member states to provide children with a decent standard of living, education, health and housing. And it also calls upon them to pay special attention to disadvantaged and disabled children. In particular, under the material aspects of children's well-being, the Convention holds, among a number of other common views concerning important matters, that states should "ensure the provision of necessary medical assistance and health care to all children with emphasis on the development of primary health care" (Article 24). It also holds that states should "in case of need provide material assistance and support programmes, particularly with regard to nutrition, clothing and housing" (Article 27).

Despite the adoption of the Convention on child rights, however, many states including many in the EU do not necessarily provide for the effective guarantee of these rights. That is, although many member states have indeed approved the Convention in affixing their signatures, almost as many have failed so far fully to implement the Convention.

For example, increasing restrictions in France on the reunification of children with their parents and other family members do not appear to be in conformity with the relevant articles of the Convention. Moreover, very recent changes in French immigration laws have drastically reduced the number of children eligible for legal entry into France on the grounds of family reunification. And yet many children urgently requiring proper health care in France are illegal "residents," if that is the correct administrative terms for many chronically sick street children. Still more, these new laws also include a number of measures that increase the ease with which poor immigrant children who are in France illegally may be expelled, with or without their parents. All of these restrictions have a major impact on the health of children and on their supposedly guaranteed access to proper health services in full conformity with the 1989 Convention to which France is a signatory nation.

Besides these renewed concerns in the EU in late 2009 with the full implementation of measures to ensure respect for children's rights including regular access to proper health care, the rising wave of A(H1N1) viral infections (so-called "swine flu") in the EU and increasing mortality rates among many children as well as adults was also a cause for serious renewed reflection about the necessity for elaborating an eventual common European health policy. For different starting points for the various EU member states' plans for inoculation of especially those most vulnerable to the virus including children complicated the effectiveness of these campaigns. Further, differences in the kinds of vaccines to be distributed, the methods of distribution, the assigning of priorities to certain groups of the population, the authorisations of different kinds of health professionals to inoculate people, and so on added substantially to the problems with different effective distribution calendars in different EU member states.

Moreover, as the first wave of virus infections developed, EU member states continued to differ widely in the kinds and quantities of information they were distributing so as to encourage the population to benefit from the new vaccines. Thus in the UK and in Sweden many people sought vaccination from the very beginning of the vaccination campaigns, whereas in France most people remained poorly informed about the reliability of the initially available vaccines and hence were reluctant to be vaccinated early in the campaign. They were especially reluctant to have their children vaccinated. And of course the many poor children in France as well as the street children in Paris, Marseille, and Lyon for example had other concerns than how to get protection against something many of them had hardly heard of.

After the early weeks of the vaccination campaigns in many of the member states of the EU, it seemed once again evident that, without an eventual common European health policy that would finally harmonize all the persisting differences among member states in delivering proper health care especially to children, children's rights even in the EU and not just in the poorest countries of Africa and Asia and South America would be honoured only in the breach. It also was evident that even in those countries which are among the most affluent in the world today guaranteeing at least children's rights to proper health care sometime soon was not going to happen.

In France, the important polling group, TNS-Sofres, reported the results of a November 19, 2009 poll conducted among the members of both the French National Assembly and the Senate. At least in those informed, intelligent, powerful, and resourceful groups, children's rights including their right to proper health care came but eleventh in priority of subjects requiring action.[203] Disagreements about just what should be the principled bases for common health policies and about how we might come to know just principled bases and thereby reach consensus seemed to be among the reasons for the persistence of such a low priority for guaranteeing access to proper child health care.

Here then by way of interlude is a further concrete example of the need for overcoming the obstacles to reaching consensus about an eventual European common social policy. As we noted in the first chapter on "Orientations," such a harmonized policy might include common policies about such particular and persistent problems as widely differing current EU member states' immigration policies and health policies.

Perhaps now by way of reminding ourselves of the still largely untapped verbal and conceptual resources at our disposal in the European high modernist poetry of suffering for re-articulating moral intuitionism today, we might look again at a further example of that poetry. This will allow us then to sketch out our plan for second thoughts in Part Two of our inquiries.

The Night-Time Heaping of Ashes

In 1944, with the outcome of a world war still uncertain and the falling V-2 bombs driving strangers into forced intimacy in the subways and air raid shelters of London, the volunteer fire watcher and church warden, T.S. Eliot, published his *Four Quartets*.[204] First appearing in separate sections from 1935 to 1942, this extraordinary work of poetic maturity both catches up the meditative movements of *Ash Wednesday* (1930) and transposes into a new key the "foresuffered" pathos of many of the central thematic concerns in both *The Waste Land* (1922) and its coda, *The Hollow Men* (1925).

Four Quartets begins with a garden scene. Earlier, *The Waste Land* had begun with representations of the memory of the hyacinth girl in a garden of hyacinths. Then, the poem's speaker affirmed, "(...) I knew nothing, / Looking into the heart of light, the silence." Now, the first of the *Four Quartets* begins with the representation of a rose garden whose door was never opened. And the speaker once again, as in *The Waste Land*, although in a very different sense, talks of knowing nothing, more exactly, of not-knowing.

> Footfalls echo in the memory
> Down the passage which we did not take
> Towards the door we never opened
> Into the rose-garden. My words echo
> Thus, in your mind.
>
> But to what purpose
> Disturbing the dust on a bowl of rose-leaves
> I do not know.[205]

Coming to appreciate critically this not-knowing requires looking back at Eliot's poetic drama.

In 1935, after a number of experiments with the idea of recreating a viable contemporary form of poetic drama, Eliot accepted a commission to compose *Murder in the Cathedral* for the Canterbury Festival. As his subject Eliot selected Thomas Becket, Archbishop of Canterbury from 1162–1170. Although a number of connected themes were of interest, such as the conflicts between Church and State, the spiritual and the secular, the past and the present, religious ritual and classical tragedy, Eliot chose to focus his play on the uncertain notion of Becket's martyrdom. What made the notion uncertain was the difficulty of answering the question whether Becket was an authentic martyr, having been murdered for his Christian faith, or whether he was merely an apparent one, having provoked his own murder by unnecessarily defying his king.

But Eliot's success in dramatising Becket's conflicting motives in neither seeking martyrdom nor in fleeing from its possibility remained partial only. For the play did not entirely succeed in communicating to audiences the felt complexities of such a difficult subject. Nor does it today. Still, the poetry of many scenes in the play continues to attract critical appreciation. And much of the most remarked poetry appears in the set choral pieces delivered by "the poor women of Canterbury."

At the very moment when the four Knights are killing Becket before the consecrated altar of Canterbury Cathedral – murder and sacrilege together – the chorus, as in the plays of Aeschylus and Sophocles, cries out. And, in lines that recall Eliot's poetic figure of the Fisher King in "The Waste Land," their cry is a question and an answer. "Where is England? Where is Kent? Where is Canterbury?" the Chorus cries out. "O far far far far in the past," the Chorus answers; "and I wander in a land of barren boughs: if I break them, they bleed; I wander in a land of dry stones: if I touch them they bleed."[206]

The Chorus rushes on to mark out a major and still obscure distinction between the painful, concrete, but limited sufferings of everyday life, and a kind of truly painful, abstract, and unlimited suffering that knows no parallels, that has no bounds – an infinite suffering.

> We understood the private catastrophe,
> The personal loss, the general misery,
> Living and partly living;
> The terror by night that ends in daily action,
> The terror by day that ends in sleep;
> But the talk in the market-place, the hand on the broom,
> The night-time heaping of the ashes,
> The fuel laid on the fire at daybreak,
> These acts marked a limit to our suffering.
> Every horror had its definition,

> Every sorrow had a kind of end:
> In life there is not time to grieve long.
> But this, this is out of life, this is out of time,
> An instant eternity of evil and wrong.
> We are soiled by a filth that we cannot clean, united to supernatural vermin,
> It is not we alone, it is not the house, it is not the city that is defiled,
> But the world that is wholly foul.[207]

Given the complexities of any critical and sustained philosophical talk about meanings as we saw in chapter three and will see again in chapter eight, and given the importance of poetic representations of not-knowing, the void, and nothingness in Eliot's mature work, what would ever count as a reasonable interpretation of this high modernist poetry of suffering, of a truly painful, abstract, unlimited, unending, indeed infinite and ineradicably evil defilement?

Poetic Significance

Much of the dissatisfaction with Eliot's *Murder in the Cathedral* in 1935 – when the horrific suffering under Stalin's Yezhov Terror was still escalating, the technologies and bureaucratization required for the Holocaust were still in the future, and the firestorms at Hamburg and Dresden, Tokyo, Hiroshima and Nagasaki had yet to be imagined – has only increased. The woodenness of the plot, the smugness of the characterizations, the artificialities of the stagecraft, and the now very widely unintelligible liturgical rhythms and symbolisms (introits, versicles, and the *Dies Irae*) – all conspire to make many of the regular revivals tedious and tiring.[208]

Yet many thoughtful readers keep returning to Eliot's choral poetry in this very imperfect play. And they keep scrutinizing not so much its shifting and varied roles in the drama of Becket's somewhat priggish struggles with his conscience and his soul. Rather, they puzzle over the sense and the significance of what this choral poetry often seems to be saying and showing. Much of that scrutiny continues to focus on the passage we have just reviewed. How is this sense and significance to be construed so as to allow for reasonable interpretation? Here – to take an example – is one distinguished critical interpretation.

> "The real drama of the play," the critic writes, "is to be found where its greatest poetry lies – in the choruses. (...) In the great chorus before the martyrdom [the women of the chorus] identify themselves with a whole world of groaning and travailing. The monstrous act they (...) witness is not an aberration, an eccentricity; it is an expression of the universal malice and corruption. (...) They have to pierce deeper, beyond all agents and forms of evil, beyond death and judgment to 'Emptiness, absence, separation from God.' In the face of the intensity of the *Dies Irae* chorus, the ecstasy of penitence and shame that breaks out with the cry "Clear the air! clean

> the sky! wash the wind! take stone from stone and wash them," and the final chorus of praise, criticism of the presentation of the hero seems irrelevant (...). We identify ourselves with the women of the chorus; their experience communicates itself to us, and gives us the feeling we have been not spectators but sharers in a mystery. We live through a *peripeteia*, we experience a great discovery. We pass with them through horror, out of boredom, into glory.[209]

This critical interpretation, however admirably situated in the movement of one of the most accomplished readings of Eliot's poetry, with its echoes of Eliot's other plays such as *A Family Reunion* (1935) and the poetry of *The Waste Land*, *The Hollow Men*, and *Ash Wednesday* together with anticipations of the central themes in *Four Quartets*, invites nonetheless further reflection. For example, just what is the experience of suffering to which the women of the chorus are taken to be referring? How are we to understand the women's communication of this experience to us the spectators? What would it mean to say that receiving this communication enables us to "live through a *peripeteia*" (a reversal), and to "experience a great discovery?" And just what is the discovery a discovery of?

We need to distinguish two sets of problems here. In the first case, we have the various problems – meaning, sense, reference, significance, and so on – that arise from our attempts to understand certain central expressions in the choral poetry. For example, what exactly are the women of the chorus saying when they chant, both ritually as in a Greek chorus and liturgically as in a Good Friday lamentation, "(...) this, this is out of life, this is out of time, / An instant eternity of evil and wrong"? It is not evident what "this" is. Nor is it evident how "this" can be "out of time," especially when the expression "out of time" seems to be put in apposition not to "out of life" but to the paradoxical phrase "an instant eternity." In short, the sense and significance of these poetic expressions is problematic.

When we turn for help with such matters even to those critical interpreters whose work has achieved a very large consensus, we find a second set of related problems about meaning, sense, significance, and so on. These problems arise from our subsequent attempts to understand certain expressions in the interpretation of the poetry. Thus, the distinguished English critic of a generation ago, Helen Gardner, writes of the "experience" of the women of the chorus that is said to be communicated to us the spectators in such a way that we come to "share in a mystery." She then goes on to add that the spectators of a poetic drama, who have become participants in a mystery, "live through a *peripeteia*" and "experience a great discovery."

But we do not understand here enough of what the critic would seem to be saying. Is the "reversal" the same thing as the transformation of the spectator into a participant? Or, more traditionally, is the "reversal" something the spectators remember in the fortunes of the hero, perhaps the changes in Becket's consciousness of the motives for his actions? Further, are we to understand that "the experience" the chorus communicates turns out to be the same as "the experience" of a great discovery – both spectators and chorus come to realize the same thing – or are they different? And, in either case, what is "the experience?"

The turn to critical interpretation here, however, while it does not succeed in unlocking the sense and significance of such central expressions in the poetry of suffering as "this, this is out of life, this is out of time," nevertheless raises a question. Just how can a critical interpretation that fails to specify satisfactorily questions of meaning in both cases be taken as rational and reasonable? A very different approach to these issues of sense and significance than that of the critics is one that we began to explore in the Anglo-American or analytic philosophical reflections on modernity of Charles Taylor and Stephen Toulmin in chapter one. We will find it useful to pursue those reflections further in chapter eight in the complementary Continental or hermeneutic reflections of Hans-Georg Gadamer and Paul Ricoeur. Here however we need now to identify more sharply three further matters that will require second thoughts in our next series of three chapters on Montale, Valéry, and Eliot in Part Two.

Swine Flu in Europe

Why should the 27 different states of the EU require a common health policy? One quite important reason arises from the fact that most serious diseases do not respect national borders. Thus as I write, European states just like other countries around the world are struggling to stockpile and to distribute in a fair and reasonable way novel, rapidly produced, and so far but summarily tested vaccines to counter the very recent pandemic caused by the newly emergent flu virus A(H1N1) 2009.

This entirely new virus belongs to the family of viruses that can be lethal for human beings. It includes the Spanish flu virus, H1N1, responsible for the pandemic of 1918–1919. That virus killed at least 30 million people. Members of this family of viruses include eight genes, two of which code for the proteins, hemagglutiniae (HA) and neuraminidase (NA).[210] These proteins serve to identify different members of the family H1N1 such as A(H1N1), H3N2, and so on.

The twentieth century witnessed three very lethal pandemics. Besides the Spanish flu, a new pandemic began in 1957 with the emergence in the south of China of a new flu virus called the Asian flu, H2N2. Thanks to antibiotic treatments this virus killed far fewer than the virus responsible for the Spanish flu extraordinary mortality rates. Nonetheless, the H2N2 virus was responsible for the death of roughly two million people. This virus also infected some people in Europe. The third and last twentieth-century pandemic began in 1968 with the emergence of H3N2 first identified in Hong Kong and called accordingly the Hong Kong flu. The H3N2 flu was responsible for the death of one to two million people, mainly children. And this virus too also infected many people in Europe.

New viruses are always emerging thanks to continual natural mutations in genes, but only some of them affect human beings. Moreover, only a small proportion of the viruses that affect humans are responsible for very high increases in normal mortality rates among human beings. And still a smaller number of the flu viruses that are lethal for human beings spread world-wide thereby becoming pandemic.

In the 1990s different kinds of swine, avian, and human viruses circulated in Asia, the Americas, and in Europe, including the human H3N2 flu virus. And around the beginning of the present century in 2000 the evolution of the flu viruses went through an important new phase. The three different antecedent types of viruses recombined in North America to form, especially from the antecedent H1N1 swine virus, a new swine virus, H3N2. Then, apparently in the Spring of 2009 in Mexico on a sub-standard and unregulated pig farm, the new swine virus H3N2 recombined with both a North American swine virus and a Eurasian swine virus to give rise to the new human flu virus, A(H1N1).

This is the virus that has become a pandemic. As I write in December 2009, the virus is currently continuing to propagate worldwide every six weeks across distances that, according to the head of the World Health Organisation (WHO), Dr. Margaret Chan, previous human flu viruses had taken six months to cover.[211] Current estimates are that in densely populated countries like those in Europe the number of newly infected persons will reach 30% of the populations. Since the new vaccines are becoming available only in December 2009 no one is yet able to provide reliable estimates of the expected European mortality rates to come. (Some of these remarks of course will need revision once new information becomes available.)

In this type of situation no one European country can manage to protect its population adequately without cooperation with other European countries. But health policies in general, and new policies governing the production, access, onset of massive vaccination campaigns, and the distribution details of vaccines with or without so-called "adjuvants," with or without lengthy enough and reliable scientific testing and government approval, with or without public debate as to priorities, differ very widely. Thus Sweden began its massive vaccination campaign on October 12 whereas France began on November 12 only. Canadian services report long lines of people waiting patiently for vaccination, despite the news of very important side effects from one substantial lot of vaccines, whereas in France a mere 10% of professional health workers showed up for early vaccination before the official onset of the national campaign.[212]

In France the government has made all the major decisions, including those about persons having priority for vaccination and those about distribution (pharmacists were not consulted at any time), without any public debate whatsoever. "The public's underwriting such decisions, which could prove to be very difficult," the director of *L'Espace éthique* for the public assistance programmes of the Paris hospitals writes, "justifies a transparent debate, clear explanations, and the putting into place of procedures that guarantee respect for the commitments undertaken and persons' rights, especially the rights of those most vulnerable."[213] But many informed members of the European Parliament coming from many other countries in the EU would very probably disagree with the underlying assumptions of such representative critical comments in France.

And hence the reticence and continuing difficulty of achieving not only consensus about a common EU health policy even in the face of a serious pandemic but also about a common EU social policy in the extended aftermath of the most serious financial and economic crisis in almost a hundred years. Thus the question remains as to just how such a consensus can be achieved without renewed critical inquiry into the superficial articulation so far of the principled bases of an eventual common EU social policy.

Part of the linguistic resources for rearticulating such principled bases in such ways as to achieve consensus more readily, I have been suggesting, may be found in the extraordinary verbal richness of some of the European high modernist poets of suffering and passage.

In Part Two of this essay we will try to develop some second thoughts about our interim findings in Part One. Thus, we will return to our general theme of the nature and kinds of moral intuition and look in more detail at the three sub-themes of moral discourse, moral knowledge, and moral motivation in the work of the European high modernist poets of suffering, Eliot, Valéry, and Montale once again. This time, however, we will proceed in reverse order so as to view some of that work with the benefits of somewhat different backgrounds. Thus we start in our next chapter with the task of developing second thoughts about Montale and moral motivation this time, however, under the heading of ethical emancipation and with the benefits of our first readings of the three poets already in hand.

PART TWO

SECOND THOUGHTS

CHAPTER FIVE

Montale and Ethical Emancipation from Suffering

After the brief "Interlude" to pull together several of the most important preliminary results in the first readings we developed in Part One, we now move on to the further task of developing some second thoughts about our major themes in Part Two. In the interests however of preserving a certain continuity in our reflections, we do well to reverse the order of our inquiries in the first half of this philosophical and meditative essay and proceed from Montale's poetry and the question of ethical liberation back through Valéry's poetic prose about moral perceptions to finish with Eliot's puzzles about moral discourse.

In our second set of investigations, then, of Montale's poetic representations, we may take our further discussion of moral motivation as mainly discussion of what actually structures or patterns our distinctive responses to the varied ways in which moral values present themselves. Some of those responses we will surmise with the help of Montale's work would seem to result in something like what we may call here with help of our second cardinal expression, "ethical emancipations."

Some Terms

In everyday common English parlance, some native English-language speakers use the word "emancipation" to refer mainly to releasing someone from "control or restraint, esp. a legal or political one." Others, however, use this word to refer mainly to causing someone "to be less bound by social conventions, moral restraints, intellectual prejudices, etc."[214] This second use is the more pertinent one for our purposes.

Note that informed speakers speak and write of emancipating someone in more general senses than they speak and write of "liberating" someone. "Liberating" someone from something usually refers to freeing someone from social conventions, where the expression "social conventions" is mainly taken narrowly as sexual conventions.[215] By contrast, "emancipating" someone from something may indeed include the notion of freeing someone from such social conventions as sexual ones, but more often the expression "emancipating" has a broader extension.

Thus, emancipating someone includes a broader understanding of social conventions than mainly sexual ones. Moreover, besides social conventions talk of emancipating someone may often include, as we noted, the additional notions of intellectual prejudices and moral restraints. Still more, emancipation is usually associated mainly with the double sense of freedom, the notion of someone emancipating someone not only from something but also for something.

In the ethical domain in particular, this broader notion of emancipation rather than the narrower one of liberation is more appropriate. For often, when persons respond to the self-presentations of some external and objective moral values in certain situations, the actual responses that flow from the patterns of our beliefs, desires, and intentions in those actions we undertake can sometimes prove to be overly constrained as a result of their merely following after certain conventions, rules, obligations, and duties.

Sometimes, however, certain moral situations may require fuller responses that open out more freely onto the domain not just of the moral but also of the ethical, not just of the obligatory but also onto that of the ideal. In such situations one may perhaps speak of someone emancipating someone else from responding on the bases of moral constraints only in behalf of rendering them capable of being able to respond also on the bases of ethical ideals as well.

After our reflection on Montale's poetic representations of moral motivations in the previous chapter, we may now pursue some further reflections on Montale's poetic representations of ethical emancipation. That is, we will start with the provisional idea that some moral motivations may succeed in freeing some persons from, say, undue moral constraints with sometimes the further effect of freeing them for, say, a greater responsiveness to certain ethical ideals.

Metaphysically Reasonable Readings

After having already considered in first readings of Montale just what makes an interpretation epistemically rational, we may now consider the idea that makes an interpretation metaphysical is its incorporating a more than merely procedural and instrumental idea of reason, a substantive and regulative idea of reason as well. And in some but certainly not all cases of interpretation, as here with the interpretation of Montale's poetic representations of an abstract suffering in the poems of *Ossi di seppia*, a more than merely epistemic interpretation, a metaphysical interpretation is required in order to address adequately the fact of a choice being required among competing goals for the interpretation.

What exposes the need to consider something other than the usual goals of explicating or elucidating a poem by the selection of appropriate means is the requirement that the interpretation must render a definite account of something presented as indefinite. That requirement appears when whatever the poem is about on some plausible construal remains essentially indeterminate.

Alternative aims for interpretation, besides the elucidation of the poem and thereby making explicit or discovering the subject, are constructive. Thus, the interpreter may have to construct the poem's subject. For in some cases, such as interpreting the subject of the poetry of suffering, that ambiguous subject of the poem may very well be a void and the nothingness that can have no definite, determinate content prior to its receiving one in an interpretation itself – "nothingness at my shoulders, the void behind me."

Consider two central ideas. The first is that an interpretation of much of Montale's European high modernist poetry of suffering, and of so much poetry like it, requires the exercise of a substantive and regulative understanding of reason. This understanding is necessary for determining, however provisionally, an alternative goal to the otherwise standard interpretive goals of explication and elucidation that turn on the exercise of procedural and instrumental understandings of rationality. And second, determining a plausible alternative goal for interpretation here in the case of the European high modernist poetry of suffering requires filling out the void that the poem seems to be about with the help of Kant's reflections on the discipline of reason.

In terms of these two issues, then, we may choose to construe some rational interpretation not so much in terms of explication and elucidation but in those of conceptualization and construction. More simply, some interpretation is rational in that, by incorporating a substantive and regulative understanding of reason, the interpretation is a rendering and not just an elucidation.

As we have seen in the details of Montale's work, many of his poems present complex situations whose core remains indeterminate. For despite our capacities to explicate and to elucidate many aspects of those situations, at least two absolutely essential elements usually remain unarticulated. Neither the nature of the speaking subject nor the subject of his central discourse is addressed explicitly enough.

Moreover, it is not a question of simply amending the interpretation to include what has been left out. For much of the poetry presents nothing definite or determinate enough that would accommodate mere explication and elucidation alone. Whatever means those standard goals usually rely on, whether careful paraphrase, or contextual considerations, or linguistic analyses, or rhetorical scrutiny, or whatever, are irrelevant. What the poetry is often about is essentially incomplete. And once the indeterminate character of an essential aspect of this poetry is grasped, then the effective choice of means must wait upon reconsideration of just what goals are to be entertained in place of the customary but now provisionally suspended ones of explication and elucidation.

Choosing new goals, however, requires the exercise of a very different set of intellectual capacities than exclusively procedural and instrumental reasoning. For the goals of a reasonable interpretation of poetry like Montale's, where so much seems to turn on comprehending such things as the possibility of a *varco* arising from a void both within and without, requires conceiving of other goals than the customary ones. The void that in some obscure sense is both the speaking subject and the subject spoken about cannot be simply explicated and elucidated. The void rather must be conceptualized and in some strong sense constructed. Such operations however call for a substantive and regulative understanding and exercise of reason and not just a functional one.

But how are we to construe this very general kind of talk in such a concrete context as Montale's poetry of an abstract suffering? Without making any claims as to actual influence on Montale or on other instances of the European high modernist poetry of suffering, we do well to pursue here Montale's own earlier interests in Kantian ideals and Kantian reason. We should not overlook the fact that, from his childhood on, Montale had a largely autodidact's fascination with philosophical issues, a fascination that his elder sister, herself a student of philosophy, ceaselessly encouraged.

In his pre-critical work, the *Observations on the Feeling of the Beautiful and the Sublime* (1764), Kant distinguished three kinds of sublime (*das Erhabene*).[216] The sublime is, Kant writes, "of different kinds. Its feeling is sometimes accompanied with a certain dread, or melancholy; in some cases with quiet wonder; and in still others with a beauty completely pervading a sublime plan. The first I call the terrifying sublime, the second the noble, and the third the splendid."[217] Kant adds that whatever its kinds the sublime "must always be great (...) [and] simple" (48).

If we remain for the moment with this pre-Critical tripartite division of the sublime, as opposed to the much later double division of the sublime into the mathematical and the dynamical in Kant's 1790 *Critique of Judgment*, how can we initially characterize the void we find so often not just in Montale's poetry but in that of Rilke, Eliot, Valéry, and others?

This void is centrally represented as great and simple, Moreover, there is something terrifying about it that corresponds to Kant's reference to a celebrated eighteenth-century description of eternity (Kant cites A. von Haller's *Ueber die Ewigkeit* 1736) as stimulating a kind of "mild horror" (50). But there is as well something of the noble about the apprehension of the void that corresponds to another of Kant's examples, namely "a description of complete loneliness" in a short story in the *Bremen Magazine* of the time that Kant says inspires a "noble awe."

The passage Kant cites reads: "I saw the Angel of Death come over me like a whirlwind. He struck me before I could plead to be spared his terrible stroke. I was petrified, as I perceived that my destiny throughout eternity was cast, and that to all the good I had done nothing could be added, and from all the evil I had committed, not a thing could be taken away" (48, Kant's note).

This image is indeed great, simple, and terrifying – even awesomely noble – think of the German modernist sculptural work of Ernst Barlach's avenging angel, "Die Rache." Of course we could go on to try to nuance this initial determination of the void as an instance of the sublime in both its terrifying and noble aspects, notably by specifying the nature of that experience for the interpretive reader with the help of the extraordinary discussions of the sublime in the *Critique of Judgment*. But our concern is not with the void as such. Rather, we are reflecting on just what understandings of reason are at work when reflective interpreters impute to central yet indeterminate places in the literary work of art implicit contents about something so elusive as, in its proper Kantian senses, the sublime.

If, as interpreters, we say that Montale's nothingness elicits the *varco* ideal as the negative sublime in its guise as both the terrifying and the noble, I think we are by that very determination of what the poem presents as indeterminate both positing the contents of our interpretation, its subject, and simultaneously positing ourselves as interpreters, its interpretative subjects.

In these contexts, however, talk of "positing" is no longer very familiar.[218] In a pre-critical work he wrote just one year before his first work in aesthetics, *The One Possible Basis for a Demonstration of God's Existence* (1763), Kant explains that positing is identical with being in general or existence.[219] And being or existence can be expressed either relatively or absolutely depending on whether being is expressed in the case of a judgment, "x is p," or in that of an existential proposition, "x is (exists)." In the first case a predicate is said to be posited with respect to a subject – the predicate is posited relatively. In the second case, "the thing itself," Kant writes, "together with all its predicates, is posited absolutely" (74).

At the end of his career, working on the *Opus postumum* shortly after 1801, Kant elaborates the notion of positing once again, but this time in the difficult and unfinished terms of his doctrine of the subject's self-positing (the *Selbstsetzungslehre*). This doctrine has to do with how the subject "makes itself into an object of experience."[220]

Kant's complete doctrine here, despite misguided attempts to link Kant's reflections with Fichte, in fact reaches back to passages in the *Critique of Pure Reason* (the First Critique), for example, Kant's claim in the "B" version of the transcendental deduction there that "the 'I think' expresses the act of determining my existence" (B 158 a). Later, in the "Paralogism of Pure Reason" in the First Critique, Kant refines the notion of positing with respect to the proposition "I think" (B 420 ff). He writes, for example, "the 'I think' precedes the experience which is required to determine the object of perception" (B 423).

One of the commentators on Kant's doctrine of self-positing writes that, for the later Kant, "knowledge of my own existence can only consist in the thoroughgoing determination of the given manifold, and in the positing of a certain set of representations, united under the concept of the empirical self, as outside the concept."[221] "Outside the concept" because when it is a matter of thinking its concept, the object is not thought in connection with its conformity to what Kant calls in the First Critique, the universal condition of possible empirical knowledge in general," but with respect to the object's "belonging to the context of experience as a whole."[222]

Now if we move from talk of the "I think" to a supposition of the subject's self-positing in the "I interpret," then Kant's mature reflections here come to an extraordinary focus on the substantive and regulative aspects of reason. We can see the point if we keep in mind our central concerns with rational interpretation of the European high modernist poetry of suffering of Montale when we explore briefly Kant's claim in the First Critique that "the synthetic unity of apperception is (...) the highest point to which we must ascribe all employment of the understanding" (B 134).

Before refining these initial ideas, however, we need to get a fuller understanding of just what the object of interpretation is in this still rather vague talk of varco as both passage and breakthrough. That is, we need to return to the linguistic and conceptual richness of Montale's poetry.

A Double Transcendence

Consider then briefly another of the central poems in a major chord of Montale's *Ossi di seppia*, a collection Montale organized in musically thematic rather than in just chronological ways. And consider as well what could satisfactorily account for the reasonableness of one of its most informed interpretations.

> Don't take shelter in the shade
> of that green thicket,
> like the windhover swooping, streak
> of lightening in summer heat.
> Time now to quit the canebrake
> stricken as though with sleep
> and gaze at the forms of a life
> that powders away.
>
> We pass in a shimmer of dust,
> mother-of-pearl, a glare
> that ensnares the eyes,
> undoing us nearly.

Still, you sense it, in these dry waves
lazing in this hour of distress
let's not throw our strayed lives
to a bottomless abyss.

Like those enclosing cliffs
that seem to fray
in a webbing of haze,
so our charred souls

where illusion burns
in a flare of ash
vanish in the bright air
of one certainty: light.[223]

When situated in the thematic movements of Montale's suite of poems, William Arrowsmith believes this lyric, "Non rifugiarti nell'ombra," is about "aspiration towards *varco*," aspiration towards "breakthrough" or "passage" (201). In particular, he interprets the lyric as an exhortation addressed both to someone or something figured as a small falcon and to himself. And the burden of the exhortation is to overcome the inertia, security, and timidity of the shady world below, and to dare, in the clarity of the bright air above, the sunny light, to "gaze [*girardare*] at the forms of a life / that powders away [*si sgretola*]" (201).

Central to this interpretation is the notion of a double transcendence, a complex movement of positive and negative, upwards and downwards. The movement is first upwards towards a Dantesque spiritual light, an ascension beyond the impermanence of life to the eternity of the inward forms of life. The white light of the noonday Mediterranean sun dissolves the shadows of the outward forms of things to leave open the possibility of a vision into the inner form of things.

Arrowsmith interprets the poem as beginning "with a typically Montalean negative, but it is one that contains a strong, not merely wistful, positive imperative. Thus in the first stanza the poem's '*tu*' is adjured not to abandon her natural domain. (...) By the last stanza, however, this injunction becomes not merely a passionate yearning for *varco* but a momentary illusion of *varco* almost achieved" (202). Arrowsmith takes this momentary illusion as the "soaring imagination['s]" glimpse of a positive transcendence, of a "shared life (...) lived at peak intensity" (202).

Besides this passage (*varco)* upwards, this ascension towards the possibility of a positive transcendence, the poem also presents the idea of a passage downwards, a descent towards a negative transcendence. The crucial images here are those of the "bottomless abyss." And the key connotations arise from the resonant Italian word, "*randage*" (but not, as Arrowsmith points out, from its English translation, "stray") of lonely and futile errancy. "Transcendence," Arrowsmith offers, "is negative as well as positive. *Varco* is a 'passage' that leads down as well as up" (202).

Finally, on the evidence in the fourth stanza strongly suggesting that the speaker in the poem decides on directing his aspiration upwards towards the light of the inner forms of things instead of downwards towards their dark annihilation, Arrowsmith proposes a very different reading. The basis of this alternative is presumably what Arrowsmith understands from the rest of Montale's work, not just in *Ossi di seppia* but in the poetry as a whole.

That understanding is comprehensive. For before his death in 1992 Arrowsmith succeeded in translating, although not publishing, all of the work Montale himself had arranged and published in book form. What then is the only indirectly supported conclusion of Montale's double transcendence?

"Ultimately of course," Arrowsmith writes, "either form of transcendence is [for Montale] destructive, since, for Montale, we become, and remain, human only by enduring the conflicting claims made upon the psyche by the two warring transcendental extremes." (203). More explicitly, Montale's poetry can be reasonably interpreted as endorsing neither a positive nor a negative transcendence. For each kind of transcendence is mortal. "If the 'death' implicit in downward transcendence is obvious enough, it is equally present in its upward form."

Arrowsmith concludes by citing Montale's prose to support this latter claim that positive transcendence is also mortal, that 'death' is just as present there as in negative transcendence. Montale writes: "The transcendental 'I' is light that illuminated only a very small space in front of us, a light that carries us towards a non-individual, and therefore nonhuman, condition" (cited on p. 203).

We find here in Arrowsmith's interpretation of "Non rifugiarti nell'ombra" a complex, richly evidential, and eminently plausible interpretation of a difficult European high modernist lyric of an abstract perhaps even spiritual suffering. Suppose once again, however, as we did earlier with Calvino's interpretation, we narrow the scope of Arrowsmith's interpretation and for our purposes restrict the interpretation to the following representative set of propositions.

Montale's "beautifully crafted lyric of aspiration towards *varco* ('breakthrough' or 'passage') varies and widens the intricating [*sic*] themes of the suite [of poems, *Rottami*] (...) By the last stanza, however, this injunction [*i.e.*, the negative imperative in the first stanza] becomes (...) a momentary illusion of *varco* almost achieved. For an astonishing instant, the soaring imagination catches a glimpse of the miracle – that transcendence that, for Montale, occurs only when shared life is lived at peak intensity. (...) But transcendence is negative as well as positive. (...) Ultimately of course either form of transcendence is destructive, since, for Montale, we become, and remain, human only by enduring the conflicting claims made upon the psyche by the two warring transcendental extremes" (201–203).

The question now is under just what construal of rational interpretation in terms of both goals and means can we account for not just the rationality but also the reasonableness of Arrowsmith's interpretation.

Representing the Ethical

In 1925, not long after publishing his still influential essay on "Style and Tradition" and after signing Benedetto Croce's reply to the "Manifesto of Fascist Intellectuals," Montale, we noted earlier, published his *Ossi di seppia*.[224] The carefully composed book of poems, with its several lyrical suites juxtaposed with individual lyrics, seemed to refer, in sumptuous fictional representations, to something like the Ligurian seascapes of Montale's youthful vacations south of Genoa at Monterosso, the landscapes that so affected Paul Valéry as well.

But this impression of a studied representational artistry was not unambiguous. Formally taking its distance from the mellifluous rhythms of D'Annunzio while retrieving Dante's harsh and strong rhymes, the "*rime aspre*" of the *Inferno* and the earlier "*rime petrose*" of the four Lady Pietra *Canzone*, *Ossi di seppia* began a critical exploration of European high modernism and its perduring legacies that would persist throughout Montale's long life and work.

Much of that exploration centred on the fractious relations, freshly controversial in our post-modern era today, between poetry and life, interpretation and reason. More centrally, Montale's finest poetry sought to articulate a profound yet obscure sense of a great and abstract suffering, the deep pathos of things and of ourselves.

Although sharing with Croce an antifascist insistence on a separation between politics and art, Montale challenged Croce's partly prescient but sinister views of modernism as a species of cultural nationalism, a preparation for Fascism. Instead, working against the attractions of the regional Ligurian poetry of even his poet friend, Camillo Sbarbaro, and finally leaving the marine seascapes of Liguria for Florence's "*terra firma* of ideas, tradition, humanism," Montale insisted on the cosmopolitan, European character of modernism.[225]

This larger understanding of modernism, on view in both the poetry and the extensive prose of Montale as well as in the give and take with the avant-garde of his times[226] – the structures of Debussy's piano preludes, the characterizations in the novels of Italo Svevo, the etchings of Giorgio Morandi, and the plays of Pirandello – is what we need to recall as we try to develop second thoughts about Montale's moral intuitions and his European high modernist poetry of suffering.

The suggestion here is that our cultural situations today, however diverse whether in Europe, North America, and Japan, call surprisingly for renewed and thoughtful attention to the conceptual resources of a now quite unfashionable understanding of critically reflective interpretation centred on the inescapably demanding interactions between art, life, and reason.

Mimetic Re-enactments

Much of the excellent historical and sociological work that is continuing to change our understanding of both the modern and post-modern eras shows that Europeans and perhaps others still share today the residual social, cultural, and historical elements of the privileged moments of high modernism in the arts. For even in the post-modern critical and artistic strategies that now clamour for all our attention, European high modernism must be presupposed as a foil, a contrast.

Yet we hesitate to consider literary works of art today in any strongly representative vein; we hesitate to interpret the poetry of Montale's *Ossi di seppia*, Eliot's *The Waste Land*, and even Valéry's poetic prose representations in his voluminous *Cahiers*, with our own lives and communities in view. We hesitate for fear of succumbing to some strain of a supposedly naive aesthetic and moral realism, of moral truths arising from the nature of things rather than from human beings.

Whatever may be at issue in such work as *Ossi di seppia*, we have learned to say often (but not always) in an instrumental, relativistic, and self-reflexive post-modern vein, whatever the visions of those interactive dissolutions between the physical and the metaphysical, "the stretching out of the rocks," "the suffering of the stones," such work, intelligent people keep telling us, creates its own inviolable space. Poetry, just like any substantial achievement in the arts, can teach no one any lessons after Auschwitz.

Poetry neither offers nor exacts thoughtful reflection. Enough, we keep saying, that such work shine forth intermittently in its occasional perfection, in its "quiet equilibrium," reflecting no more than "bright arid seas," endlessly representing and referring to nothing other than itself.

Yet to construe Montale's poetry, or any work of art in no other than its own self-referential and formalist terms in such a minimalist post-modern spirit, is to violate not only that distance between politics, morals, and literature on which both Montale and Croce insisted mistakenly. It is also to forego the rich linguistic and conceptual resources of a mimetic reflection on moral discourse, perception, motivation, and emancipation. Such a mimetic reflection comprises a set of critical practices that, classically after Aristotle, construes poetry and works of art generally as indeed more philosophical than history. For some poetry may make something like universals manifest by enacting exemplary representations of actual situations such as those we face today in the new Europe.

Moreover, some of these representative enactments can, in ways that today we may be losing the interest, attentiveness, and sustained concentration to fathom, properly refer beyond themselves. At times, such representative enactments may be, as perhaps we have glimpsed here and there in this essay, profoundly ethical.

For far from always functioning instrumentally for achieving certain private and fugitive satisfactions, some poetic representations of speech and action as those on view in much of the European high modernist poetry of suffering may set up imaginative, strongly cognitive, and social explorations of alternative ethical goals and their possible consequences in the minds of readers and interpreters.

The Disappearing World

Recall another of the disparate voices of *Ossi di seppia*, "Forse un mattino (...)". (1923). With these reflections as backgrounds, consider briefly its peculiar evocations and the issues that arise from trying to account for the reasonableness of such an interpretation.

> Perhaps one morning while going along in the air of glass,
> arid, looking back, I shall see, with the terror
> of a drunken man, the making of a miracle:
> nothingness at my shoulders, the void behind me.
>
> Then as on a screen, suddenly, trees houses hills
> will assemble themselves for the usual deception.
> But it will be too late; and I shall go on, quiet,
> with my secret, among the men who do not turn.[227]

Since several of the nuances here are important for our interpretation, consider a more recent version of the same poem.

> Maybe one morning, walking in air
> of dry glass, I'll turn and see the miracle occur –
> nothingness at my shoulders, the void
> behind me – with a drunkard's terror.
>
> Then, as on a screen, the usual illusion:
> hills houses trees will suddenly reassemble,
> but too late, and I'll quietly go my way,
> with my secret, among men who don't look back.[228]

This is a sobering voice, subtle with its ironies and allusions, a voice that for all the familiarities of its modernist images of movie screens and wasteland cityscapes insists on a careful hearing.

The poet represents the speaker as musing, in one of the late Jamesian inner monologues Montale admired, about some future enlightenment, a negative epiphany. The speaker imagines the possibility of his miraculously seeing, while taking an ordinary morning walk, not just what is in front of his eyes but what stands invisible both at his shoulders and behind his back.

This impossible circumspection will change the speaker's perception of things and the world in such a way that, henceforth, despite the resumption of his normal everyday perceptions, he will possess unlike other people the secret that the reality of things and the world itself is actually a real fiction. Coming to such a realisation, however, will fill the speaker with terror, a terror as in the drunkard's apprehensive ruminations, of the loss of reason.[229]

Such a speculative paraphrase of course does an injustice to many of the salient features of this poem – its calculated place in a meticulously articulated book, the deliberateness of its metrics and rime schemes, the calibrations of its assonances and dissonances, its studied interconnections with other poems that explore similar images, metaphors, and themes, and especially the peculiarly remote significance of its major and abstract concerns with perception, knowledge, and reason.

Montale's work, as his celebrated English translator has written, is "instinctively, unconsciously philosophical and, like the Italian mind generally in the first half of the century, suffused, often unawares, with Crocean idealism, saturated in its categories of thought."[230] Any reasonably satisfactory attempt at interpretation of such work needs to bring the philosophical aspects of this poem into focus.

This mimetic reflection, incorporating strong claims about poetry's capacities to represent and to refer to more than itself, to imply real and not just fictional authors, to exhibit some determinate, stable, and decidable meanings, to allow evaluative and not merely descriptive criticism, even to manifest genuine pathos – this is the view that continues to suffer neglect and even denigration today in much recent, powerful, and influential post-modern work – work inspired by linguistic formalisms, varieties of post-structuralism, strains of deconstruction, cultural criticism, Lacanian inspired re-appropriations of Freud, and so on – work at the very centre of post-modernism and literature.

But whatever the genuine merits of these other reflective strategies – and they are many although they still require fresh and thorough assessment – perhaps we have done mimetic thinking about the literary arts an injustice. Perhaps in a time of historical, cultural and even social disarray, we have not been attentive enough to the voices in such works as Montale's *Ossi di seppia*, voices that may resonate even today in our still perplexing interactions with the suffering in many persons' lives.

Part of that inattention arises from certain unexamined strains in post-modernist relations with literature. And one of the most important of such tensions is the constrained and unduly restrictive understanding of reason and rationality that often leads to post-modernist attacks on the representational and referential powers of some literary works of art.

Montale on Moral Motivations: Second Thoughts

Before recapitulating some of the issues here in our return to the very idea of modernity in our next chapter, we may pull together here some of these further reflections on moral motivation, ethical emancipation, and Montale's poetic representations of abstract suffering. Perhaps we may take this first set of second thoughts as the first of our tentative conclusions about moral intuitionism in the European high modernist poetry of suffering and emancipation.

(C1) Much of Montale's high modernist poetry of an abstract personal suffering may not improperly be understood as offering in part poetic representations of patterns of belief, desire, and intentions that continue to structure much moral motivation even today.

(C2) Some of these poetic representations of moral motivation would seem to call attention to certain moral situations where ordinary life is unduly constrained by the immanent demands of everyday moral norms, obligations, duties, and constraints.

(C3) Other of these poetic representations would seem to present images of release from such undue restraints.

(C4) Moreover, sometimes some of Montale's high modernist poetic representations of suffering appear to offer reflective persons today fictional characterisations of characters who propose to emancipate others from certain unduly restrictive immanent moral constraints so as to be capable of aspiring towards the realization of some partly transcendent ethical ideals.

(C5) That is, some distinguished instances of the European high modernist poetry of suffering offer reflective persons today in Europe a novel perspective on the nature of both moral motivation and ethical emancipation that may sometimes open out onto both moral intuitions into external objective moral values and also onto the necessity of achieving freedom for responding not just to moral norms only but to ethical ideals as well.

CHAPTER SIX

Valéry and the Visual Perception of Suffering

We need now to return for second thoughts to Paul Valéry's richly nuanced poetic meditations on worlds, bodies, and minds with a view to concluding with some further formulations about the nature of ethical intuitions and moral knowledge.

Moral Intuitions and the World

Whether or not there is a satisfactory philosophical criterion for identifying competent moral observers, as we were discussing among other things in our first readings of Valéry, and whether or not there is a distinct species of perception that is moral as opposed to all perception being empirical,[231] we need to look more closely at more of Valéry's work. Our plan is to examine such less familiar materials to try to get a better understanding of just what we are talking about when we talk about moral sentiments, moral feelings, moral intuitions, and even so-called "moral perceptions."[232] Are all such matters to be understood exclusively as moral contents?[233]

In what follows we will proceed on the assumption that what some moral epistemologists today call moral perception may be taken for our specific purposes here as very closely related to moral intuitions.[234] And for a rough working hypothesis, let us proceed with the idea that several of the European high modernist poetic representations of apparently moral perceptions in the extraordinary notebooks of Paul Valéry provide reflective persons even today with challenging ethical materials for reflection. These materials, moreover, are usually of a broader scope as well as articulated with more suggestive linguistic and conceptual richness for rethinking our ethical situations in Europe today than the much plainer texts and examples that moral philosophers all too often unduly restrict themselves to examining.

On one of many occasions when Valéry speaks of Mallarmé, his "*maître*," Valéry writes: "I saw Stéphane Mallarmé for the last time on July 14, 1898 at Valrins. After lunch he brought me to his 'office' – four steps long, two wide, with a window open onto the Seine, and the forest beyond the foliage completely torn with light, and the slightest tremblings of the shining river reverberating [*redits*] weakly on the walls."[235]

The conjunction of work and world in this passage is less important than the suggestion of a mysterious collaboration between the two. "*Redits*," says Valéry, "re-spoken," "re-said," as if the world is speaking a language of its own – as if a language of the world occasionally sets up an echo in the human milieu, in the work room, in the poet's study, in his listening, in his repetitions.

And towards the end of the same privileged text where Valéry celebrates both the master poet Mallarmé and poetry itself, the suggestions of the world's profuse vitality are filled out at length. "We went to the countryside. The 'artificial' poet picked the simplest flowers. We loaded our arms with cornflowers and poppies. The air was on fire; the splendour absolute, the silence full of dizziness and exchanges, death impossible or indifferent, everything formidably beautiful, burning and sleeping, and the images on the earth trembling. In the sun, in the immense form of the pure sky, I was dreaming of an incandescent circle where nothing distinct subsisted, where nothing endured, but where nothing was passing away either as if destruction itself, barely accomplished, was destroying itself. I lost the feeling of the difference between being and non-being."[236]

The "exchanges" that fill the silence of this extraordinarily rendered scene – a prose poem of European high modernist literary art – are ambiguous. They refer to the communion between two poets like that between a father and a son. And they also refer to the resonances between each of the poets and the physical world. This second set of exchanges is reinforced once again by the suggestion of slight movements in the air, the shimmering phenomena of a country day irradiated and finally evanescent with a burning, a blazing sunlight.[237]

The physical world for Valéry, then, is not just a world full of movement; these movements themselves may seem at times to speak. Their occasional sounds seem here to address the poet as if the rustling of flowers and water were voices.

This picture of course is impressionistic in the painterly sense.[238] But the impressionism here – with the intimations of death, of indeterminacy, of eternal return, of transmutation, of silence – this impressionism is a post-impressionism. The naivety of catching the physical world in the play of a new optics and a fuller understanding of perception is already too self-conscious. And the "Dernière visite à Mallarmé" both anticipates a leave-taking from a Newtonian world already questioned in Valéry's readings of Maxwell, of Faraday, soon of Cantor, and later of Einstein.[239]

This vibrant and resonant image of the physical world recurs throughout Valéry's work as it also does in that of Montale. The sea in Italy in 1877, for example.[240] Or the ecstatic passages in the *Dialogues*, especially in "Eupalinos" when Socrates is speaking. And there are the quick unstudied jottings in the personal notes, for example in Spain in 1924 near the Escorial.[241] Here, to close the circle and to echo the familiar theory, world imitates art.

Valéry rarely tried to move beyond these descriptions of world. Though at times he speculates on the fullness and superabundance of the world – its density, its resistance to order, its irregularities, its resistance to any understanding of physical laws as more than conventions – Valéry is consistently skeptical about the value of theories in this domain. He nourishes his interest in the physical world with careful but finally amateur studies in the mathematics and the new sciences of his time.

Later in life he frequents a number of laboratories. He listens patiently and with genuine interest to the explanations of experiments. He concerns himself with the scientific details not just of sensation and, interestingly, of perception but of physiology as a whole. But throughout these continued enthusiasms Valéry remains faithful to his initial doubts which he now extends beyond abstract matters to empirical matters as well.

This resistance to theory accounts for Valéry's refusal to think of "the world" in philosophical terms such as "real" or "existence" or "being."[242] Valéry criticizes these terms in several places, especially in *Cahiers* 19. "The words 'exist' or 'being' are vague," he writes, "[the expression] 'I am' without any attribute makes no sense" (19: 538).[243] In another text much earlier he writes: "deification of the verb, 'to be,' there you have the half of philosophy" (11: 810).

And, as a critic points out, Valéry entertains the same suspicions about the word "real."[244] The word makes sense only when used in definite contexts but never when used alone. "The word 'real' is defined each time by its context," Valéry writes (11: 403). And elsewhere: "(...) 'real' has no meaning" (9.553) The consequence is that such an abstract idea is useless. "We have no need for a general notion of 'real,' etc. (...) which corresponds to nothing more than a scholarly and dialectical demand" (20.16).

When such terms are used concretely, however, Valéry construes their referents as indications of a peculiar inexhaustibility in the world. This excess – and this is a point especially important for our concerns with capturing more fully the nature of moral knowledge arising from intuitions – both saturates sensation and overflows the perceptive processes. At least in this guise, the world is always something other; it is more than we can sense and perceive. "The idea or the will hidden in the notion of reality," Valéry writes, "is this: there is something more in every real thing that even the sharpest and fullest perception can do nothing but make more elusive. And therefore the vicissitudes of perception change nothing about the *quid*. No perception can exhaust it" (11.188).

Thus, Valéry construes the world largely by contrast with what can be known, strictly speaking. The world is an inexhaustible and fugitive fullness of movement and solicitation. Whatever we can come to know of this world is always incomplete. "At dawn," Valéry writes in 1927 at Grasse, "the cypress offers itself. This golden house appears – what is it doing? It is constructing itself at each instant" (12.189).

Some philosophers such as the phenomenologists, Brentano, Max Scheler, Dietrich von Hildebrand, and Paul Ricoeur, have held similar views about the quite specific manners in which values and especially moral values present themselves to perception and intuition. They present themselves, say, perhaps more abundantly as Valéry does here: that is, moral and ethical values may offer themselves to our intuitive capacities in some of the ways the cypress tree offers itself to our visual capacities. But can we also say with Valéry that moral and ethical values construct themselves at every instant in our morally intuitive grasping of them? Or may we understand such constructions in terms of the ways in which such values offer themselves to us rather than in the nature of the values themselves? Are what we may be said to grasp in moral intuition, say the self-presentations of moral and ethical values, real?

After these reflections on the world, consider finally for now several of Valéry's further reflections on the second cardinal element of his trinity, the body.

The Four Bodies

What we refer to when we speak to other persons say physicians of our bodies we refer to as "my body." Although we are accustomed to speak of the body as if it were a thing, it is evident that a person's body cannot be a thing in the sense in which, say, the body of an animal is a thing. For this "thing" belongs to us in a distinctive way; "it belongs to us a little bit less," Valéry writes cryptically, "than we belong to it."[245]

Neither is "my body" properly characterizable as an object. Nor as an event. Nor can the body's spatial location be perceived unambiguously. Nor can its temporal qualities, especially its postures. This body then, "my body" as Valéry insists, is never completely at our disposal; it is only partly available. The body "obeys or disobeys, accomplishes or hinders our plans. Our strengths and surprising weaknesses come from the body. They are linked with that more or less sensitive mass, as a whole or in part, that sometimes charges itself bruskly with impulsive energies that make it 'act' in virtue of who knows what interior mystery, and that sometimes seems to divine within itself the most burdensome and most unchangeable weight."[246]

Besides this mysterious sense of "my body" there is also what we might call "the other's body," my body as seen by others. Of course I also see my body – directly as well as indirectly in portraits, in mirrors, even in still waters as Narcissus does.[247] But Valéry wants to claim that the body I see is not the body I am. The former is surface only, and exterior; it can exist for the eye alone. The latter is surface and depth, an exterior and an interior; it exists even for the blind.

My smile achieves its distinctive form in "the other's body" but my pain arches its back in my body alone. The other's body then "(...) is the one that has a form and that the arts apprehend, the one on which fabrics, costumes, and woven textiles ajust themselves. This body is the one that sees love or that wants to see love, anxious to touch love. It knows no suffering; [in the face of suffering] it makes merely a grimace."[248]

But talk of an interior here is ambiguous. For we easily confuse bodily states with bodily parts, brain phenomena with mental phenomena. Accordingly, Valéry insists on a third body, call it "the scientists' body," the body of the liver, the kidneys, the heart. We can know this body only through direct observation, dissection, and all the machinery of the medical sciences. The scientists' body is the body of Descartes, Newton, Harvey, Gilbert, and Claude Bernard.[249]

Finally, Valéry suggests a fourth sense, what we might call "the imaginary body," although Valéry himself remarks with his usual skepticism that the expression "the real body" would do just as well. Valéry develops this notion from speculation on several problems with the idea of "the scientists' body." Take the case of pain. Does the scientists' body experience pain? Is pain a brain phenomenon and hence a subject of neuro-physiological observation either now or in the future? Or is pain a brain state at all?

Such familiar questions today are traditionally philosophers' questions. They seem to have no other claim on our attention other than their curious property of being perennial – questions philosophers and no one else either know how to answer. But, Valéry asks, were someone to know how to answer such philosophical questions about mind and body, exactly what would he or she have to know? "I call 'the fourth body,' " Valéry replies, "the unknowable object whose knowledge would resolve in one sweep all problems because these problems imply [this object]."[250] The fourth sense of the word "body" then, what Valéry calls "the imaginary body," is an idea we would require to solve mind-body problems which neither the movements of the first kind of body nor the shapes of the second nor the quantities of the third address.

Thus, the fourth body is one of those things for which we lack words and yet which may exist. It is a theoretical entity this "imaginary body," but of a special sort. For as a skeptic Valéry holds that, whatever the progress of our sciences, whether such a body exists cannot be known.[251] But if this is the case for the "imaginary body," what of the case of consciousness?

Consciousness and The Mind

"The mind," Valéry writes, "is at the mercy of the body. (...) Our true lights emanate from the body."[252]

For our purposes several aspects only of mind require some description here. We may begin by glossing Valéry's word "*esprit*" provisionally in English as "consciousness" instead of "mind" or "spirit," and proceed by noting four of its characteristics.[253]

Like world, consciousness for Valéry first of all is a whole.[254] Accordingly, consciousness is multiple, a variety of separate activities, each caught up in the play of order and disorder.[255]

But, as the same passage suggests, consciousness is also a ceaseless activity, a play therefore not just of various dispositions, capacities and powers, but a constant play. At one point, in the "Introduction to the Method of Leonardo da Vinci," Valéry writes: "The human characteristic is consciousness; the characteristic of consciousness is a process of perpetual exhaustion, of detachment without rest or exclusion from everything that comes before it, whatever that thing might be – an inexhaustible activity, independent of the quality as of the quantity of things which appear and by means of which the man of intellect must at last bring himself deliberately to an unqualified refusal to be anything whatsoever."[256]

For the activity of consciousness is not only incessant; it is also circular. Nietzsche appears here as elsewhere in Valéry's work, especially in the dramatic figure of Valéry's Faust in his unfinished play.[257] And, to dramatize this idea of the circularity of consciousness, Valéry takes his reflection a step or two further. "I am inclined to believe," he writes, "that a person who lived a very long time would, at the end of his round, provided that he was in such a condition that his thinking would remain rather active, take the measure of his feelings and, having finally adored and burned, burned and adored everything that deserved to exist in the sphere of his knowledge, die with a sense of completion."[258] For Valéry consciousness must come full circle.

The sketch we have so far then is of a differentiated set of various mental activities achieving ultimately an intermittent unity in an endless circle. There is as yet no representation of anything like moral intuition.

Perhaps a mechanical image would help here – one from hydraulics. But despite Valéry's penchant for such figures and his fascination with the drawings of Leonardo, none is forthcoming.[259] Instead, Valéry draws a consequence. Because it is ceaseless movement, Valéry argues, consciousness cannot have any perduring object. Thus, the "man of intellect" who refuses to be anything whatsoever as Valéry hints earlier, can be taken as conforming himself to a central element of his own consciousness, its lack of any perduring object.

But Valéry's skepticism must be pushed farther. For we catch a glimpse here of something more radical, Valéry's nihilism.[260] Perhaps we may even use a critic's comment as a rough summary of Valéry's notion of consciousness. "Valéry's nihilism is a nihilism before which nothing ceases to pass, but one which seems to be able to make contact with each one of these things only by means of the same process with which it detaches itself. (...) The spectacle is of a sadness so vast and so general in its causes that it reaches an inhuman purity. In the intellectual order there is no tragedy so unjust than that of the faculty of thought itself arriving by its own acuity at nothingness and at its own self-annhilation."[261]

Mind then, rooted in the body like a copse of cypress trees in the sailors' cemetery at Sète where Valéry insisted on being buried and where today a museum celebrates his life and work, is not one thing. Mind for Valéry is many activities moving ceaselessly in what would be an endless repetition were we circumspect enough to grasp it. Yet mind is also many activities coalescing here and there in self-conscious moments only to dissolve instantaneously before any perduring object can assume more than a momentary form. This is the mind that through body only is opened out into a world that forever surpasses it.

Perhaps some of these images of the ceaselessly moving mind's occasional moments of coalescence especially about such intensely experienced moral matters as Valéry's own intellectual and affective insufficiencies could be taken as images for those momentary stays against confusion we sometimes refer to as moral intuitions? We will have to explore that possibility in our next section.

For now, we have before us world, body, mind – a whole if not the whole – each element with its dark side which no observation can ever attain – the fullness of the world, the imaginary body, and the possible object of self-consciousness. This is the general intellectual landscape in which Valéry sets the movement of his own poetry and poetics.

Desires and Mental Acts

Whatever qualifications may be required for Valéry's discussion of world, body, and mind, we need to explore Valéry's work especially on mind, consciousness, and desire. Consider briefly just one of these themes in more detail, the obscure notion of desire.

To begin, recall two points. First, Valéry as we noted is shaken early in his creative life by the experience of no longer being master of himself. This experience is provoked by his encounter with the Montpellieraine, the woman who continued to exercise a strange power over his imagination for some time. The biographical context thus provides some fullness to what the word "desire" refers here.

Second, Valéry makes a striking conceptual point in his 1920 "Avant propos." Speaking of the poetic ideal of the symbolist poets he writes: "One might think first off that we were the simple victims of a spiritual illusion. (...) But a desire cannot be illusory. Nothing is more specifically real than a desire qua desire. The same is true of Anselm's God – his idea and his reality cannot be disassociated. (...) One has to suppose on the contrary that our way was indeed unique; we were touching with our desire on the very essence of our art."[262] Even though the analogy Valéry wants to establish between mental and real existence of desire and the mental and real existence of God is unworkable, Valéry's comment underscores the fundamental importance of desire in his work.

Desire provides Valéry with a way for distinguishing between two of his loves, poetry and philosophy. The distinction turns no longer on defects of philosophy but on the respective interest of both philosophy and poetics. Thus in the 1937 lecture at the International Congress in Asthetics Valéry writes: "I believed that I saw in Leonardo a thinker, in Spinoza the manner of a poet or an architect. Doubtless I was mistaken. Nonetheless, it seemed to me that the form of the exterior expression of a person was sometimes less important than the nature of his desire and the manner in which he structured his thoughts."[263] For the mature Valéry, what characterizes the philosopher is the order of thought, whereas what characterizes the poet is the order of desire.

Two years earlier in "Questions de poésie" Valéry used the notion of desire to distinguish between two kinds of discourse. Valéry wants to contradict d'Alembert's (1717–1783) claim that only what is good in poetry is what is excellent in prose by drawing attention to what some poets actually do. Thus he writes: "Others (...) have tried by analyzing desire and poetic pleasure and their connections more and more precisely to construct a poetry that could never be reduced to the expression of a thinking nor to translate itself into other terms without perishing."[264] Desire here is the source of what is unique, untranslatable, and even inexpressible in any other form than poetry.

"Desire" then is not an abstract word empty of any real meaning for Valéry, the way "being" is, but a sign of some real power felt in the mind, the body, and the world. Is this power to be linked mainly with the capacity to intuit morally salient features of persons and things in the world? Further, desire is of the very essence of poetry. For desire is constitutive of poetic states of mind and distinguishes both the irreducible activity and discourse to which we apply the name of "poetry." Is this constitutive power also to be linked with the capacity to apprehend such salient features in sufficiently rich linguistic terms?

These initial points are seen in more relief when we notice a distinction Valéry draws between two kinds of poetic desire. For desire is both a theme of poetry and an incentive for poetry. The second is of most interest for us.

Valéry speaks of desire as an incentive in the 1939 Zaharoff lecture when he writes that according to some, "the principal and the most charming object of [the poet's] desire must be to communicate the impression of how a creative emotion is born and how it comes to be born happily. By virtue of its surprise and its pleasure this impression may indefinitely protect the poem from all later criticism." Desire in this context is more an intention than an emotion.

Valéry discusses a second kind of poetic desire in his 1921 dialogue, "Eupalinos ou l'architecte." Thus at one point in the character of Socrates Valéry writes: "Here I am, says the constructor. You are the matter, you are the force, you are the desire; but you are separate. An unknown work has isolated you and prepared you according to its means. The Demiurge pursued his designs which do not concern his creatures" (II: 145). Desire in this context becomes a theme of poetry.

In the same dialogue, however, Valéry focuses again on the figure of Socrates (II: 97). Desire here is not just a subject matter; it is in fact the source and origin of that set of mental acts which results in poetry. The creative capacities themselves derive from this state of desire. The important point for us is to see that the capacity for carrying through to completion certain kinds of intuitive mental acts, such as the apprehending of the self-presentations of objective moral states, can be linked with creative acts of literary imagination.

But what are the connections between desire and poetics? To see these connections we need to recall that indefinable area at the origins of poetic activity which Valéry thinks resists conceptual analysis. Valéry describes this origin as disorderly, arbitrary, infinite, unstable, and so on.

Does Valéry say more about these matters? Yes. For the connections between Valéry's poetics, his reflections on the "the action that does something" ("*l'action qui fait*"), and that phenomenon of desire that is at the origin of this action lies in these fuller descriptions. Begin then once again, but this time with mind, and move from mind to the body and the world.

Valéry's descriptions of mind as we know are almost innumerable. But he describes some features of mind much less often than others. Consider for example the notion of the accidental as opposed to the deliberate.

In his 1919 text, *Notes et digressions* on Leonardo, Valéry writes of several key traits.[265] The clarity, the precision, the exactness, the simplicity – all these traits which Valéry celebrated in his heroes, his fictions, and his reflections are, however, but one side only of his meditations on mind.

The importance of the accidental can be seen in Valéry's discussion of analysis. In the same text, for example, he talks of Leonardo pursuing his analyses but also in some sense being led by them. The critical point here is not the truism that some thinking is not perfectly lucid, but the importance sometimes of the accidental in achieving lucidity and, especially, of accidental analyses leading the mind into unsuspected domains.

Another recalcitrant element in mental life we might call the phantasmagoric, the domain of monstrous thoughts which appear and disappear in an ongoing horror show to which we pay as little attention as we can.[266] The notion is hallucinatory. It is also supported by the testimony of painters, the drawings of the disturbed, the discourses of the mentally ill. Thus for Valéry the mind is not just the locus of clarity; it is also the domain of the accidental and the phatasmagoric.

Related to this extended description are the many references Valéry makes to dream states where the play of associations seems to elude even the most persistent attempts to find an order. The mind not only sleeps; it sleeps deeply as the physiologists have taught us to say. And the dream states which arise in deep sleep exhibit an opacity, a density, an almost chemical viscosity that still resists any finally satisfying analysis.

Valéry is suspicious of any talk of mystery here. He will not blink the phenomena.[267] But what Valéry denies here is perhaps more interesting than what he affirms.

Consider one further feature of mind which Valéry locates in his lunar landscape of the oneiric, the phantasmagoric, and the accidental. Valéry wants to emphasize not just the peculiar movements of mind but its apparent absence of limits, its distinctive infinities.[268] Mind's infinity, the suggestion here goes, is paradoxically a closed one, a child of Cantor's reflections but not of Aristotle's. Yet the infinity at issue here while closed is nonetheless an infinity. And thus, like the accidental, the phantasmagoric, and the oneiric, it opens ultimately onto even darker recesses than those of the mind; all four lead us back from the mind to those other obscurities, those of the body.

The movement from mind to body goes by way of what Valéry calls the sensibility. "Actually, it is only sensibility that interests us," Valéry writes in 1919.[269] And in an aside from 1936 he glosses the sense of this very general term with the help of a philosophical phrase which has its own difficulties. "I am someone who never opposes," he writes, "who does not know how to oppose intelligence to sensibility, reflected consciousness to what is immediately given,"[270] as if the transition itself between mind and body was itself both real and yet finally imperceptible.

In 1935 however, in his "Notion générale de l'art," Valéry describes sensibility more fully. Sensibility, Valéry wants to hold, is part of the organism's incessant activities, not of immediate but of more long-term self-preservation. Sensibility contrasts with those activities that ensure immediate self-preservation and with the activities of the mind. The second contrast is more important. Thus, sensibility is opposed to "intellectual activity properly speaking, for it consists in a development of sensation that tends to repeat or to prolong what the intellectual tends to eliminate or to iron out."[271]

Once this contrast is drawn Valéry distinguishes further the action of sensibility and its capacity. The distinction is especially important and requires citation in full. "Sensibility (...) has a horror of the vacuum. It reacts spontaneously against what stimulates it. Each time that a temporal extension that is idle or lacks any preoccupation imposes itself on someone, sensibility brings about in that person a change of state marked by a kind of emission that tends to reestablish the equilibrium of the exchanges between the power and the act of sensibility. The tracing of some decoration on a surface that is too bare, the birth of a song in a silence that is too noticible, these are the responses, the complements that compensate for the absence of stimuli – as if this absence that we express by a simple negation was acting positively on us."[272]

Sensibility then is a two-sided phenomenon, partly a receptive capacity for activity and partly an activity in its own right. Once again, Valéry's striking description highlights those interfaces where sensibility works upon mind and where the world works upon sensibility, as in another lengthy passage where Valéry discusses further the activities of sensibility.[273]

Mental Acts and Poetic States

Were we then to take up a perspective on Valéry's intellectual landscape such as the one which I have been trying to sketch here, where could we locate the movement of his poetry and the crystallization of his poetics?

Valéry distinguishes two senses of the word "poetry." Thus, in his 1937 lecture at the *Université des Annales*, "*La Necessité de la Prose*," he writes: "Poetry is a particular action founded on language. Poetry also has a more general meaning. (...) the word designates a certain state that is both receptive and productive."[274] Thus the word, "poetry," refers to both an action and a mental state.

Valéry presented a fuller account of this distinction ten years earlier at the same university in his lecture, "Propos sur la Poésie." The mental state in question is specified as a particular emotional state. And the action at issue is identified as a species of representation.

Poetry, Valéry writes here in reversing the order of the later account, "designates first of all a certain emotional genre, a particular emotive state that can be provoked by quite diverse objects or circumstances. We say of a landscape that it is poetic; we say the same thing of a certain circumstance of life; and we say it also of a person. But the word 'poetry' also has a second, more narrow sense. In this sense poetry makes us dream of an action, a strange occupation whose object is to reconstitute the emotion that the first sense of the word designates.[275] Poetry thus is the act of reconstituting a previously experienced emotional state with the help of the artifices of language.

One further touch must be added to what is here only a sketch. For Valéry the end of poetry is not the act of representation as such but the communication of this representation to another person in such a way that this person may share the emotional state which the poet had originally experienced and then reconstituted. Thus, in the Zaharoff lecture at Oxford in 1939 Valéry writes: "The function of a poet is not to experience the poetic state – that is a private matter.

Rather, the function of a poet is to create a poetic state in others. A poet is recognized by the simple fact that he changes the reader into someone 'inspired.' "[276] Poetry in this perspective is the production of peculiar kinds of artifacts, namely those that induce poetic states. "A poem," Valéry says in the same lecture, "is a kind of machine for producing poetic states by means of words".[277]

Such a notion of poetry raises of course several questions, questions for example about the way Valéry conceives an emotional state, about the nature of its reconstitution, and also about the role of the reader in the elaboration of this reconstitution. But formulating such questions and, even more, trying to answer them is premature until we have a fuller understanding of what Valéry's views actually are.

Some idea of why these critical questions are premature can be gained from recalling Valéry's summary definition of poetry in his notes on literature published in 1929. "Poetry," he writes there, "is the attempt to represent or to restore with the help of articulate language those things or that thing that cries, tears, caresses, kisses, sighs, and so on try obscurely to express and that seem to want to express those objects in what they apparently have of life or of presupposed purpose." And Valéry adds to this account a gloss on "that thing": "That thing is not otherwise. It is of the nature of this energy that it spends itself in responding to what is."[278] This account raises serious doubts about just what poetry is to represent, whether a mental state like a particular emotion, or some feature of the world which has provoked this mental state.

Valéry's related comments on the origin of the act of poetry reinforce this ambiguity. For Valéry refuses to restrict the objects of presentation to one kind of thing only. In 1937 he writes: "The poet wakens in a person on the occasion of an unexpected event, an external or internal event: a tree, a face, a 'subject,' an emotion, a word. And sometimes what gets things started is the will to express something, a need to translate what one senses. But sometimes on the contrary what starts things going is an element of form, the sketch of an expression that looks for its cause, that looks for itself in the space of my soul (...) sometimes something wishes to be expressed, sometimes some means of expression wants to be at the service of something."[279]

The object of representation then, although always a mental state, is differentiated by reason of its own intentional object. The mental state is both a response to some inner or outer provocation and a production of a species of intentional object. But can we get clearer about the nature of this mental state?

Essential to the poetic state is a harmonious relation among representations. Valéry characterizes this relation as a resonance. And he understands this relation by analogy with the different relations which connect representations in dream states."[280]

Valéry then attempts to distinguish between ordinary emotions and poetic emotions. The first are clearly distinct states of mind for Valéry, whereas the second are confused states of mind in the sense that more than one emotion is involved. Further, the second but not the first are accompanied by what we might call some feeling for the whole.[281]

Now, the confusion that underlies the *naissant* sensation of the whole in poetic emotion is not just the mixture itself of different "ordinary" emotions. Rather, Valéry seems to hold that each of these individual emotions as well as their conjunctions involve numerous what we may call cacophonies. And these must be eliminated before the harmony Valéry wants to insist on actually arises.[282]

Thus, the harmonious mental states which the poet enjoys and which he or she seeks to reconstitute are peculiarly mixed emotional states. The initial harmonious conjunction of these mixed states are, we might say, orchestrated such that a sense of the whole arises. To simplify, what distinguishes poetic emotion is the sense of the whole. And this sense appears when the poet orchestrates the passion into a harmonious emotional state.

Mind then is linked with world. For the world continually interrupts the mind's attempted dialogue with itself. And mind is linked with body too. For Valéry construes the emotional harmonies of poetic states of mind as peculiarly suited to what he calls the primary forms of sensibility.

These forms Valéry usually leaves unexplained. But his underlying idea is clear. For part of what Valéry means by a poetic emotion is the awareness of one's sensory capacities working in a kind of marvellous conjunction such that our perceptions are heightened. What one perceives is not the sum of one's different sensory capacities – but that sum enhanced by the harmonization of its essential elements. The picture we have then, as radio astronomers might say in a description Valéry would appreciate, is not just the image our instruments have produced, but the image now "computer enhanced."

The peculiar mind-body connection which poetry involves comes clearer when we consider the role speech plays in poetry. For Valéry the major figure is the voice. In his opening lecture on poetics at the *Collège de France* in 1937, "Première leçon du Cours de Poétique," Valéry wrote at length.[283] There he put unusual stress on the performance of poetry – just reading the poem mentally is out of the question. The force of Valéry's description of poetry is caught in his phrase, "a prolonged hesitation between sound and sense." This movement, which Valéry often compares to that of a pendulum swinging between its two extremes, is not just mental then. The movement of poetry is embodied; it is vocal.

In the landscape of the whole which Valéry calls the relation of world, body, and mind, where then is poetry?

Poetry both as a state of mind and as an action is found in the intersections. As a state of mind poetry appears where world and mind overlap, at those indeterminate points and moments when the world arises into the mind like a suddenly agitated Mediterranean tide surging into the crevasses of the sea cliffs above the rocky inlets, the *calanques*. And as an action poetry appears also in the interfaces between mind and body, at those indefinite places where we not only speak our minds but where we understand ourselves speaking, where we as it were overhear our language speaking in our own voice.

Were we to privilege any one of these varied intersections among world, body, and mind, Valéry would insist on body as the central point of exchange. The world breaks into the mind only because the mind is embodied and thus, while always distinct, the mind is already a part of the world. And the mind realizes its projects in the world only because of the same embodiment.

Thus, for Valéry the mind and the world come together and break apart in my body. More specifically, poetry effects its transmutations through the voice. The voice gives the mind a purchase on the world and the voice lets the world emit its alien undertones whenever we listen to ourselves speaking.

Seeing Moral Qualities

We need now to stand back from the linguistic and conceptual richness of Valéry's poetic representations of many aspects of poetic perception and moral knowledge in the many volumes of his *Cahiers*. And when we take our task as trying to achieve some kind of useful overview, we quickly come upon the central matter in these many reflections of the nature of certain kinds of perceptual processes as opening onto apparently a direct and immediate access to things as they are.

Were we to take inspiration from an account of perceiving like Valéry's, then moral intuiting might be seen as sharing with perceiving generally a similar access to things as they are, but more particularly as opening out onto the self-presentations of moral qualities. One helpful way of understanding such a supposition is to recall several pertinent features of philosophical accounts of the perceptual process itself.

Standardly, when we perceive something of any kind whatsoever, we not only perceive the thing as a whole; we perceive it also as having different properties or qualities.[284] These different properties of things are what allow them to be categorised under general headings as belonging to a particular class of things. Moreover, these different properties may appear not just in one thing but in several things at the same time. Still more, some of these properties may appear as essential to the nature of the thing itself whereas others may appear as merely accidental.

Philosophers have busied themselves with the differences between these two basic kinds of properties from Aristotle disputing with Plato about the existence of "forms," to Ockham arguing with Aquinas about the nature of universals and particulars, right up to the beginnings of modern philosophy in Hobbes's quarrels with Descartes about substances and accidents and Hume's difficulties with Berkeley about which properties might be taken as primary and which as secondary. For our purposes one of the most fruitful disputes about properties occurred in the eighteenth century when the Scottish philosopher, Thomas Reid, argued against both Berkeley and Hume.

A century previously, in the midst of the rise of the new empirical sciences in the work of Boyle and others, philosophers like Locke took over the view that the most basic properties that can explain just what things are are not the properties that observers directly perceive. When we inquire into the nature of things, the properties that we directly perceive are secondary properties, whereas those that finally enable us to explain things are primary properties.

Secondary properties are mainly the specific objects of individual external senses in the way, for example, that the colour of my sofa is the specific object of my individual sense of vision. By contrast, primary properties are mainly the objects of more than one sense in the way, for example, that the size of my sofa is the object of both my sense of vision and my sense of touch. Secondary properties as immediate sensory qualities are much more dependent on individual senses than primary ones are.

Locke and Boyle differed on many points in this general discussion, including on just how many primary and secondary properties there are and on just which properties may properly be taken as primary or secondary. Berkeley focussed this dispute on whether either primary or even secondary properties are objectively real properties of things and hence strongly independent of our thinking about them, or not.

Much of the discussion centred on what the perceiving mind was immediately aware of, and whether the immediate awareness apparently involved in some perceptual processes basically delivered merely ideas of some properties or the properties themselves. And many philosophers both in Valèry's time – recall his abiding interests in mathematics and the sciences – and in our own – recall the discussions today about the nature of such things as the still merely postulated elementary particle called "the Higgs boson" – have continued to reflect on these finally quite elusive issues in connections with the twentieth century replacement of Newtonian science with quantum physics and its branches.

How then can at least some perceptual processes be properly understood as actually dealing with some objectively real properties of things? Reid argued that the so-called way of ideas for arriving at a satisfactory account of scientific knowledge, as for example Hume's theory of impressions and ideas, had misled both Berkeley and Hume just as it had misled Locke, Boyle, and Descartes. For the word "idea," which Descartes took over uncritically from the medieval Scholastic philosophers, needs to be understood as fundamentally ambiguous. That is, the word "idea" can mean either thinking, i.e., that species of mental act whereby a person arrives at a particular conception of something, or the result of that thinking, i.e. the thought itself.

Reid proposed an alternative view, one he argued remedied such a fatal ambiguity in the way of ideas and opened up a new way to understand knowledge. He first elaborated his views in terms of what he called a "common sense" philosophy, a form of philosophical realism that took more seriously than his predecessors "the commonly shared unreasoned principles" of non-philosophers,[285] in his *Enquiry into the Human Mind on the Principles of Common Sense*, published in 1764 when he succeeded Adam Smith in the Chair of Moral Philosophy at Glasgow. He proceeded to develop related views in great detail in his 1785 *Essays on the Intellectual Powers of Man* and in his 1788 *Essays on the Active Powers of Man*.[286]

In the areas with which we are most concerned here, philosophical ethics, Reid was a moral intuitionist. He argued that persons naturally develop a capacity not just to feel what is morally right and good by the operations of some kind of "moral sense," as eighteenth "sentimentalist" philosophers like Shaftesbury and Hutcheson held. Rather, persons naturally develop a capacity to make true or false judgements about such moral matters as what morally we owe to other persons, as to what is their moral due.[287]

All too briefly, here is a representative summary today of Reid's subtle views on the topic of most interest to us here, the relations between the perceiving of moral qualities and their intuiting as a similar perceiving of aesthetic qualities figuratively represented in some high modernist poetic writings of Valéry.

Reid held that the "sensations of primary qualities of objects speak to us like words, affording us 'natural signs' of the qualities of things. The mind passes naturally over a word to consider what it signifies, and in like manner it passes over its own experience to consider directly the qualities they signify. This is so for 'original perceptions' of primary qualities; perceptions of secondary qualities have to be acquired."[288]

What makes for some of the subtlety of Reid's view is his use of analogies between the ways in which some primary properties or qualities present themselves to observers and the ways in which some words come to us from others. For just as some words are natural signs, so too some primary qualities are natural signs. Moreover, Reid also assumes a subtle distinction between the sensation of primary qualities and secondary qualities, and the perceptions of primary qualities only. Finally, not all perceptions of primary qualities are what Reid calls "natural"; only what he calls "original perceptions" of primary qualities are natural.

Thus, "[w]hen I see a tree," a helpful example of how Reid's view works goes, "I do not receive a mere idea of a tree; my vision of the tree involves the judgement that it exists with a certain shape, size, and position. The initial furniture of the mind is not a set of disconnected ideas, but a set of 'original and natural judgements.' These make up what Reid calls 'the common sense of mankind.' "[289] The key point here is Reid's rejection of any idea as a substitute for primary and secondary properties as objective intermediary between the mind and the world. Note too the accent here on "original and natural judgments" which helps us to see that part of those "original perceptions" we just considered are natural judgments and not ideas.

To carry through such a resolution and analysis, however, requires being clear about the basic distinction between sensation and perception. For philosophers today the word "sensation" refers mainly to the sensory phases of dealing with the environment and one's body in different ways. By contrast, the word "perception" refers mainly to the conceptual phases of the direct or indirect extraction of information about things or facts from the environment and one's body.[290]

With this distinction in hand we can better appreciate Reid's contention that "the mind is so constituted that sensation automatically causes belief in external objects. The belief is neither inferred nor rational but is caused by the occurrence of the sensation."[291] Thus the sensing of an external object naturally causes a belief in the external existence of that object. And the combination of sensation and belief yields perception. Note however that Reid distinguishes between the sensation of primary qualities or properties and that of secondary ones. Only the first and not the second bring about "clear conceptions of the external qualities causing them."[292]

Reid argued that sensations as such cannot "represent" external physical properties, as Descartes and Locke held, because sensations do not resemble such properties. And, since sensations are essential with beliefs to perceptions, perceptions cannot represent external physical properties either.[293] Reid also argued that sensations as such cannot "be taken for" external objects, as Berkeley and Hume held, because common sense intuitions show that sensations are substantially different from external objects. In short, sensations naturally signify external objects; they do not represent them. Or one might say that for Reid sensations are intrinsically non-intentional.

In one critically important case for our concerns, however, and especially for appreciating the significance for fresh consideration of moral intuitionism today of the repeated examples both in Valéry's notebook entries and in the sketches often accompanying them on the manuscript pages, the case of our sensing and perceiving visible figures in vision, Reid makes an exception. For contrary to his original view of perception, Reid holds that "we directly perceive what he calls 'visible figure,' which is a real figure projected onto the retina, a figure representing the spatial relations of the parts of an external object. [Yet W]e have no sensation of visible figure."

Reid thus preserves his fundamental principle that sensation is unlike anything external, while asserting that we are directly aware of something – a visible figure – "which does represent something external."[294] Reid wants to take his "visible figure" or seen figure as objective and mind-independent. By way of considering a basic objection to Reid's views at the beginning of our final chapter, we will come back to this fascinating case.[295]

Valéry on Moral Knowledge: Second Thoughts

We need now to formulate some of our second thoughts on moral intuitionism and suffering with respect to our second theme of moral knowledge and perception in Valéry's poetic representations in some of his *Cahiers*. Perhaps we may then say, again in a provisional fashion only by way of concluding our second thoughts on Valéry, something like the following.

(C6) Some moral states of affairs present themselves indirectly to reflective readers of such high modernist poetic representations of personal moral suffering as some of the figurative descriptions on view in Valéry's voluminous *Cahiers* in such ways as to raise basic issues about the nature of how persons perceive the properties or qualities of moral states of affairs.

(C7) These indirect self-presentations of human suffering mainly consist in what seventeenth and eighteenth century British philosophers called primary as opposed to secondary qualities.

(C8) Such primary qualities as the properties by which intellectual and affective personal suffering may be properly said to differ from physical pain are not merely sensations incorporated in those perceptions that can lead to genuine moral knowledge; they are also the related perceptions that necessarily include with the sensations the pertinent beliefs as well.

(C9) Among the contents of the beliefs that accompany perception are particular true and false judgments about moral matters that bear on external and objective states of affairs including objective moral values.

(C10) These true and false judgements included naturally in the perceptions of many moral situations mediate interactions between the world, the body, and the mind.

CHAPTER SEVEN

Eliot on Moral Discourse and Suffering

We already discussed Eliot's high modernist poetry of suffering in chapter two with the help of a close look at some of the persistently difficult issues involved in understanding the cardinal notion of literal meaning. There we formulated several initial findings with the help of some of Donald Davidson's sustained reflections on so-called deviant uses of language. We then proceeded with both our first readings and, after an Interlude, with second thoughts about the high modernist poetry of suffering in Valéry's poetic prose and in Montale's poetry. Now we need finally to return for second thoughts to Eliot's poetry and to reconsider several still unresolved issues regarding literal meanings.

Meanings and Truths

In one of his many important papers the distinguished English philosopher, Michael Dummett, has commented extensively on Davidson's views.[296] These comments both clarify several of Davidson's ideas as well as provide a comparative perspective on meaning that is quite useful for our concerns with the European high modernist poetry of suffering. Dummett's comments also bring into focus one of Davidson's radical and yet deeply puzzling claims. The claim follows from Davidson's apparent inability comprehensively to explain linguistic communication with the help of a set of linguistic principles flexible enough to accommodate the literal or first meanings of deviant expressions that occur very often in poetic and dramatic uses of language.

That important claim runs: "There is therefore no such thing as a language, not if a language is anything like what many philosophers and linguists have supposed it to be" (445). And of course such a claim invites the query as to just how, if not linguistically and philosophically, a language is to be construed.

Dummett offers a summary of the argument for this claim, a summary that includes several precisions that we may borrow for dealing with our concerns with rationally and reasonably interpreting literal meanings in some perhaps deviant poetic utterances. "The apparatus of prior and passing theories, or, as I have called them, long-range and short-range theories," Dummett writes, "is required to explain the phenomena of malapropisms and of deviant and unfamiliar uses. (...) It is also sufficient to explain linguistic communication in general. But neither the short-range nor the long-range theory has the right form to be described as a theory of a language. Hence the notion of a theory of language is not needed for the philosophy of language, but only that of language" (466).

Earlier in his comments Dummett calls attention to a pervasive ambiguity in Davidson's talk of a "prior" theory. For "prior" can mean either one's own "linguistic propensities," that is, the antecedent theory participants bring to either a conversation or an interpretation and subsequently modify. Or "prior" can mean the already modified theory in each stage of the conversation or interpretation that continues to undergo revision. To simplify, a "prior" theory in the first sense is brought to the interpretation, whereas in the second sense a "prior" theory is already included in the interpretation. The second sense, Dummett thinks, is the operative one in Davidson's views.

Throughout, where Davidson and Dummett speak of a conversation or a reading, we of course have to keep in mind for our purposes an interpretation, say of some of Eliot's literal meanings of expressions in his poetry. In continuing to speak of interpretation, however, we need to take care. For, as Dummett points out in calling attention to Wittgenstein's remarks in the *Investigations* (Section 201), Davidson often uses the expression, "the interpreter," too broadly.

Thus, to keep this philosophical discussion bearing directly on our concerns with interpreting such passages as Eliot's talk of "nothing" in *The Waste Land* dialogue, we need to shift our attention from the relation between this poetic passage's obscurities and the interpreter's elucidatory aims to the prior interpretive relation between the represented speakers and hearers in the dialogue. In this case, the prior theory is construed as the hearer's "theory about how, in general to understand S [the speaker] when S addresses H [the hearer]; and this theory may obviously change in response to what S says in the course of the particular conversation" (459–60).

This first clarification about "prior" theory leads to a second clarification about the operative sense of a "passing" theory. Thus, the hearer's passing theory needs to be construed as "a theory about how to understand specific utterances of S made during that conversation" (460). A passing theory may incorporate surmises about how to understand particular non-standard utterances the speaker may make during the conversation without the evolving prior theory incorporating them. For however it evolves, the prior theory remains a theory about how to understand the speaker in general and not any particular speaker.

Consequently, Dummett thinks he can sharpen this distinction between prior and passing theories by substituting for it talk of long-range and short-range theories. Thus, if we turn to the speaker, a long-range theory is not to be taken as comprising what the speaker believes prior to the theory of the hearer. Rather, the speakers "initial long-range theory comprises his expectations concerning how, in general, it is disposed to understand S when S addresses H."

These expectations are to be taken as "certain suppositions about what, at that moment, are H's long-term dispositions to understand in particular ways what S says to him" (460). And the speaker's short-range theory is better described, not as the passing theory that the speaker intends the hearer to use, but as relating to "how he intends, and expects, H to understand particular utterances he makes during the conversation, when he does not intend, or expect, H to incorporate his interpretations of those utterances into his long-range theory" (460).

Thus, part of what this revised distinction brings out is Davidson's own persistent concern, not so much for articulating shallow differences between what a speaker means and what his words mean, but deeper differences "between what a speaker, on occasion, means, and what his words mean" (Davidson, 434).

Common Languages and Idiolects

With this background in view we can now better appreciate the general concern that provoked Davidson's reflections on malapropisms. As Dummett sees the matter, "Davidson is concerned with (...) a hearer's understanding of a word or phrase in a sense unfamiliar to him. A speaker cannot attach a meaning to an expression, Davidson says, unless he intends his hearer to understand him as doing so, and he cannot intend him to understand him thus unless he has a reasonable expectation that he will" (461).

Moreover, Dummett goes on to distinguish the different features of the phenomenon in question. "The phenomenon occurs in three kinds of cases," he writes: "that in which, unknown to the speaker, the hearer is unfamiliar with the expression; that in which the speaker inadvertently makes a deviant use of a word (a malapropism); and that in which his deviant use is deliberate. In the third case," Dummett continues, "he will drop clues prompting the hearer either to modify his long-range theory, or to adopt the correct short-range theory, as the case requires, and may therefore well succeed in conveying his meaning. In the first two cases, he has a false long-range theory concerning the hearer, that is, a false idea of the hearer's long-range theory, but the hearer may still succeed in understanding him as he intended" (461–462).

This general concern is the clue to understanding something that Davidson seems to have confounded. For Davidson sometimes seems to confuse the notion of a natural language such as English or French with a particular speaker's use of a language at a particular time and place, with a particular use of an idiolect, a speaker's individual speech habits.[297]

For Davidson, an idiolect is more fundamental than a language in the sense that a common language is to be understood "as a range of overlapping idiolects." But, even more precisely, as Dummett writes, "we must take a language in the fundamental sense to consist, not of the general speech habits of an individual at a particular time, but, rather, his habits of speech when addressing a particular hearer at that time" (469).

Although Davidson favours the notion of an idiolect over that of a common language, despite his attention to communication between speakers and hearers his concern is curiously non-interactional. On his view, communication is more an exchange of monologues than a dialogue. "In his [Davidson's] picture," Dummett writes, "there is no interaction, no exchange of the roles of speaker and hearer: the hearer remains mute throughout the conversation, or, rather monologue" (462). Conversely, this incomplete picture of the communicative situation reflects rather well the fictional scene that Eliot represents poetically in *The Waste Land.*

A final distinction is now called for in the case of linguistic communication since, as we have seen, more than one theory is at issue. When Davidson uses the term "theory," as for example when he speaks about an "interpreter" or hearer having a theory at any particular moment in a linguistic interaction, he does so "only because a description of the interpreter's competence requires a recursive account" (441). But, as both Ian Hacking and Dummett have pointed out in different ways, this talk of "recursive" is misleading. For "recursive" can be construed either as "effectively decidable" or as "specified inductively." The latter sense and not the former is the one that Dummett takes to be the operative one.

Now, once again, when we take these precisions back to our concerns with trying to interpret the meanings of non-standard uses of puzzling expression like "nothing" in *The Waste Land*, we find further clarifications. Thus, the amended talk about long-range and short-range "theories" (in the precise sense of inductively specified descriptive accounts of meaning) opens up several ideas. For when we shift our attention to the long and short-range theories of the hearer, taken now as the critical reflective interpreter, we can construe the interpreter's antecedent attitudes more loosely. We can take them now not so much as beliefs but as expectations and suppositions as to how the poet intends his expressions and those of his fictional characters to be understood. These intentions, moreover, can be either standing intentions or occasional ones.

Furthermore, we can make a similar shift in focus, this time from talk of the speaker to talk not just of the hearer but of the interpreter in reflecting on the three cases distinguished above.

Thus, the interpreter's puzzlement about the sense and significance of a particular expression in the poem can arise either because of the interpreter's unfamiliarity with the expression (recall Eliot's occasional, and notorious, uses of Sanskrit terms in *The Waste Land*), or because of inappropriate scrutiny of inadvertent deviant uses of a word (perhaps the opposition between capitalized and non-capitalized uses of "nothing" in the mental reply "Nothing and nothing"), or because of inattention to deliberate deviant uses (an interpreter's overlooking, say, the missing interrogative mark in the *Collected Poems* but not in the first edition of the imperative question "Why do you never speak" – period). Nonetheless, several issues here still need more attention.

Interpretations Broad and Narrow

One question arises here as to whether the long-range and short-range theories are both supposed to be theories of the utterances of a speaker or of something else altogether.

Any theory that is about another theory we may call a second-order theory; a first-order theory is a theory about anything else except another theory. Thus Davidson's theories about both the speaker's and the hearer's long-range and short-range theories are second-order theories. Of course Davidson may rejoin that we don't have theories about these, merely expectations. But Dummett argues that, in order to avoid an infinite regress, Davidson needs to provide a first-order theory and has not done so. And, most importantly, this missing first order theory, Dummett holds, cannot be a theory of meaning.

To isolate this crucial point Dummett distinguishes among "a language, a theory of meaning for that language, and a second-order theory" (467). His discussion is nuanced and hence we do well to recall Dummett's points at some length. "A language is an existing pattern of communicative speech," Dummett writes. "It is not a theory, but a phenomenon. A theory of meaning for that language, as conceived by Davidson, is a theory of the content of expressions belonging to it – what that content is and how it is determined by the composition of the expressions. It does not itself employ the notion of meaning, but can be recognized as an adequate representation of the meanings of words and expressions of the language. It serves to explain how the language functions, that is, to explain the phenomenon of speech in that language; but it does so only indirectly."

Dummett goes on to adduce some justification for these views. In doing so he introduces some nuances. "This is so," he claims, "because the theory itself contains no reference to speakers or to their beliefs, intentions or behaviour, linguistic or non-linguistic. Instead it uses theoretical terms such as 'true' applying to certain expressions of the language. In order, therefore, to assess a theory of meaning for a language as correct or incorrect, we must have some principles, implicit, that make the connection between the theoretical notions and what the speakers of the language say and do."

These principles," Dummett continues, "are not regarded by Davidson as part of the theory of meaning itself: they are presumably constant over all theories of meaning and all languages. We may call them the linking principles. Save in their presence, it will make no sense to speak of believing or disbelieving a theory of meaning, since they alone (...) provide a criterion for its being correct."

Finally, Dummett concludes by showing the difference between a first and a second-order theory. "A second-order theory is of a quite different character. If it is a long-range theory, it consists of a set of beliefs about what expressions of some language mean, or about what certain individuals intend or take them to mean; if it is a short-range theory, then about what certain utterances were intended or taken to mean" (467).

These lengthy comments are helpful but several questions remain. One is whether the linking principles referred to here "connect the theory of meaning to the linguistic practice by imputing theories to the speakers" (467). For, unlike Davidson, Dummett thinks that we need to distinguish between a broad sense and a strict sense of "interpretation."

In the strict sense, interpretation is what Wittgenstein calls a *Deutung*. This strict sense is what Davidson propounds when he explains that, when Mrs. Malaprop says "a nice derangement of epitaphs," she means "a nice arrangement of epithets." Interpretation in the broad sense however is a way of understanding, an *Auffassung*, or what Mrs. Malaprop herself may understand by "a nice arrangement of epitaphs."

We also need to distinguish between second-order theories about what the long and short-range theories of both speakers and hearers comprise, and theories of meaning. Does Mrs. Malaprop have a second-order theory about some belief, or does she hold some theory of meaning?

Sorting through such issues requires explicating the linking principles. As Dummett continues at some length:

> Only the linking principles, when made explicit, will reveal whether a theory of meaning for a language is genuinely an object of knowledge, in some mode of knowledge, on the part of everyone who knows that language. Independently of whether it is or not, however, someone's knowledge of the language may be schematically represented by attributing such a theory to him. In knowing the language, he thereby attaches to expressions belonging to it the meanings they have in that language. The theory of meaning purports to provide the only possible analysis of what it is for those expressions to have those meanings. The speaker himself may be ignorant of that analysis: but, by attributing to him the corresponding theory of meaning, we simultaneously represent him as attaching those meanings to the expressions and

> supply an analysis of their having those meanings. In the same way, a second-order theory is not literally to the effect that such-and-such a theory of meaning is correct, or is the theory held by a certain individual. Its literal content is that certain expressions have certain meanings, or that some individual intends them to have or takes them as having those meanings. Since a theory of meaning makes explicit what it is or would be for them to have those meanings, however, the second-order theory can be represented as a theory about that theory of meaning (468).

But at least one further question needs answering. If we identify the first-order theory with a theory of meaning, as Dummett wants us to do against Davidson, what exactly is to count as the language at issue?

Here Dummett urges us to take the relevant sense of "a language" (what he calls elsewhere "a pattern of communicative speech") as referring to a natural or common language such as French or English or a dialect. That is, Dummett wants us to reject Davidson's construal of "a language" in terms of different overlapping idiolects.

Such a choice of course still means that a theory of meaning would have to deal with deviant expressions because no speaker of a common language or a dialect has perfect mastery. Here the task of a theory of meaning will be to "give the meanings that its words and expressions in fact have" in the speaker's use of a common language or a dialect while treating the speaker's idiolect as a second-order theory. In short, on Dummett's view a "common language is related to an idiolect essentially as the rules of a game are related to a player's beliefs about what they are" (469).

Part of this crucial disagreement here focuses on just which of the many roles a language plays is to be taken as primary. In particular, is a language's communicative role or is a language's cognitive role to be taken as primary? Dummett puts the matter this way: "Language is both an instrument of communication and a vehicle of thought; it is an important question of orientation in the philosophy of language which role we take as primary."

We can welcome Davidson's attention to the communicative function of language, since we are disposed to take that as its primary role "language is a vehicle of thought because it is an instrument of communication, and not conversely. And yet it is an error to concentrate too exclusively on communication. Wittgenstein is well known to have taken language primarily as a social activity; and yet his challenge to say one thing and mean something else thereby has to do with language in its role as a vehicle of thought" (470–471).[298]

Behind this cautionary reminder lies Dummett's concern that Davidson has constructed a theory of linguistic communication by focusing his attention mainly on the admittedly numerous but nonetheless exceptional cases instead of on the ordinary ones (472). The result is the relative neglect of theories of meaning as first-order theories in the interests of indulging the fascinations of second-order theories of speakers' and hearers' meanings.

Clarifying Matters

What then are the major clarifications that emerge from these considerations of an alternative discussion of interpretation and meaning when we look back at some further representative work in contemporary Anglo-American philosophy of language?

The substitution of talk about long-range and short-range theories for prior and passing ones brings to the fore, in the literary instances we are mainly interested in, a poet's general expectations about the interpreter's perduring dispositions to understand expressions in particular ways and vice versa. This precision also foregrounds the poet's particular expectations and intentions with regard to a particular poem. The poet would have the reader understand specific expressions there without the reader having to modify his long term dispositions. The stress falls on distinguishing between what the expressions mean, and not on what the poet means but exactly on what the poet means in using these expressions on this occasion.

Moreover, when the poet uses normal expressions deviantly, the presumption should be that the poet writes neither inadvertently nor ignorantly but deliberately, perhaps even leaving clues for the reader's interpretation. Further, the criticism of the monologue character of Davidson's account of spoken linguistic communication actually brings out one of the crucial asymmetries between spoken and written communication. Unlike spoken communication, written communication almost always allows of no proper interaction.

As for the reader, the task is to interpret (in the strict sense of providing minimally an account of a particular expression's literal meaning instead of resting content with its loose apprehension) the poet's language. The word "language" here is to be construed as the poet's specific patterns of literarily represented speech addressed to an implicit reader of a particular poem, rather then as the poet's own habitual speech habits. And the reader's strict interpretative account is minimally to be a theory of the poet's literary representations of specific language patterns in the poem in the weaker sense of "theory" in which each salient element in the reader's account is inductively specifiable.

Besides these precisions we need to notice finally a major disagreement between these closely related accounts. Are we to understand the literal meanings of the central expressions that interest us as a function of the primacy we choose to award to some account of truth? Or are we to understand the literal meanings of those central expressions by proceeding primarily from some theory of meaning?

To return to our example, when Eliot literarily represents a fictional conversation in which one character asks "What is the wind doing?" and the other replies mentally "Nothing again nothing," how can competent readers be properly said to succeed in reflectively interpreting the literal meanings of these expressions? Do they succeed when, to simplify, they provide inductively specifiable accounts of how it is such expressions as "Nothing again nothing" mean what the poet with his readers in mind expects and intends the words to mean on this occasion while construing meaning after truth? Or is it rather the converse, that is, when competent readers construe truth after meaning?

With the help of this second representative discussion of meaning and truth, we may now articulate informally several further elements in our concern with literal meanings in poetry and rational interpretation as follows:

1) The poet's long-range theory may be taken to include general expectations about and intentions with regard to a critical reader's interpretive dispositions to construe both normal and deviant expressions the poet addresses to him or her in particular ways. And the poet's short-range theory is similar, except that in this case the poet neither intends nor expects the critical reader to modify his or her own long-range interpretive dispositions.
2) The interpreter's long-range theory may be taken as comprising general strategies as to how a critical reader is to interpret an individual poet, and his or her short-range theory as comprising particular strategies as to how a critical reader is to interpret a specific work of the poet.
3) Finally, a reflective interpretation of the meaning of a literary work is an inductively specifiable account of specific patterns of expression in a specific text where the account itself, deriving form a first order theory where "meaning" is primitive, includes discussion of the putative truth of such expressions.

When taken at least summarily, some elements in several distinguished current philosophical accounts of interpretation and meaning do provide us then with helpful considerations in trying to interpret the meaning of such perplexing expressions in the high modernist poetry of suffering as the different uses of "nothing" in *The Waste Land*. In particular, four points need highlighting.[299]

The notion of an "interpretation" as a process centred on specific patterns of the various uses of expressions in a literary work that tries as well to accommodate both the writer's and the reader's intentions strikes a helpful balance between formalist and pragmatic considerations. Second, that a rational interpretation must be articulated in such a way as to be inductively verifiable is also a needed hedge against many impressionistic or subjectively intuitive readings of literary works.

Moreover, a distinction between long-range and short-range intentions and expectations on the side of both writers and readers underlines clearly the need to direct a rational interpretation to very specific aspects of an extremely complex phenomenon. This phenomenon might be taken as the shifting senses of just what is to be understood as the literal meanings of poetic utterances.

Finally, an insistence on careful and sophisticated rival accounts on making explicit the presuppositions of a rational interpretation with respect to the priority of either questions about meaning or questions about truth is a sobering reminder. For, however specific a rational interpretation's ends, the expressions in which the interpretation itself is formulated require critical attention in their own right.

These positive reminders however arise against a background that requires continued scrutiny. For the initial question to which many of these contemporary accounts are addressed as answers – what is it for words to mean what they do? – is quite general, whereas the questions to which the reflective interpretation of the putative literal meanings of expressions in passages of a high modernist literary work is addressed are much more specific. This difference suggests that some of the elements in the general philosophical views on language are not so pertinent to the understanding of poetic utterances in works like Eliot's *The Waste Land* as they may at first appear. For several crucial points remain troublesome.

In the specific contexts of our concerns with both the language in which some moral situations are represented as well as the language in which we articulate just what makes such situations moral, the key notion of "theory" seems equivocal for it is applied to very diverse matters. We are all too often being continually urged to develop a "theory" of linguistic communication, a "theory" of long-range and short-range expectations and intentions, a "theory" of literal versus non-literal meaning, a "theory" of interpretation, a first-order and a second-order "theory," even a "theory" of meaning and a "theory" of truth. But surely this is just too much theory. In reflective literary appreciations can we talk of "theory" in any other than a systematically misleading way?

One serious difficulty here then is our inability so far to characterize the appropriate sense in which an account of interpretation and meaning that might inform our understandings of reflective with regard to poetic expression is "theoretical."

A second problem arises about the important distinctions in many contemporary philosophical views between literal versus non-literal meanings and normal versus deviant expressions. Just how these distinctions relate is not evident. The presumption here is that some normal and deviant uses of language can be taken to exhibit both literal and non-literal meaning.

But in attempting to understand central instances of the high modernist poetry of suffering, so much of which is fragment, gloss, and pastiche, talk of normal and deviant uses of language seems moot. And trying to elaborate an understanding of meaning on the basis of a problematic notion of the literal that leaves no room for other central features of poetic uses of language, for example the symbolic, seems foolhardy. However useful these distinctions can be made, they surely cannot stand alone without further discussion and supplementation in the detailed particular contexts of interpretations of literary works of art.

Finally, the central disagreement even within related contemporary philosophical views about the respective primacy of either a theory of truth or a theory of meaning still needs resolution if we are to provide the notion of rational interpretation in the literary domain with coherent and consistent conceptual underpinnings. Are we "first" to settle the meaning of the poet's talk of "nothing" in *The Waste Land* before we raise the question of its truth? Or rather must we "first" settle on what "truth" comes to in works like these before we can address questions of meaning? Simply to assert that addressing questions about truth is evidently subsequent to determinations of "meaning," even in poetic discourse, would be overly hasty.

Part of the difficulty here, just as in the previous cases of theory and different uses of language, lies in taking sufficient care with the peculiar domain of discourse that is at issue. Questions about the nature of meaning and truth, and disagreements about their respective priority, may accommodate more than one kind of reasonable discussion depending on whether the pertinent domain is logical, mathematical, scientific, humanistic, and so on.

Or are we to take the persistent disagreement here as pertaining to all domains of discourse in exactly the same respect? This seems unlikely. Thus, at least one central problem about the nature of literal meaning in the representation and in the articulation of moral situations remains outstanding. And that problem is to specify just how these quite complicated matters of meaning and truth are to be understood when it comes specifically to interpreting and understanding puzzling kinds of apparent literal meanings in poetic utterances like, memorably, "Is there nothing in your head?" and "I can connect nothing with nothing."

Conventions and Meanings

The basic problem that undercuts these discussions of interpretation and meaning is that neither of these accounts alone, nor their problematic conjunction, nor any other alternative analytic account meaning seems to be able so far to withstand sustained philosophical scrutiny.

Stephen Schiffer has exhaustively argued this very point. He writes: "if one were to make a list of all the things philosophers have in mind when they talk of 'theories of meaning or intentional content,' then I would claim that there are no two theories satisfying the descriptions on that list."[300] To see the force of this synthetic remark, we need only to recall just what kind of things figure on Schiffer's list.

At the outset,[301] Schiffer describes a hypothetical philosopher of language who has views very much like his own. Moreover, these views also coincide roughly with most of the views still at the centre of much analytic philosophy of language today. Keeping in mind our more particular concerns with what is to count as a reasonable interpretation of the meanings of poetic uses of language in representative instance of the distinctive European high modernist poetry of suffering, we may articulate these views roughly as nine hypotheses. I will list them with brief comment only.

A. "There are semantic facts: some marks and sounds have meaning, some are true, some refer to things, and so on" (xv; 1–2). Specifying the meaning or significance of Eliot's uses of "nothing" in *The Waste Land*, however, needs to be distinguished from the more difficult task of specifying their truth and their reference. Moreover, is the specification of such meanings necessarily the recognition of "semantic facts?"
B. "Every natural language has a compositional meaning theory: a finitely statable theory that specifies the meaning of each word and syntactic construction of the language in a way that determines the meaning of every expression of the language" (xv; 2–3). Yes, but we need to be clear, as Dummett points out, about what counts as a "theory" here. Still, can the meaning of every poetic expression, even deviant ones, be determined, if not recursively, even by inductive specification?
C. "A correct compositional meaning theory for a language is also a compositional truth-theoretic semantics for the language: that is, it determines a truth condition for every utterance in the language that has one" (xvi; 4). But, similarly, why is every utterance said to require truth conditions? Can some well-formed utterances, say in poetry, sometimes lack such conditions?
D. "It would not be possible to account for a human's ability to understand utterances of indefinitely many novel sentences of a language without the assumption that the language had a compositional semantics" (xvi; 4-6). Fine, so long as we can agree on how to answer some of the questions that arise from the scrutiny of particular utterances about the nature of compositional semantics itself.
E. "Humans have beliefs and other propositional attitudes with content" (xvi; 6). And one propositional attitude is interpretation.
F. "Someone's present belief, say, that she is reading, is identical with some internal state of that person's" – some novel state-token "that is that belief" (6). But this won't do unless we can specify fully what vague talk here of "internal state" comes to. And that seems unlikely.
G. "The rational theory of propositional attitudes: believing is a relation to things believed, to values of the variable 'Y' in the schema 'X believes Y' which things have features that determine the intentional features of beliefs" (xvi; 7–10). Similarly, for the propositional attitude of "interpreting," talk of "features" here, especially for the case of rational interpretation, needs specifying.

H. "Semantic and psychological facts are not irreducibly semantic or psychological, but can be revealed to be facts statable in sentences devoid of semantic, mentalistic, and intentional idioms" (xvi; 10–11). Such a claim seems overcommitted to an unexamined and still implicit understanding here of "objectivity."

I. "The Gricean program [[302]], Intention-Based Semantics, is essentially correct, and thus the semantic reduces to the psychological in the style of that program" (xvi; 11–13). Maybe, but, as Grice himself conceded, much remains to be done.[303]

Now this rather long list, we recognize, is easy to quarrel with, especially since many of the items require the careful exposition that Schiffer provides at length if they are not to be misunderstood. Moreover, without being prepared to disavow the list in its entirety, Davidson and Dummett would be quick to distance themselves from some of these claims. Nonetheless, the list remains serviceable. For it reveals with unusual clarity the basic presuppositions that underlie virtually all substantive work in analytic accounts of meaning to date.

As the detailed treatments of these views bring out,[304] these presuppositions in different degrees underlie in particular many of the Davidson and Dummett views that we have taken as representative. Most interestingly, these presuppositions appear to be precisely the ones that finally fail to hold up. After claiming that "there are no true theories satisfying the description" on his list, Schiffer writes: "the questions being asked in the philosophy of language that would require positive theories as answers all have false presuppositions" (265). Or, as he generalizes earlier in his book, "the questions that now define the philosophy of language have false presuppositions" (xx).

This general point includes a more specific one that we need to make explicit. On the basis of protracted individual discussions of each of these nine hypotheses, Schiffer argues that what would qualify as a positive theory of meaning (by contrast with his negative view) is unavailable because of the false presupposition, a Wittgensteinian point, that there are such things as meanings.

Moreover, the meaning of a sentence, *pace* Frege, is not a function of the meaning of its parts. Consequently, no compositional theories of meaning will work either. Further, the relational theory of semantic compositionality and presuppositional attitudes fails as well. Again, just because semantic parts turn out to be irreducible does not entail that a theory of meaning cannot consist either of the results of reductive analysis of semantic idioms. Finally, the Davidsonian assumption that a theory of meaning is a constructive theory of the form a "meaning theory" would have for a natural language is not required to explain how speakers "can effectively determine the meaning or meanings of an arbitrary expression."[305] In short, all positive analytical theories of meaning, at least on Schiffer's thorough investigations, are seriously flawed.

Perhaps Schiffer is, in some important respects, wrong. He may well be. But whatever the qualifications on which a Davidson or a Dummett might insist, we are still left with the prospect of trying to work with a seriously compromised set of descriptive views about meaning. And to the considerable extent that these descriptions, or ones very much like them, must underlie the plausibility of the stimulating but non-descriptive speculative views about meaning in, for example, hermeneutic accounts that we will be considering in our next chapter where we return to second thoughts on modernity, our initial problems here with the analytic views about interpretation and meaning are dangerously compounded.

Having Foresuffered All

At the outset of these investigations into moral discourse and literal meaning, I noted that the passage with which we began occurs in the large, variegated, and complex contexts of Eliot's poem as a whole. Inside that context we find Eliot's perplexing talk of "nothing." But his various uses of this expression are themselves part of a larger set of concerns that seem, at least in part, to elude many of the analytic philosophical reflections here on interpretation and meaning.

Eliot's *The Waste Land* needs to be understood as embodying a particular conception of poetry that has been described as a "dynamic projection, by means of compressed and patterned language, of specific finalities and intensities of emotionally and sensuously charged awareness."[306] Moreover, this compressed and patterned language has an astonishing richness that still eludes much philosophical reflection on language.

Eliot's practice, the same critics have specified, "was to draw on – to mimic or brilliantly adapt – a staggeringly large number of the non-literary ways in which language is spoken or written or chanted or sung (and to borrow whatever he needed from the literary tradition as well). (...) He used language not for narrative or dramatic purposes of character illustration or suspense and resolution, but first and foremost to build the poem's tonal centres" (160). These tonal centres are mainly to be understood in Eliot's own terms in his 1953 piece, "The Three Voices of Poetry," as either "the voice of the poet talking to himself – or to nobody," or "the voice of the poet addressing an audience," or "the voice of the poet when he is saying, not what he would say in his own person, but only what he can say within the limits of one imaginary character addressing another" (cited, p. 160).

These complexities of tone and voice, however, when taken together with the extraordinary range of ordinary and literary uses of language, whether contemporary or traditional, underlie many of our difficulties even today in reasonably interpreting the meaning of Eliot's poetry. And these difficulties are only enhanced when we focus particular attention on just how we are to understand Eliot's poetry of suffering, to comprehend, for example, the shadow behind one's walking in the morning and the shadow ahead of one's walking in the evening, and all in some as yet uncomprehended way foreseen by a Tiresias.

> (And I Tiresias having foresuffered all
> Enacted on this same divan or bed;
> I who have sat by Thebes below the wall
> And walked among the lowest of the dead.)

But of course Eliot does not say that Tiresias foresaw the endless questions and torturous answers in the dialogue we noted – "Do / You know nothing?"– or the very different affirmations in the memory of the hyacinth girl – "And I knew nothing." Rather, Eliot represents Tiresias (but in parentheses) as saying that he has "foresuffered all." And we also recognize in the complexities of both contemporary philosophies of language and the very different complexities of Eliot's high modernist poetry of suffering that we do not yet know enough about what reasonably interpreting the meaning of such expressions might finally come to.

Eliot on Moral Discourse: Second Thoughts

We need now to pull together some of these reflections on moral discourse and literal meaning in Eliot's poetry of suffering. Perhaps we may conclude for now, in a tentative and provisional way only, some second thoughts on Eliot, and, in adding them to some of our second thoughts on both Valéry and Montale, propose for further reflection something roughly like the following.

(C11) Some moral states of affairs present themselves indirectly to reflective readers of such high modernist poetic representations of moral suffering as Eliot's *The Waste Land* as obliging sustained personal responses not just in their literary and aesthetic appreciations but more profoundly in their individual and communal lives.

(C12) These poetic representations of moral suffering consist essentially in the exhibiting of the contents of certain intrinsic and objective moral values that the poet succeeds in reconfiguring by means mainly of non-literal descriptions of plausibly lifelike moral states of affairs.

(C13) While some reflective readers can satisfactorily describe the contents of these configured moral presentations in plainly descriptive language, elucidating both the obligatory and ideal character of the moral substance of these intrinsic and objective moral values on view in some of their poetic representations requires making use of more than plainly elucidative language.

(C14) Such figurative uses of language in the elucidation of these moral contents may be referred to as a matter of moral discourse.

(C15) Contemporary reflection on values in Europe today requires fresh, critical reconsideration of the sources of such values not just in certain normative events and in certain normative texts including works of European high modernist poetry; it requires as well sustained efforts to elucidate such often still sedimented values in more figurative terms rather than exclusively in non-figurative ones.

CHAPTER EIGHT

Residues and Surfeits of Sense

In the previous three chapters we were able to make space for second thoughts about the fruitfulness of the extraordinary linguistic resources to be found in the European high modernist poetry of suffering for helping to work towards consensus in ongoing EU debates of principled bases for an eventual common European social policy. In this chapter we return for second thoughts to our earlier considerations in Chapter Two about the senses of modernity today, for much still remains obscure about the modern intellectual backgrounds of such debates. There we looked in particular at two different philosophical readings of modernity within contemporary Anglo-American philosophical reflection. By contrast, here we will take up two readings of modernity within contemporary continental philosophical reflection.

Poetic Languages

Although Hans-Georg Gadamer presented his most influential discussions on Europe in a collection of essays,[307] much of his reflection on philosophy and literature is to be found in *Truth and Method* (1960). He also discussed questions about the meaning and truth[308] of literary works of art and especially poetry in many of his other works.[309] Some of the most important essays are to be found in *The Relevance of the Beautiful*, a collection that includes shorter work arising almost entirely from some of his subsequent and extensive reflection on the various strengths and weaknesses of *Truth and Method*.

In "Aesthetics and Religious Experience," an essay he first published in 1978, Gadamer took up once again, although only in passing, one of his many formulations about the relations between truth and literary works of art.[310] As so often elsewhere, Gadamer's thorough background in the study of Greek philosophy and philology suggested a starting point in classical literature, in particular in the epic poetry of Hesiod (*Theogony*, lines 26–28). If the muses always inspire the poet with ambiguous sayings that mix what is false with what is true, then the question arises, "what sort of claim to truth is coupled with the poet's freedom of invention?"[311]

Gadamer's concern here is to stake out some of the limits to exclusively "formalist" considerations in the arts.[312] His view is that poetry is always something more than the sum of its formal components. And this something more includes above all matters of meaning and truth. Poetry consists in "presenting something true through the formal mastery of language" (143, Gadamer's emphasis).

Just what this "something true" is Gadamer does not clearly say. He adds however that poetry "communicates a content and elevates that content into a vivid and tangible presence so that it entirely fulfils us" (144). Whether this "something true" is to be identified with a tangible fulfilling presence Gadamer does not say either. Still, he clearly emphasizes here the primacy of truth over meaning.

In an important earlier essay, "The Relevance of the Beautiful" that he first published in 1977, Gadamer already provided a more detailed discussion of truth and poetry.[313] Recalling here Heidegger's work, especially Heideggers's many essays in his 1959 collection, *Unterwegs zur Sprache*, on such German poets as Hölderlin, Georg, Trakl, and Rilke, as well as Heidegger's more general reflections in "The Origin of the Work of Art," Gadamer reflected on how works of art might be said to do something more than manifest meaning. Agreeing with Heidegger's rather obscure claim that art communicates truth in a complex double movement of both concealment and unconcealment, Gadamer argued against "idealist" accounts of art. Not all the meaning that a work of art manifests can be recovered, *pace* some idealist views, just because any response to a work of art is necessarily finite. Consequently, no matter what does become manifest, the artwork always conceals something of its meaning.

This concealed residue however is not to be identified with a residue of meaning only. As Gadamer says after Heidegger, part of what the artwork conceals is its facticity, "the fact that a particular thing such as this exists" (34).[314] Whatever meaning a work of art may be said to manifest, then, is not solely a matter of meaning. Rather, something more than meaning, the claim here goes, makes itself uniquely manifest to human understanding (37). The facticity of the artwork "represents an insurmountable resistance against any superior presumption that we can make sense of it" (34). In short, a work of art may be said both to communicate meaning and to manifest "something true." This "something true" Gadamer takes as the possibility of undergoing and having a certain kind of experience, an experience of "the kind of truth that we encounter in the experience of the beautiful" (18).

Gadamer provided a further context for these mainly but not exclusively Heideggerean reflections on art, truth, and experience in a still earlier essay first published in 1971, "On the Contribution of Poetry to the Search for Truth."[315] Here his accent fell strongly not on the Greek classical starting point of reflections on artworks and truth but on the German classical culmination of these reflections in Goethe and Schiller. Moreover, instead of talk about content versus form and experience versus concepts, he centred his discussion on truth and poetic language. Gadamer argued "that poetic language enjoys a particular and unique relationship to truth" by reason both of the "legitimation" that poetic form confers on content and of the fact that not all poetic form is always adequate for its content (105).

Gadamer's stress on language in these essays showed an unusual approach. Instead of moving, as many Anglo-American philosophers have, from general considerations about the nature, elements, structures, and so on of linguistic communication to the particularities of poetic uses of language, Gadamer argued that, because "poetry is language in a pre-eminent sense," the nature, elements, and structures of poetic language should be taken to determine our understanding of linguistic communication.

The basis of his argument here was the observation that linguistic communication, as the various phenomena of conversational discourse show, involved basic presuppositions. Among these presuppositions are: (a) "that we do not know everything already;" (b) that "what we think we know is capable of becoming questionable;" (c) that we are ready "to allow something to be said to us" (106); and (d) that "there is something clearly in question for us so that what is said must [*sic*] be taken as an answer" (113). And the point of his argument was to put us on our guard about taking the communicative elements of language as the most basic ones.

Building on this analysis Gadamer went on to distinguish between two different "hermeneutic situations," the experience of language in "genuine dialogue" and the experience of language in poetry. The first experience is with speech, especially in speaking with one another. "When we speak to one another," he writes, "we do not so much transmit well-defined facts, as place our own aspirations and knowledge into a broader and richer horizon through dialogue with the other" (106). The second experience of language is with understanding poetry: "When we read a poem, it never occurs to us to ask who it is that wants to say something to us or why. Here we are wholly directed toward the word as it stands. We are not recipients of some form of communication that might reach us from this or that person. The poem does not stand before us as a thing that someone employs to tell us something. It stands there equally independent of both reader and poet; detached from all intending, the word is complete in itself" (107).

These reflections led Gadamer to a different formulation of the relations between poetry and truth than those that arose from his initial reflections on Hesiod. There Gadamer's question arose out of a tension within the doctrine of poetic inspiration between truth and falsity in what is inspired versus truth and falsity in what is created. His question now, however, is no longer about what claim to truth can be coupled with the poet's invention, but about "in what sense there can be truth in such a word," i.e., in the poetic word taken above as "complete in itself."

When we return to some of the perplexing uses of poetic language in the European high modernist poetry of suffering, we note immediately the pertinence of some if not all of Gadamer's reflections here. Thus, the contrast Gadamer wants to promote between concepts of meaning and truth on one level and experiences of meaning and truth on the other connects nicely with Gadamer's emphasis here on interpretation as trying to articulate the occurrences of a certain obscure experience.

Similarly, Gadamer's concern to invert the usual subordination of sense and significance of poetic discourse to the demands of a prior and quite general theory of linguistic communication finds an echo in his stress on a certain sympathetic identification with certain speakers in certain poetic works as some kind of prior condition that must be met before the meaning of these works can be apprehended.

Finally, Gadamer's reflections on interpretation, whatever their difficulties, do imply a central awareness of the importance of his distinction here between the experience of language in conversational dialogue and the very different experiences of language in poetry. In poetry, utterances are no longer mere means for interpersonal communication. Rather utterances here are ends of some sort that characteristically call attention to their quasi-independent status. Despite these helpful initial points, however, more detail from Gadamer proves useful.

The Primary and the Secondary

In the same essay from 1971 "On the Contribution of Poetry to the Search for Truth," Gadamer develops further his notion of a certain completeness in poetic uses of expression that links them to their conversational ones. He points out that the history of both the epic and the drama illustrate that "not everything can be expressed in a poetic way in every age" (107). Thus the initial formulation of his lead question yields a more perspicuous one: what does "truth" mean and what kinds of truth are implied by "the fact that certain forms of expression are possible [in a particular era] while others are not." More succinctly, "what does it mean to say that certain forms of poetic language are no longer 'true'? What is the meaning of 'truth' here?" (107–108).

Despite some problems with these formulations, Gadamer tries to answer his questions about privileging both meaning and truth rather than just one or the other exclusively. Thus, he calls attention to a key distinction between what he calls a primary and a secondary meaning of the Greek word for truth, *aletheia*. Something is true in the primary sense, Gadamer thinks, when it is "open": that is, when speaking with one another "we tell the truth" in the sense that "we say what we mean." By contrast, something is true in the secondary sense when "something shows itself": that is, when something shows itself to be just the thing it really is, when something [as it were] " 'says' what it 'means' " (108).

In the first case, persons say what they mean; in the second, things show what they are. In each case the Greeks spoke of some thing being true, whether the thing be an utterance or a material entity. This is the perspective from which Gadamer goes on to speak of "the truth of things."

For Gadamer, poetic language includes "poetic words," or what he calls later "poetic statements" (*Aussagen*). These "statements," where the word "statement" is understood in a non-conventional way, exhibit a kind of completeness reflected in the legal uses of the word "statement," for example when a witness makes a "statement" before the court. Moreover, poetic statements also exhibit an autonomy in the sense that, unlike the statement of a witness, the poetic statement "bears witness to itself and does not admit anything that might verify it"; it requires no "external verification" (110).

A poetic statement is "true," Gadamer now asserts, "in the sense that it discloses [something], producing this self-fulfilment" (112). And what a poetic statement discloses is "a specific content intended in a particular way [that] comes to stand in a poem by means of its emergence as a true word" (113).

This discussion of poetic statement yields a final reformulation of Gadamer's initial question about poetry and truth. The question now is no longer about poetic creativity, poetic inspiration, and claims to truth. Nor is it about the relation between the completeness and autonomy of poetic statements and truth. Rather the question now is: what is the relation between truth and poetry and "the fact that what the word [i.e., a poetic statement] evokes is always there"? (113)

Gadamer here eschews any further extended discussion and offers his response immediately:

> It does not matter whether we are concerned with specific themes that are expressed in our own or at any other time, for the decisive thing is that the word [i.e., a poetic statement] summons up what is 'there' so that it is palpably near. The truth of poetry consists in creating a 'hold upon nearness.' (...) the poetic word brings the transience of time to a standstill. It too 'stands written,' not as a promise, nor as a pledge, but as a saying where its own presence is in play. (...) The word of the poet does not simply continue [the] process of *Einhausung*, 'of making ourselves at home.' Instead it stands over against this process like a mirror held up to it. But

> what appears in the mirror is not the world, nor this or that thing in the world, but rather this nearness or familiarity itself in which we stand for a while. This standing and this nearness find permanence in the language of literature and, most perfectly, in the poem (113–115).

In short, Gadamer's later work raises questions about truth and meaning in poetry – think of the European high modernist poetry of suffering that we have been considering throughout this essay – by calling attention to the limits of both a certain "formalism" and a certain "idealism." In the first case, part of what analyzing the formal components of a literary artwork leaves unaddressed are matters of truth. And in the second, part of what an idealism cannot address according to Gadamer is the necessarily finite character of any response to an artwork. Something more is always on hand. And this something more is always the facticity and contingency of the artwork's relation to both truth and meaning. Accordingly, Gadamer sees in any thoughtful experience one may come to have with a work of art a "double movement" of manifestation and concealment.

Besides this first major theme of a double movement, Gadamer articulates as well his views on the primacy of language as poetry over language as communication. Unlike some philosophers of language however different such as, for example, Davidson and Dummett and Schiffer some of whose views we considered earlier, Gadamer wants to subordinate the elements and structures of linguistic communication in spoken dialogues to the features of poetic communication in interpretation. For Gadamer thinks that features of poetic language, and in particular features of poetic "statement," are the authentic sources of meaning and truth in poetry.

Thus, for Gadamer the pertinent features here of poetic communication are basically three. The first feature of poetic statement is the completeness of poetic language in the sense of the links among poetic statements, their history, and their quasi-legal irrevocableness. The second is the autonomy of such statements in the sense that such statements require no further supporting evidence than their own peculiar character. This feature comprises the unique capacity of poetic statements to both "summon" and to provide a hold on the "nearness" of things against an inexorable impermanence. And the final feature of poetic statement is the insistence on linking meaning with truth.

These three major features of poetic statement, Gadamer believes, give rise to a construal of truth in terms of both what is said in these statements (i.e., what poets say in the poetic statements when they say what they mean) and what these statements show (i.e., what the peculiar features of poetic statements allow of something to become manifest in the double movement of concealment and unconcealment). Whatever meaning such statements may properly exhibit arises from the residual "truth" of these statements, whatever of the world may or may not partly come to stand in the speaking of language itself in poetic statement.

Informally then, and rather roughly, with many examples of the distinctive European high modernist poetry of suffering and passage in mind, perhaps we may now provisionally formulate these views in some such terms as these.

1) Poetic language both manifests and conceals meaning in such a way that the necessarily contingent response to any work of poetic art always must leave some meaning concealed.
2) The fact that the attempt to interpret any poetic artwork provokes a realization of an irretrievable residue of meaning gives rise to a recognition of the finitude of human understanding.
3) What is finitely and hence necessarily imperfectly apprehended in a poetic work of art is mainly the "something true" that poetic language vividly presents and communicates through some of the perfection of its formal properties.
4) Poetic language includes "poetic statements" exhibiting a completeness and autonomy that are key elements for understanding this "something true" in a double sense. This double sense comprises, first, what the poet succeeds in saying when he or she says in a particular way what he or she means; and, second, something showing itself in a particular way as the thing it most authentically is in what it makes manifest of its meaning in language.
5) This double sense, however, is more than a complex content. For it arises in those statements that bring fugitive things to a stand in the saying and showing of poetic language, and thereby brings the reader into a new and near familiarity with what things genuinely are.

To return to one of our initial examples from our opening section on Orientations, the meaning of Eliot's difficult uses of expressions like "Do you know nothing? (...) You know nothing" is necessarily subordinated to whatever of the world may or may not partly come to stand in the way language itself seems to speak in these poetic expressions. And when a critic propounds an interpretation of such poetic language, as in the section, Interlude, where Helen Gardener talks of the women in the chorus of Eliot's play, *Murder in the Cathedral*, "identifying themselves with a whole world groaning and travailing" and of ourselves needing to identify with these women in order to share in the mystery of this experience, we need not demur. For in attending to the demands of interpreting Eliot's poetic language the critic may also use language in such a way as to try to bring to a stand in his or her interpretation what makes itself manifest in the poetry.

The Sedimented and the Supplemented

Gadamer's discussions of meaning and truth in the experience of literary artworks is a major element in a second contemporary hermeneutic reflection on such questions in the work of Paul Ricoeur.[316] Although Ricoeur saw two of his works, *The Rule of Metaphor* (1977) and *Time and Narrative* (1983–1985), as parts of a whole, in fact the latter work incorporates some important qualifications in his views.[317] For besides introducing some needed nuance, this work brings out more clearly than the former one does several key relations between questions of meaning and questions of truth. We may consider these in turn.[318]

In the first volume of his *Time and Narrative*, while discussing what he sees as a gap between historical and narrative explanation, Ricoeur recalls Husserl's investigations of Galilean and Newtonian science in his unfinished and posthumously published *The Crisis of the European Sciences (1934–1937)*. There Husserl was concerned with "the genesis of meaning," a notion Ricoeur wants to use to specify historical explanation. Ricoeur speaks accordingly of the genesis of meaning as "the meaning of the noetic intention that forms the historical character of history and keeps it from dissolving into the other types of knowledge" (1.179–180).

Ricoeur's point is that before meaning is articulated in the structure of a particular kind of explanation, meaning is already sedimented in the world of everyday action and interaction. Meaning arises out of a social and cultural social world, a world of immediate "lived experience" as Husserl liked to say, one that is prior to scientific knowledge. The mediate articulation of meaning then always refers back to the immediate inarticulate meaning immanent in the basic world of interaction (1.182).

If the genesis of meaning lies not in knowledge but in action, any particular narrative, as Ricoeur writes, "has its full meaning when it is restored to the time of nature and of suffering in mimesis" (1.70). Thus the unreflected domain of action not only is the source of meaning; it also comprises an antecedent fullness of meaning to which subsequent articulations of meaning refer.[319] This fullness of meaning is sedimented in the symbolic mediation of action.

Ricoeur understands "symbol" here largely after Ernst Cassirer's use, i.e., as part of "cultural processes that articulate experience" (1.57).[320] However, he stresses the public aspect of such processes, the way in which actions become readable as subject to rules as norms. Consequently, although immanent in action, the fullness of meanings sedimented in action is publicly accessible by reason of the symbolic mediations of action.

As Ricoeur notes, "the symbol introduces a twofold relation of meaning into the gesture as the behaviour whose interpretation it governs. We may take the empirical configuration of a gesture as the literal meaning bearing a figurative one. At the limit, this meaning can appear, in certain conditions neighbouring on secrecy, as a hidden meaning to be decoded. That is how any social ritual appears to strangers, without any need for turning their interpretation towards something esoteric or hermetic" (2.43–44).[321]

These two notions of the genesis of meaning and of a fullness of meaning mediated symbolically lead to a third, the idea of an increase of meaning that Ricoeur discusses in the final volume of his trilogy. Although he finds the idea of retrieving the origin of meaning, and thereby not just a fullness but an increase of meaning, in Heidegger's analyses of time and temporality (3.79), Ricoeur nuances these analyses by choosing to talk about "a supplement of meaning" (1.93).

As he went on to point out much later in his phenomenological description of reading, Ricoeur's talk here of an increase or supplement of meaning is to be understood in terms not just of a fullness but of an indeterminate and inexhaustible surfeit of meaning in the symbolic mediation of action. "What the work of reading reveals," Ricoeur claims, "is not only a lack of determinacy but also an excess of meaning. Every text, even a systematically fragmentary one, is revealed to be inexhaustible in terms of reading, as though, through its unavoidably selective character, reading revealed an unwritten aspect in the text. It is the prerogative of reading to strive to provide a figure for this unwritten side of the text" (3.169). Thus the symbolic mediation of action that literary texts represent and readers configure has an inexhaustible meaning potential (cf. 3.227).

Throughout his trilogy Ricoeur keeps returning to qualify some of his own distinctive philosophical concerns with the help of comparisons and contrasts with Gadamer's work. One of the most important discussions occurs late in the third volume where Ricoeur takes up the crucial senses of the hermeneutic notion of "tradition." Commenting on how Gadamer's controversial proposal that some truth-claims are only mediated by the past in the sense that before we actually evaluate such claims we are already inside particular historical traditions, Ricoeur writes:

> the question of meaning (...) cannot be separated from the question of truth except in abstraction. Every proposal of a meaning is at the same time a claim to truth. What we receive from the past are, in effect, beliefs, persuasions, convictions; that is, ways of holding for true; to use the insight of the German word *Für-wahr-halten*, which signifies belief. (...) it is this tie between the language-like realm of traditions, and the truth claim bound to the order of meaning that confers a certain plausibility on the threefold plea [of Gadamer] for prejudice, authority, and, finally, tradition. (...) the pre-judged is thus a structure of the pre-understanding outside of which the "thing itself" cannot make itself heard. (...) as for authority, it signifies (...) the increase that the claim to truth adds to mere meaning, in the context of "holding-for-true". (...) [and as for tradition] we are carried along by it before we are in a position of judging it, or of condemning it (3.222–223).

The point of this extended comment is that any initial attempt to put oneself at a distance with respect to any set of truth claims is a mistake just because of what tradition here is taken to be. "Through tradition," Ricoeur summarizes, "we find ourselves already situated in an order of meaning and therefore also of possible truth" (3.223). Consequently, the transmitted contents of a tradition as bearers of meaning include certain truth claims that already bring with them a "presumption of truth." For we receive such claims with an initial confidence as to their well-foundedness and warrantability before we set about the task of public argument and discussion of these contents (3.227).[322]

Just as in the case with Gadamer so too here with Ricoeur, these reflections on meaning are helpful in the contexts of our concern with articulating a broader, less constrained account of meaning so as to allow for rational interpretation of the European high modernist poetry of suffering. When we return, to take one example only, to some of the perplexing elements in our application of Gadamer's reflections on interpretation to the painful poetic exchanges in Eliot's *The Waste Land* in chapters two and seven, Ricoeur's stress here on the genesis of meaning in action is pertinent. An interpretation cannot be deemed unreasonable just on the grounds that some of its uses of language can seem to be as obscure as the poetic expressions they are meant to elucidate.

The interpreter sometimes must try to fashion an idiom that takes seriously the complex ways in which meanings arise not just in poetic representation of states of affairs but especially of dynamic situations. Here the interpreter is keenly aware that the poetic language of the obscure exchanges in the poem is provoked by situations that occur not just in fiction but in life. Whatever sense and significance of so many poetic lines about "nothing" may have is inextricably linked with the simultaneous unfolding of a situation that cannot be understood as exclusively literary.

In the case moreover of his poetic drama, *Murder in the Cathedral*, which we discussed briefly in the Interlude, the poetic expressions are themselves embodied in a tragic and liturgical choral commentary that provides still more of the complex contexts for the sense and significance of these expressions. Given these complexities, we need to allow the reflective interpreter who appreciates the need to articulate an appropriate account sufficient speculative room for experimenting with fresh uses of ordinary critical terms. But before attempting some formulations, we need somewhat more detail about the substance of Ricoeur's views.

Referring Empirically and Non-Empirically

Ricoeur's reflections on the reciprocity of questions about meaning and truth when seen in the context of a hermeneutic understanding of tradition need to be kept in view when we turn to his more detailed reflections on the difference between historical and fictional narratives. Ricoeur sees these two types of narrative as closely related by reason of their common "mimetic" procedures, a polyvalent term Ricoeur carefully analyses into different senses. These procedures are taken to be the common "configurating operations" in the two basic types of narrative, whereas the difference for Ricoeur lies in their different relations to "the questions of truth" (2.3).[323]

Historical narrative alone "can claim a reference inscribed in historical reality" (1.82). Yet, in trying to retrieve the traces of past events, historical narratives need to make use not just of what Ricoeur calls empirical reference but also of a non-empirical, metaphysical reference that characterizes imaginative construction. Conversely, fictional narrative while centred on the use of metaphysical reference needs, for example in its reliance on normal uses of the past tense, to proceed as if it were using empirical reference as well.[324]

Consequently, Ricoeur speaks of an "interweaving of referential modes" while insisting nonetheless on a distinction between empirical and non-empirical modes of reference (1.82, 1.85, 1.92). This distinction serves to introduce an asymmetry between the two kinds of narrative such that the reliance on empirical reference in historical narrative privileges that kind of narrative's relation to truth claims (2.158). As Ricoeur writes later, "only historical narrative claims to refer to a 'real' past, that is, to what actually happened" (3.5).

Ricoeur's major concern, however, throughout the detail of these three volumes is with meaning and interpretation in the special case of temporality. His controversial thesis is that "time becomes human to the extent that it is articulated through a narrative mode, and narrative attains its full meaning when it becomes a condition of temporal existence" (1.52).[325] Thus, when Ricoeur talks of truth claims, tradition, and reference, his interest lies in showing that "what is ultimately at stake in the case (...) of the truth claim of every narrative work is the temporal character of human existence" (1.3).

Ricoeur thinks that narrative fictions raise problems that are simpler than those that lyric poetry presents. The reason he provides, however, is somewhat obscure. These problems are simpler, he writes, "because the world [i.e. in narrative fictions] (...) is apprehended from the angle of human praxis rather than from that of cosmic pathos. What is re-signified by narrative is what was already pre-signified at the level of human acting" (1.81). And these problems are more complicated than those lyric poetry raises because of the asymmetry between fictional and historical narrative "with respect to [narrativity's] referential intention and truth claim" (1.81). This asymmetry is what pushes Ricoeur to propose the interweaving of the two kinds of reference we have already noted, empirical and non-empirical.

Part of the background for these views is to be found in Ricoeur's glosses on what precisely it means for a fictional narrative to be "true." The pertinent sense turns out to be a "concern for being true – in the sense of being faithful – to reality, or for equating art and life." (2.11). And this notion itself Ricoeur sees as involving the further idea of "verisimilitude" not just as a resemblance to truth but as an image, "a semblance of truth" as well (2.13). Thus the relation between fictional narrative and truth is caught up in a tension between truth as a faithfulness to the real and truth as a semblance of this real.

Yet Ricoeur himself leaves the door open to a certain criticism of his work here, particularly of his preference for fictional narrative over lyric poetry. Thus, at the very end of his second volume he writes: "Only after a theory of reading has been proposed (...) will fictional narrative be able to assert its claims to truth, at the cost of a radical reformulation of the problem of truth. This will involve the capacity of the work of art to indicate and to transform human action" (2.160).

But this reformulation itself may testify to something already gone awry in the initial understanding of fictional narrative and truth that provokes the reformulation. And the reformulation to which Ricoeur is finally brought turns out to be none other than the inseparability of questions about truth from those about meaning, the very issues with which we began.

In summary, Ricoeur calls sustained philosophical attention to the genesis of meaning in the pre-reflective lived world of action by contrast with the reflected represented world of knowledge. Meaning here exhibits a peculiar fullness in the symbolic mediation of the lived world of action, for example in ritual and festival (think of the Canterbury Festival at which Eliot's *Murder in the Cathedral* was first performed). And because of its symbolic mediation, meaning even at this pre-reflective level is not private and hence is publicly accessible to some degree.

Like Gadamer however, Ricoeur argues for a certain excess of meaning, an inexhaustibleness of meaning that at any one historical moment must partly elude all of our cognitive strategies (including reflective critical interpretation) aimed towards getting at the truth of things. These strategies themselves exhibit certain "structures of pre-understanding" that, among others, comprise tradition. Consequently, we are already implicated in certain traditions before we deploy any particular effort at interpretation, just as we already are part of a pre-reflective lived world of action. Thus whatever putative claims to truth we set out to examine may be said to bring along with them a certain antecedent presumption of truth. In this regard, not just meaning but truth itself in some hermeneutic sense arises out of a pre-reflective and pre-cognitive domain.

The many strategies we habitually use to understand both meaning and truth include both historical and fictional narratives. For Ricoeur, as we have seen, each of these has a somewhat different relation to truth although each is taken to be complementary to the other. Thus Ricoeur speaks of an intertwining of two referential modes, empirical and non-empirical reference, in both history and fiction.

Since, however, history primarily makes use of empirical reference, Ricoeur privileges historical over fictional narrative and over lyric poetry. And he argues that the sense of truth at issue in the empirical reference of historical narrative is truth both as a faithfulness to the real and as a semblance of the real. But, just as in the case of meaning so too in that of truth, Ricoeur construes the real in terms of the priority of the pre-cognitive and the pre-reflective over the lived world of action. Consequently he argues for the necessity to overcome any merely abstract separation between questions of meaning and those of truth.

Informally then, and rather roughly once again with our examples of the distinctive European high modernist poetry of suffering in mind, perhaps as we did with Gadamer's views we may now provisionally formulate Ricoeur's views here in some such terms as these.

6) The meaning of a reflective critical interpretation arises out of our immediate, unreflective, pre-cognitive, social and cultural world of interaction in the symbolically mediated, public fullness of lived experience prior to scientific theorizing and knowledge.
7) Articulations of interpretive meaning always refer back to this genesis of meaning in an inexhaustible fullness.
8) Questions of meaning are so closely connected with questions of truth that they can be separated only in abstraction.
9) For raising one kind of question already involves the raising the other, since in the lived world of human interaction we are already situated within traditions that incorporate presumptions of both meaning and truth.
10) In the case of lyric poetry, as in those of both fictional and non-fictional narrative, we find an intertwining of both empirical and non-empirical reference such that talk of truth is subject to the tension between truth as faithfulness to the real and truth as semblance of the real.

Accordingly, when we return again to the European high modernist poetry of suffering, we find that a rational and reasonable interpretation cannot separate any final understanding of the meaning of such poetic "statements" from their truth. And that is the case, if Ricoeur is right, because sources of these questions must be finally situated in the symbolic mediation of the pre-reflective and pre-cognitive world of lived as opposed to represented experience.

Blocking the View

While respecting the important differences between these two representative hermeneutic accounts, just as we did much earlier between two representative analytic views, we need finally to ask just how satisfactory these views are. In particular, we want to know how adequate these hermeneutic views of meaning are when confronted with the difficulties of interpreting central works of the European high modernist poetry of suffering such as those we have been examining here. Consider finally then still another high modernist work.

> Never, not for a single day, do we have
> before us that pure space into which flowers
> endlessly open. Always there is World
> and never Nowhere without the No: that pure unseparated element which one breathes
> without desire and endlessly knows. A child
> may wander there for hours, through the timeless
> stillness, may get lost in it and be
> shaken back. Or someone dies and is it.
> For, nearing death, one doesn't see death; but stares
> beyond, perhaps with an animal's vast gaze.
> Lovers, if the beloved were not there
> blocking the view, are close to it, and marvel (...)
> As if by some mistake, it opens for them
> behind each other (...) But neither can move past
> the other, and it changes back to World.

Before looking more closely at these lines from the Eighth Elegy of Rainer Maria Rilke's *Duino Elegies* (1923),[326] we do well to notice several general points here that make reflectively interpreting these lines perhaps more complicated than many of those we considered from Eliot or from Valéry or from Montale with which they are broadly related.

Rilke's lines here first of all are presented in an English translation only, one of many translations into English of these elegies and no doubt not the last. Each generation of poets, to take the English speaking world only, finds it necessary to translate all over again such cardinal texts in European high literary modernism, just as Eliot's poems continue to be translated throughout the non-English speaking world. The fact then that these lines are translated and indeed will continue to require translation is one major difficulty for interpretation.

Another initial feature of these lines is their situation not just within a section of an extended lyric like the lines of Eliot lines that form part of one section only in his *The Waste Land*. Rilke's lines are part of an extended poetic sequence whose very complicated compositional history stretches out over at least ten years.[327] The further difficulty here then is how to interpret such lines in sufficiently large yet nuanced enough terms to do justice to both their complex setting and their complex history.

Finally, unlike the other examples that share this term, these lines do not include several of the especially puzzling expressions in Eliot's earlier poetry and poetic drama, expressions like the term "nothing" or "I do not know." But without using such expressions, these lines nonetheless directly suggest this negative motif with the unusual conjunctions of "Never, not" and "never No-where without the No."

Moreover, these lines also suggest the negative motif indirectly: consider the evocative series of contrasted expressions such as "pure space," "world," "pure unseparated element," "timeless stillness," "death," "beyond," "vast," and "opens." Thus, still another difficulty for interpretation here, when compared with the already demanding examples from Eliot, is dealing perspicuously and judiciously with direct and indirect suggestions in poetic uses of negative expressions.

After reflection, I think we can see how the hermeneutic account of meaning and truth that we have recalled in some detail can make several important contributions to the task of dealing effectively not only with these initial general difficulties for interpretation but with particular ones also For example, the notion of poetic language as "poetic statement" enjoying a certain primacy and priority over the uses of language in everyday communication is provocative.

This notion suggests that whatever categories we bring to the task of rational interpretation should not derive exclusively, as many Anglo-American accounts would have it, from a reflection on the presuppositions of linguistic communication. Rather, interpretation needs to proceed as well with a clear focus on the "autonomy" and "completeness" of poetic language as such.

This suggestion of course is not uncontroversial. But it does serve at least the purpose of warning against various kinds of linguistic reductionism where poetic language is subordinated, inevitably, to the explanatory strategies used in the analysis of non-poetic language.

The hermeneutic account is also helpful in assembling salutary reminders for rational interpretation about the inexhaustibleness of meaning as arising out of the ongoing pre-reflective world of lived experience. Meaning on this view can never be fully articulated without leaving a dynamic residue. Moreover, the inexhaustibleness of meaning is situated in the symbolic mediations of pre-cognitive interaction. Thus, in the case of poetry, sustained interpretive attention must be devoted not just to literal versus non-literal meaning but especially to symbolic meaning. How this is to be done is not spelled out. But the stress on the fullness of symbolic meaning in a pre-reflective world must be addressed.

Besides these reflections on language and meaning the hermeneutic account also provides a suggestive discussion of reference and truth for rational interpretation. The emphasis here not just on empirical versus non-empirical reference in, say, "poetic statements," but on the "intertwining" of these kinds of reference calls attention to a complex set of issues in the interpretation of the poetry of suffering that analytic accounts pass over too quickly.

Moreover, the reminder from both Wittgenstein and Heidegger of the importance of distinguishing between what "poetic statements" may say with respect to truth and what they may show is quite useful. For it provides a way of dealing with the problem of how poetic language often seems to mean more than it says either to its author or to its interpreters.

The further distinction, however sketchy, between say poetic truth as faithfulness to the world versus poetic truth as a verisimilitude of the world may be developed perhaps as different kinds of a showing that is particularly pertinent when dealing with how symbolic uses of language refer. Finally, the hermeneutic claim that questions of meaning and questions of truth are inseparable except by way of abstraction remains a cryptic but nevertheless suggestive point about the need to address both issues even when dealing mainly with only one or the other in poetic interpretation.

Despite these instructive elements in the hermeneutic accounts however, a number of serious deficiencies seem evident. Without protracting our criticism or trying to make it complete, we need to point out at least some difficulties with the three major issues just looked at.

Thus, with regard to the primacy of poetic language as "poetic statement," just what the hermeneutic account is getting at remains extremely unclear. Putting us on our guard about imposing in an uncritical way on the analysis of poetic language certain conceptual categories derived form the uses of language elsewhere is one thing. But to assume, as these hermeneutic views appear to, that there is something quite specific called "poetic language" (not to mention "poetic statements") that can be clearly delineated from non-poetic language is something else. The long, difficult, and continuing development of different schools of structuralist linguistics shows, among many other considerations, that the notion of "poetic language" in the hermeneutic account is far too general to be of much theoretical use for interpretation.

Similarly, however useful the welcome emphasis in the hermeneutic views on symbolic uses of language and the care taken to show the different senses in which "the symbolic" is at issue, talk of the extremely elusive notion of meaning in terms of inexhaustible potential and the pre-cognitive structures of the lived-world remains too general for the interpretation of European high modernist lyric poetry.

Of course the reply may well be, if we require more detailed analyses, we need only to look at the endless analyses Husserl furnished in his *Logical Investigations* or in *Formal and Transcendental Logic* or in *Experience and Judgment*.

But just what remains philosophically convincing today in this impressive work is not even clear to Husserl specialists much less to those interested in the European high modernist lyric and the poetry of suffering. So we require a fresh attempt not only to take the critical measure of the basic presumption here of a coherence in the notion of a pre-reflective, pre-cognitive world but to specify the overly vague talk of the inexhaustibleness of meaning precisely in the domain of the literary arts. Otherwise, interpretation of European high modernist poetry need not change its usual presuppositions before turning to the interpretation of the poetry of suffering.

Finally, whatever sense we may succeed in making of poetic truth as both reflection and verisimilitude, both resemblance and semblance, a saying and a showing, a bringing to stand of the fugitive "truth of things," we remain puzzled about the inseparability claim about truth and meaning. How can we reformulate this claim sharply enough that it will allow of confirmation or disconfirmation? How can we draw the relevant consequences from such a claim for the interpretation of such lines as Eliot's? And if one's aims include those of clarifying just this kind of talking about the interrelatedness of truth and meaning, how is one to proceed without begging the central questions?

Whatever the suggestiveness then of the hermeneutic accounts of meaning and truth, the genuine difficulties that still encumber these accounts raise serious problems for anyone tempted to adopt such views without further reflection. Fortunately, a good deal of contemporary work both in the Anglo-American tradition and in the continental tradition continues to prove instructive. As for us, we cannot try to survey that work here. Rather, we must now move to conclude in our immediately ensuing final section entitled "Envoi."

ENVOI

With both preliminary and then interim conclusions now in hand from the previous chapters, before ending we do well to return to the leitmotif of our essay. We first enunciated this leitmotif in our initial "Orientations" and then detailed this major theme further in the "Interlude." That leitmotif has been the suggestiveness of the linguistic and conceptual richness of some of the European high modernist poetry of suffering for achieving eventual consensus about the resources and liabilities of forms of moral intuitionism for coming properly to know and to re-articulate the principled bases of a common EU social policy. Consider then briefly a final time the need for and the difficulties in achieving a common European harmonized social policy.

Homeless in Europe

Many more persons today travel very far and very widely than in the previous generations. On their return home these people usually have stories to tell of their adventures among peoples they had met for the first time and of places they had not visited previously. Like Herodotus fashioning an occasion for recounting his adventures, such people return home from their extensive travels and often make an opportunity for recounting their adventures in great detail for the delight and instruction of their friends and neighbours.

Sometimes, however, these otherwise exhilarating stories end with sad accounts of the quite extreme poverty of so many persons glimpsed along the way. Returning from visits to the many Mogul tombs in India,[328] for example, some friends may finish their marvellous stories with distressing accounts of destitute and famished children lying in the streets of Kolkata while untouchable multitudes of sacred cows wander unbothered in their midst.[329]

But one need not travel to India to find, if not sacred cows, then both untouchable subjects and destitute children. For almost every capital city in the EU in 2009 harbours an important number of utterly destitute homeless children.[330] Yet these extremely impoverished street children continue to live precariously in the midst of extraordinary European affluence.[331] Successive governments in various EU countries come and go, each with a plan for, among so many other matters, remedying permanently the shame and the immense suffering of the destitute street children in their comfortable midst. But as in Kolkata so too in Paris: many still uncounted homeless children suffering from extreme poverty, with the retardation of normal cognitive and affective development as one of its many terrible consequences, are still finding night-time shelter only in the streets and momentarily quelling their hunger by sniffing glue and other toxic substances.[332]

This is the problem not of homeless people generally but, in even more painful particulars, the specific problem of homeless street children.[333] And the problem of homeless street children is, like the problem of generalized access of poor children to proper health care and the problem of properly integrating immigrants coming from outside the EU, one of the central social issues facing the emerging Europe.[334] Despite repeated attempts to remedy such intolerable situations in the affluent cities of the EU, why do such inhumane and profoundly unjust situations persist in the midst of plenty?

Many professional social scientists concur in citing as one of the major elements for persistent failures to remedy these situations the lack of sufficient political will to muster the requisite monies and energies to institutionalize lasting solutions. But what then is "sufficient political will?"

Most recently, and with regard to a very different matter, EU countries have demonstrated what such a "sufficient political will" looks like. They have mobilized their power, their resources, and their populations in historically unprecedented ways to face up to the consequences of the financial and economic crisis which began in the United States in September 2008 when the American government allowed the investment bank of Lehman Brothers to fail, and which then spread to Europe as well as to the entire world. After allocating hundreds of billions of dollars and euros, we are told that, thanks to the requisite political will among other things, recovery is now underway. But not a single EU country has yet demonstrated any similar requisite political will to face up to the morally unacceptable problem of the persisting destitution of its many homeless street children.

Reflecting more generally on what is to account for the apparent unwillingness of countries across the world to address effectively the globalized problems of extreme poverty today – think of the very carefully considered millennial projects of the United Nations initially projected in 2000 for realization in 2015 and now judged already to be a failure – one of France's most distinguished biological scientists has recently argued for an explanation of such ineffective action not in terms of a lack of sufficient political will but most fundamentally in terms of a lack of adequate perception. Responsible people just don't see the problem; they just don't perceive things the way they really are.[335] Like those governments and highly placed persons around the world who in fact showed themselves capable of finally remedying some problems of extreme poverty, so too those governments and highly placed persons in the EU who are capable of finally remedying the problem of utterly destitute street children in their countries perhaps just don't perceive the problem.

That is, many knowledgeable, powerful, resourceful European parliamentarians simply do not perceive what makes finally remedying the continuing problem of destitute and homeless children in the streets of some of Europe's wealthiest cities like Paris and London and Rome the terribly insistent problem it is. In short, on the evidence of their incapacities finally to solve this common problem perhaps one may not unfairly hold that their perceptions are distorted to such a degree that such persons have become morally blind to the persisting social injustice of allowing such a solvable problem to continue. Without recovering a reliable perception of the moral and ethical issues in such fundamental problems as the persisting and very grave social injustice within the EU of utterly destitute and homeless street children, inadequately generalized access to health care, very widespread inequities in dealings with increasing numbers of people immigrating to Europe, and other quite serious social issues as well, no eventually harmonized European social policy is possible.

This meditative and speculative essay in philosophy and literature has focussed on the necessities of enlarging our usual moral and ethical idioms. Our somewhat unconventional approach here has been to reconsider some only of the immense verbal resources for rearticulating our common European ethical and moral intuitions on hand in some of the European high modernist poetry of suffering and passage. For these are among the richest linguistic and conceptual resources that can open our eyes once again to perceiving reliably what should lie at the principled foundations of those shared values that must inform any finally satisfactory common European social policy.

With these reminders of our leitmotif in hand, we need now to return a last time now to some of our recurring themes in our previous reflections on modernity and the European high modernist poetry of suffering.

Modernist Poetic Re-articulations?

"Modernist poetry," one critic writes, "provides (...) a power to shape our models for reading and valuing literature and a power to establish images or models of mental activity that agents in the culture treat as basic features in their self-representations."[336] The second of these powers, literature's power to establish models, is what especially concerns those who would like to explore further the larger contexts of suffering, poetry, and philosophy.

However, talk of "models" is too strong. Yet unless we explore some of this kind of talk freshly, poetry in the post-modern period will continue to relinquish the formative role it played in the modernist era to what are often, if not always, the not-inconsequential vagaries of literary theory and intellectual fashion.

Behind these claims for poetry lies a particular appreciation of important cultural parallels between the present era and the modernist period. "We face essentially the same cultural pressures," the critic continues, "as did the modernist poets. The interpretive languages that hold authority over our social life are devoted to mapping human motives and powers of agency into the designed, manageable structures proposed by the social sciences (...) one effect (...) is a dangerously reductive image of human agency."

Another, we need to add, is an equally dangerous because similarly reductive understanding of reason as merely procedural, instrumental, and functional, as merely representing relations among our goals and the means for attaining them without reason's being able to envision novel goals altogether.

Perhaps we have yet to take seriously enough the claim that the central question of European high modernism is the meaning of its poetry. This poetry is the heir of a double not a single tradition. And both traditions can be seen in the work of T.S. Eliot with which we began these reflections: the eighteenth-century enlightenment preoccupations with action and history we find in the spatially distended dialogues, pastiche, and collages of his encyclopaedic *The Waste Land*, and the nineteenth-century romantic fixations on mythologies of the self and the natural world we find in the temporal monologues of the meditative lyrics in his *Four Quartets*.

The beneficiary of the late Eliot is Wallace Stevens with his poetics of being, self-consciousness, fictional worlds, and imagination – "there never was a world for her," Stevens wrote memorably, "except the one she sang and singing made." And the catalyst of the early Eliot is Ezra Pound with his poetics of particularity, structure, invention, and image. On the one side lies a respect for the precise, literal description of discrete objects within a classical, Augustan concern for imitation; on the other is a concern for the unending transformations of things into symbols within a romantic, symbolist, visionary humanism.

Yet only one of the strains is dominant in the high modernist poetry of suffering. This strain is not the fragmented aborted stories of Pound's *Cantos* and Eliot's *Waste Land*, but the Goethian *Ich-erzählung*, the lyric of the isolated speaker reflecting, assimilating, reaching an epiphany, the lyrical self in Montale's Ligurian "presentiment of you." This dominant species of the modernist lyric, the internalized quest romance, is, since the end of the eighteenth century, still the norm for our understanding of the lyric today in terms of "the Wordsworthian crisis lyric."[337]

Still, we might suspect that post-modernism in literature begins with the attempt to reinstate what this dominant form has excluded, namely the Poundian aesthetic with its early eighteenth-century echoes of parody, puns, playfulness, and performance-works with multiple voices. Think of Josef Brodsky's distinguished work. Yet at the centre of this post-modernist poetry are the still insufficiently analyzed notions of self-reference, self-reflection, and self-positing[338] – all arguably aspects of our proliferating and notoriously ambiguous uses of the word "representation."

These repressed figures of voice, allegory, and apostrophe resist most of our contemporary attempts to understand the lyric as a fictional representation of a personal utterance. But if no consensus on an alternative theory of the modernist lyric is yet in hand, nonetheless important changes in the conception of the modernist lyric are in evidence, especially in the shift of attention from utterances to tropes, from symbol to allegory, and from self-reflection to self-reference.

The result is a construal of the modernist lyric not as Northrop Frye's overhead utterance waiting for description and interpretation but, quite ominously, as Paul de Man's now endlessly interpretable and revisable fictional worlds – historical, ethical, literary, and personal – all arising from figure and address where the accent falls on allegory as distinction and difference rather than on symbol as intimate reconciliation.

Listen again to another of the insistent, peremptory voices of *Ossi di seppia*. Consider how this voice may continue even in the new Europe today to solicit our critical reflections on the interactions between poetry and life in times of economic, social, and cultural disarray.

> Splendour of noon outspread,
> when trees cast no shadow,
> and more and more all around appear
> in too much light, aspects darkly yellowing.
>
> Above the sun – and the dry shingle.
> My day is, therefore, not gone by:
> the most beautiful hour lies beyond the low wall
> that closes in a whitewashed sunset.
>
> Drought all around: over a relic
> of life a kingfisher hovering.
> Beyond dejection lies the bliss of rain,
> but happiness won is in the waiting.[339]

When we construe too strongly the reasonableness of an interpretation in the various domains of the arts, we usually miss something essential. When for example we interpret the distinctive European high-modernist twentieth-century poetry of suffering with an instrumental, procedural, and relativistic understanding of reason and rationality, our readings run the serious risk of imposing on such shadow-filled, obscure, and finally quite abstract work conceptions of moral discourse, moral knowledge, and both moral motivation and ethical liberation that are usually far too clear. What continues to summon us to interpret such truly memorable verbal art often vanishes "in an excess of light."

When by contrast we think of the reasonableness of such interpretation with a less stringent but finally more substantive even creative and constructionalist idea of reason and rationality in mind, one that offers a looser more ambiguous notion of language, perception, and the will, we often can catch a glimpse of what is at stake in such extraordinary work, of persons and their communities, of critics and their cultures, of nature and history all caught up in the harrowings of what seems inexorable tragedy, of meaning, truth, and freedom as "aspects yellowing darkly."

I do not yet know how to comprehend critically enough such aspects yellowing darkly. Are they only the early Ligurian voices of Montale's singing words? Could such intimations perhaps be yours? Must they be in some way mine? And, in these more than merely postmodern times, still at the beginning of a new century after the end of the most bloody of centuries – inescapable night and fog – just who is to say?

I believe, however, that all too often in Europe today, in a time of radical historical, economic, and social transformation, we continue to neglect our communities and ourselves – and needlessly – if we set aside, for too little thought and perhaps too much fashion, the still substantial resources of a critical idea and ideal of our European high modernist literary heritage.

For some sustained philosophical reflection, however unconventional, on the abstract suffering so many of these works poetically represent can open up a sometimes necessary and reflective interplay between hearing poetry and living our lives. Perhaps some of this reflective interplay between art and life is where some European communities today may find the requisite and renewed intellectual and practical resources for forging newly fruitful uses of both moral intuitions and ethical insight into the significance of our finally ineluctable sufferings as individual human beings and societies.

Several of those resources – critical, philosophical, and even metaphysical – are perhaps on view and in our hearing, however abstractly, in the works of such twentieth-century poets of suffering as Eliot, Valéry, and Montale. But not only there.

Latvian Autumn

In October 1961, the German poet of Polish and Lithuanian ancestry, Johannes Bobrowski, composed his "Latvian Autumn." His poem is neither a high-modernist work nor a post-modernist one. Like much Celan's poetry his poem is not so much a work at all but something much more indefinite, say, a piece.

Bobrowski's piece is among the distinctive twentieth-century's poems of suffering that still resonate in the deeply troubled new century that now constitutes our own specifically European times. For such pieces comprise some of the essential memories that keep returning in hard times today. Before plotting any further course some may sometime wish to embark on in possible subsequent inquiries into the possible uses of some forms of a rearticulated moral intuitionism in the emerging new Europe, Bobrowski's poem may help serve to check our bearings as we conclude.

More than ten years after his release in 1955 as one of the last surviving German prisoners of war still working at forced labour in the Soviet coal mines of the Donets Basin in Ukraine not far from what was the Voronezh Front and the destruction of Operation Citadel at the Battle of Kursk, and less than four years from his premature death at the age of forty-eight in an East Berlin hospital far from the shifting polyglot borders of his childhood and the classical and musical Baroque splendours of his youth amid the pre-war Koenigsberg cityscapes of Kant and Herder, the poet whose several works memorialize the eponymous Slavic peoples and settlements of the ancient region of Sarmatia between the Vistula and the Memel along the sandy, pine-streaked Baltic littoral, completed his beautiful and still profoundly unsettling poem, "Latvian Autumn." The second part of his poem in one of its several English translations reads:

> When the river is not awake any more,
> the cloud above it, voices
> of the birds, calls:
> We shall not come any more –
>
> Then I'll kindle your light,
> that I cannot see, my hands
> I shall lay over it, close
> to the flame, that stayed
> upright reddened by so much night
> (like the castle that came down
> over the slope, in ruins,
> like a wingéd snake
> of light through the river, like the hair
> of the Jewish child)
> and did not burn me.[340]

Now even when we consider this piece as a whole, and even after many contextual readings against the complex backgrounds of Bobrowski's work and times to which I have but alluded above, much here remains deeply evocative and profoundly enigmatic.

What is evocative is the faint promise this literary work of art offers us of arriving at a fuller understanding of the meaning of the immensity of human suffering in the midst of and in the terrible aftermaths of what have been memorably called "the European civil wars."[341] What seems promising is the hope of apprehending what has been at stake in the European twentieth-century, the bloodiest of centuries, and from now on in our new century being able to act accordingly. What is profoundly enigmatic is how we Europeans today might find another kind of liberation in breaking through to the fuller significance of such a vastness of evil that brought such suffering about.

Consider for a moment the crucial yet deeply puzzling description here of the light. "[T]he flame," the speaker in the poem says, "die Flamme, sie blieb / stehen rötlich vor lauter Nacht." "[T]he flame," the translator writes, "that stayed / upright reddened by so much night." Another translator renders the utterance differently, "the flame, it stood still, / reddish in nothing but night."[342]

This partly figurative and not just literal description of a motionless, reddish flame is puzzling because we find it persistently difficult not just to interpret such an utterance[343] in the sense of to translate it, but to interpret it in the sense of to render the sense and significance of such a flame in our own very closely related but now nonetheless different times today. Yet interpret it we must. For this puzzling expression is also crucial because its meaning controls the significance of the entire final stanza with its three linked and yet elusive similes and consequently whatever temporary rare traces of wisdom for today that we might find in such unforgettable works.

Each simile adduces some kind of likeness between what this expression describes – a red flame standing still and upright in the dark night – and, first, a bright castle falling into dark ruins, then streaks of light rippling like a snake through dark waters, and finally the dark hair of a Jewish child. And, most important, these difficult comparisons with a mysterious flame that does not burn an outstretched hand may strike many careful readers even today as pointing towards an inexhaustible ethical significance touching on the ruins of history, the ambivalences of nature, and the unfathomableness of the Shoah. Yet if we cannot reasonably render such crucial and puzzling expressions, how are we reasonably to interpret this evocative, promising, and enigmatic poem as a whole?

What makes a reading of such difficult verbal artefacts reasonable is its articulation of the poem's sense and significance in the kind of form that allows of appraisal as either objectively true or objectively false, largely speaking. Reasonableness requires plain speaking. And "largely speaking" here comes finally to parsing several of the central rational interconnections among language, perception, motivation, and ethically liberating insight, in not just objective and non-relativistic ways but also in meditative even metaphysical ways. For some of these interconnections, perhaps some on exhibit here, would seem to involve not just concrete objects like stones, or streaks of light on river waters at nightfall, or children's hair but even at times abstract objects like the obscure referents of some kinds of human suffering.[344]

Apprehending Aspects Yellowing Darkly

In the case of Johannes Bobrowski's poem, what are the appropriate uses of language for articulating such basic yet obscure moral and ethical matters apparently on view in this piece as the hazards of history, the indifference of nature, and the ineffaceable traces still among us of monstrous evils? Can such matters always be put plainly, clearly and distinctly? Can what is at stake in such matters always be put literally? Or to capture what is essential in such matters must we at times explore the non-literal and the figurative resources of language as well?

Central to argued yet meditative attempts to construe instances of the twentieth-century distinctive poetry of suffering in such varied work as that of Yeats and Eliot, Valéry and Saint-John Perse, Rilke, Machado and Lorca, Mandelstam and Akhmatova, Ritsos and Montale, Celan and Milosz, Herbert and, as here, Bobrowski, is a basic ethical intuition. The ambiguous "subject" of pieces like these – what such pieces are about – is "a negative sublime," the still unthinkable immensities of suffering and of the overwhelming vastness of the forces that continue to wreak such suffering.

Not improperly "apprehending" such subjects – rightly fearing them but rightly grasping them nonetheless – would appear to require refashioning several central connections between acting rightly and some basic construals of moral discourse, moral knowledge, and moral motivation. In particular, such connections would seem to require refashioning aspects of genuinely dark but occasionally brightening richly reconstructed poetic fictions, as – perhaps we might say figuratively for the title of this essay – Eugenio Montale's "aspects darkly yellowing."

Endnotes

1 The quite extensive literature on the general international contexts of the particular immigration problems in Europe can be usefully surveyed in K. Koser, *International Migration: A Very Short Introduction* (Oxford: OUP, 2007). See especially "The Future of International Migration," pp. 109–123. For the particular backgrounds see *Atlas des migrants en Europe: géocritique des politiques migratoirs*, ed. O. Clochard (Paris: Armand-Colin, 2009). For immigration within the EU see the discussions of recent Polish immigration to Belgium in M. Galent, I. Goddeeris, and D. Niedźwiedzki, *Migration and Europeanisation: Changing Identities and Values among Polish Pendulum Migrants and their Belgian Employers* (Cracow: Nomos, 2009), especially pp. 7–43.

2 On political and philosophical aspects of questions about human rights today see the quite recent work of C. R. Beitz, *The Idea of Human Rights* (Princeton: PUP, 2009) and of J. Griffin, *On Human Rights* (Oxford: OUP, 2009), especially pp. 149–187. See also T. Pogge, "How Should Human Rights be Conceived?" in his *World Poverty and Human Rights* (Malden, MA: Blackwell, 2002), pp. 52–70. Cf. the indispensable collection, *Les grands textes internationaux des droits de l'homme*, ed. E. Decaux (Paris: La documentation française, 2004).

3 A recent example of major changes in one of the EU countries' immigration policies is that of the United Kingdom (UK). The then Prime Minister, Gordon Brown, announced on November 12, 2009 a widespread toughening of the already demanding conditions in the UK for non-Europeans to reside there, for their obtaining a labour permit, and for new priorities to be awarded British citizens looking for work. Moreover, an increasing number of professions in the UK will henceforth be inaccessible for non-Europeans. Conditions governing the temporary immigration of Europeans have also been tightened. Cf. the detailed article of V. Malingre, "Le premier ministre britannique s'engage à freiner l'immigration," in the French daily afternoon newspaper of record, *Le Monde*, November 14, 2009. Similarly for the special case of those non-European immigrants seeking asylum, in October 2009 the Austrian parliament adopted a new law drastically restricting asylum. L. Van Eeckhout provides a detailed picture of the recent developments of increasingly similar restrictive policies in France in *L'Immigration* (Paris: Odile Jacob, 2007), especially in her chapter, "L'Union européenne: une forteresse assiégée?" pp. 57–68.

4 On the European social model see especially the regularly updated and generally quite reliable statistics of the Statistical Office of the European Community accessible at <epp.eurostat.ec.europa.eu>. See also C. Matthieu and H. Sterdyniak, "Le modèle social européen et l'Europe sociale," *Revue de OFCA (Observatoire français des conjonctures économiques)*, N° 104 (2008), 43–103; Y. Chassard and J.-L. Dayan, "Le modèle

social européen resiste," Problèmes économiques, N° 2, 982 (November 11, 2009), pp. 23–28; C. Mathieu and H. Sterdyniak, "European Social Model(s) and Social Europe," Organisation for Economic Cooperation and Development (OECD), Working Document, No. 10 (April, 2009); A. Euzéby, "Pour une approche éthique de la protection sociale dans l'Union européenne," *Revue du marché commun et de l'Union européenne*, N° 530 (July–August, 2009); *Union européenne*, (Paris: OECD, 2009), and the special issue, *L'Europe* of *Alternatives Économiques, Hors-Série*, N° 81 (2009).

5 For a more extended discussion see A. Bhalla and P. McCormick, "The European Immigration Debate," in their *Poverty Among Immigrant Children in Europe* (London: Palgrave Macmillan, 2009), pp. 49–64 which I draw on partly here. See also C. Wihtol de Winden, "L'Immigration en débat(s)," in *Le grand tournant. L'État du monde 2010*, ed. B. Badie and D. Vidal (Paris: La Découverte, 2009), pp. 176–180.

6 Different approaches to dealing with the necessary empirical bases of these discussions are usefully discussed in A. Rea and M. Tripier, *Sociologie de L'immigration* (Paris: La Découverte, 2003), especially "Migrations de travail: exploitation et mobilité sociale," pp. 33–48; and Table 3, "Population étrangère résidant dans quelques pays européens," p. 94. In general, dealing critically with statistics in the domains of social policy requires some special knowledge. See for example S. Dupays, *Déchiffrer les statistiques économiques et sociales* (Paris: Dunod, 2008), especially "Comment mesurer les inégalités et la pauvreté," pp. 70–86. Note that the French national statistics office (*INSEE*) is not fully independent from government control. One consequence is that some French statistics for unemployment and poverty sometimes have been delayed and at other times challenged for their accuracy. Cf. L. Data, *Le grand truquage: Comment le gouvernement [français] manipule les statistiques* (Paris: La Découverte, 2009), especially "Les chiffres de l'emploi et du chômage: petits arrangements entre amis," p. 23–45; and "Réduire la pauvreté ... en changeant d'indicateur," pp. 97–113. The name of the author is a pseudonym for a group of government statisticians. Cf. the recent, encouraging interview with the current *Directeur général* of *INSEE*, in *Le Monde*, November 18, 2009. One needs to note that the general problem of the guaranteeing of political independence for national offices of statistics in EU member states is not limited to the French case.

7 M. Dummett, *On Immigration and Refugees* (London: Routledge, 2001), p. 10.

8 *Ibid.*, p. 27.

9 *Ibid.*, pp. 12 and 34 respectively.

10 *Ibid.*, pp. 42–43.

11 Cf. T. Pogge, "Severe Poverty as a Human Rights Violation," in *Freedom from Poverty as a Human Right: Who Owes What to the Very Poor?* ed. T. Pogge (Oxford: OUP, 2007), pp. 11–54.

12 Cf. J. Rawls, *The Law of Peoples* (Cambridge: Harvard UP, 1999), especially pp. 113–120.

13 Cf. O. O'Neill, "Global Justice, Whole Obligations?" in *The Ethics of Assistance: Morality and Distant Need*, ed. D.K. Chatterjee (Cambridge: CUP, 2004.)

14 R. Audi, *The Good in the Right: A Theory of Intuition and Intrinsic Value* (Princeton: Princeton UP, 2004), pp. 188–195.

15 See the outstanding and thoroughly documented work of E. Marlier, A. B. Atkinson, B. Cantillon, and B. Nolan, *The EU and Social Inclusion: Facing the Challenges* (Bristol:

The Policy Press, 2007). Marlier *et al.* provide an excellent critical overview of both the distinct phases in the development of European social policy from 1974 to the present as well as of the evolution of the methods for coordination of the different policies among the gradually expanding number of member states and the mid-term reviews of the Lisbon Strategy and of the EU Social Agenda 2005–2010. See especially, "The EU Social Inclusion Process and the Key Issues," pp. 17–57. For the general contexts see B. Elissalde *et al.*, "Société(s) Européenne(s) et Europe Sociale," in their *Géopolitique de l'Europe* (Paris: Nathan, 2006), pp. 211–224. Cf. A. Lechavalier, "L'Europe sociale demeure à construire," *Alternatives Économiques, Hors Série*, n° 81 (2009), pp. 56–59.

16 Note that for the pertinent meanings of the cardinal word "suffering" both here and throughout this essay, its measurement, and its moral significance I rely mainly on J. Mayerfield, *Suffering and Moral Responsibility* (Oxford: OUP, 1999), especially "The Duty to Relieve Suffering," pp. 111–127. For the general notion of "social suffering" together with a series of multi-disciplinary essays see the special issue, "Social Suffering," of *Daedalus: Proceedings of the American Academy of Arts and Sciences*, 125 (1996). For the reflections here on literary representations of suffering see especially D.H. Morris's essay, "About Suffering: Voice, Genre, and Moral Community," pp. 25–46.

17 The main source for comparative statistical data on European levels of inequality and poverty is the Luxembourg Income Study. This data is regularly updated and is available on line at <www.lisproject.org>. Cf. *L'État de l'Union 2009: Rapport Schuman sur l'Europe*, ed. T. Chopin and M. Foucher (Paris: Lignes de repères, 2009). For historical backgrounds on European social policies in European countries see H. Kaelble, *Vers une société européenne 1880–1980* (Paris: Belin, 1988), and J.-Cl. Barbier, *La longue marche vers l'Europe sociale* (Paris: Presses universitaires de France, 2009). For a contemporary and pessimistic view see F. Denors and A. Schwartz, *L'Europe sociale n'aura pas lieu* (Paris: Raisons d'Agir, 2009).

18 For some arguments see for example some of the late twentieth century historically most important papers in the recent two-volume collection, *Global Justice: Seminal Essays*, ed. T. Pogge and D. Moellendorf, vol. 1 (St. Paul, Minn.: Paragon, 2008), especially A. Sen's "Equality of What?" 61–82, and *Global Ethics: Seminal Essays*, ed. T. Pogge and K. Horton, vol. 2 (St. Paul, Minn.: Paragon, 2008), especially D. Miller's "Distributing Responsibilities," 481–506. Both collections supplement a somewhat older collection of recent papers only, *Global Justice*, ed. T. Pogge (Malden, MA: Blackwell, 2003), including an important article for our specific concerns here with an eventual European common social policy, A. Føllesdal, "Federal Inequality Among Equals: A Contractualist Defense," pp. 242–261.

19 We will sometimes use the term "moral" as in the expression "moral intuitionism" to cover both of these distinct matters, but generally we shall try to restrict talk of the moral to duties and the corresponding rights and talk of the ethical to values and ideals.

20 B. Bailyn, *The New York Review of Books*, November 19, 2009, pp. 44–46. The citation is from p. 44.

21 On the complex relations between the individual and the social I follow here the comprehensive reflections on individual and collective responsibilities in P. Kourilsky's *Le Temps de l'altruisme* (Paris: Odile Jacob, 2009), especially pp. 114–124. As an immunologist and former head of the Institut Pasteur, Kourilsky draws many of his most fruitful reflections from analogies between and extrapolations from individual per-

sons' relations in social networks and individual cells' relations in biological networks. Cf. M.Girvan and M.E. Newman, "Community Structure in Social and Biological Networks," *Proceedings of the National Academy of Sciences*, 99 (2002), 7821–7826, and J.M. Epstein, *Generative Social Science* (Princeton: Princeton UP, 2006).

22 For some of the historical backgrounds see generally the French-German harmonized accounts in the jointly published French and German textbooks, *Histoire / Geschichte. L'Europe et le monde du congrès de Vienne à 1945*, ed. P. Geiss, D. Henri, and G. Le Quintrec *et al.*, (Paris: Nathan / Klett, 2008), especially "Permanences et mutations sociales (1815–1939), pp. 100–125; and *Histoire / Geschichte. L'Europe et le monde depuis 1945*, ed. P. Geiss and G. Le Quintrec *et al.* (Paris: Nathan / Klett, 2006), especially "Économie et société en France et en Allemagne depuis 1945: de fortes convergences," pp. 276–293. For a more particular account see for example, E. Barnavi and K. Pomian, *La Révolution européenne, 1945–2007* (Paris: Perrin, 2008), and *Visions d'Europe*, ed. B. Geremek and R. Picht (Paris: Odile Jacob, 2008). For European cultural values see O. Galland and Y. Lemel, *Valeurs et cultures en Europe* (Paris: La Découverte, 2007). For France in particular cf. the results of the latest of four nine-year studies on the evolution of values in France in *La France à travers ses valeurs*, ed. P. Bréchon, J.-F. Tchernia (Paris: Armand Colin, 2009), and the brief but trenchant article of A. Michnik, "Reflexionen über 1989," Deutschland, Nr. 2 (2009), pp. 28–29. Both should be compared with the fullest study currently available and regularly updated, "L'enquête européenne sur les valeurs" accessible at <www.europeanvaluesstudy.eu>.

23 For this emphasis on persons as knowers see S. Evnine, *Epistemic Dimensions of Personhood* (Oxford: OUP, 2008).

24 Cf. D. Sobel and S. Wall, *Reasons for Action* (Cambridge: CUP, 2009).

25 See for instance R. Audi, *The Good in the Right: A Theory of Intuition and Intrinsic Value* (Princeton: Princeton UP, 2004), and the papers collected in *Ethical Intuitionism: Re-evaluations*, ed. P. Stratton-Lake (Oxford: Clarendon, 2002), especially P. Stratton-Lake's comprehensive, "Introduction," pp. 1–28.

26 For important eighteenth-century reflections on kinds of intuition see X. Tilliette, *L'intuition intellectuelle de Kant à Hegel* (Paris: Vrin, 1995). For the importantly different uses of the word "intuition" in mathematics see C. Parsons, *Mathematical Objects* (Cambridge: CUP, 2008), pp. 138–185.

27 Today, probably the most important example of contemporary moral intuitionism is F.M. Kamm's *Intricate Ethics* (Oxford: OUP, 2007). Excluding articles in journals and emphasizing the most recent work only, thoughtful and demanding critiques of differing versions of moral intuitionism can be found here and there in K.A. Appiah, *Experiments in Ethics* (Cambridge, MA: Harvard UP, 2008), esp. pp. 73–120, A. Gibbard, *Reconciling Our Aims: In Search of Bases for Ethics* (Oxford: OUP, 2008, esp. pp. 11–32, T. Scanlon, *Moral Dimensions: Permissibility, Meaning, Blame* (Cambridge, MA: Harvard UP, 2008), *passim* under the rubric "moral principles," and some material on practical reason in C.M. Korsgaard, *Self-Constitution: Agency, Identity and Integrity* (Oxford: OUP, 2009). See also M.Zimmerman, *Living with Uncertainty: The Moral Significance of Uncertainty* (Cambridge: CUP, 2009).

28 Besides English language philosophical work on moral intuitionism, similar reflection has also marked much European reflection especially in the phenomenological tradi-

tion. In this essay, however, I have chosen to concentrate mainly on English language reflection on intuition and moral intuitionism. See however note 51 below.

29 See also J.B. Schneewind, *Sidgwick's Ethics and Victorian Moral Philosophy* (Oxford: OUP, 1977).

30 See also *Themes from G.E. Moore: New Essays in Epistemology and Ethics*, ed. S. Nuccetelli and G. Seay (Oxford: OUP, 2007).

31 See also H.A. Prichard, *Moral Writings*, ed. J. MacAdam (Oxford: OUP, 2002).

32 That is, in Moore's problematic technical idiom, not allowing of any proper articulation of the supposed relation between a moral sense datum and a moral object.

33 See also *The Philosophy of C.D. Broad*, ed. P. A. Schilpp (La Salle, Ill.: Open Court, 1959).

34 See also W. D. Ross, *The Foundations of Ethics* (Oxford: OUP, 1939).

35 For one distinguished example only see John Rawls's "Four Lectures on Henry Sidgwick," in his *Lectures on the History of Political Philosophy* (Cambridge, MA: Harvard UP, 2007), pp. 375–415.

36 See for example M.R. DePaul, "Intuitions in Moral Inquiry," *Oxford Handbook of Ethical Theory*, ed. D. Copp (Oxford: OUP, 2006), pp. 595–623.

37 P. McCormick, *The Negative Sublime: Ethics, Warfare, and the Dark Borders of Reason* (Heidelberg: Universitätsverlag Winter, 2003), pp. 7–8.

38 Recent well-informed discussion of central topics in philosophy and literature can be found in the chapters on art, literature, authors, practice, fiction, truth, and value in P. Lamarque's *The Philosophy of Literature* (Oxford: Blackwell, 2009). Somewhat older discussions that make use of the Polish phenomenologist, Roman Ingarden's, views are to be found in P. McCormick, *Fictions, Philosophies and the Problems of Poetics* (Ithaca, N.Y.: Cornell University Press, 1998) and in its more historically oriented companion, *Modernity, Aesthetics and the Bounds of Art* (Ithaca, N.Y.: Cornell University Press, 1990).

39 For recent articles see those in *The Oxford Handbook of Ethical Theory*, ed. D. Copp (Oxford: OUP, 2006), and *Contemporary Debates in Moral Theory*, ed. J. Dreier (Oxford: Blackwell, 2006).

40 *Oxford Dictionary of English*, 2nd ed., ed. C. Soames and A. Stevenson (Oxford: OUP, 2003), s.v. Note that this latest Oxford Dictionary and new standard, whose evidence for "core meanings" instead of for the overly stringent necessary and sufficient conditions of meanings derives for the first time from the 100 million word British National Corpus, is not the same as the renowned multi-volume but now outdated *Oxford English Dictionary.*

41 R.L. Gregory, "Intuition," *The Oxford Companion to the Mind*, ed. R. L. Gregory, 2nd ed. (Oxford: OUP, 2004), s.v.

42 A.R. Lacey, "Intuition," *The Oxford Companion to Philosophy*, T. Honderich, 2nd ed. (Oxford: OUP, 2005), s.v.

43 Cf. S. Blackburn, "Intuitionism (ethical)," in his *Oxford Dictionary of Philosophy*, 2nd ed. (Oxford: OUP, 2005), s.v. The notion of "objectivity" here is to be understood as a kind of minimal objectivity. "Some of our most important mental states and events have a minimal objectivity, in this intuitive sense," C. Peacocke reminds us; "a thinker's

being in the state, or enjoying the event, does not in general make the content of the state or event correct" ("Objectivity," *Mind*, 118 [2009], 739).

44 R. Audi, *The Good in the Right: A Theory of Intuition and Intrinsic Value* (Princeton: PUP, 2004), p. 202. Audi provides a wealth of detailed references on both the histories of ethical intuitionism and the contemporary revival of philosophical interest in ethical intuitionism as compared and contrasted with varieties of utilitarianism, deontology, virtue ethics, and moral realism. See also M. Huemer, *Ethical Intuitionism* (London: Macmillan, 2005), M.R. DePaul, "Intuition in Moral Inquiry," in *The Oxford Handbook of Ethical Theory*, ed. D. Copp (Oxford: Oxford University Press, 2006), pp. 624–644; and the extensive work of F.M. Kamm, especially her *Intricate Ethics* (Oxford: Oxford University Press, 2007), pp. 438–445.

45 Cf. R.M. Chisholm, *Ethics and Intrinsic Values*, ed. J.R. White (Heidelberg: Winter Universitätsverlag 2001), especially "The Things that are Intrinsically Good," pp. 25–35, and M.J. Zimmerman, *The Nature of Intrinsic Value* (New York: Rowman & Littlefield, 2001).

46 Although strongly connected in antiquity, the related and very important notions of rationality and reasonableness need differentiation. What remains controversial is just how to distinguish the two notions as distinct but not completely separate. Generally, I take the words "rational" and "rationality" mainly but not exclusively to denote formal and theoretical features, whereas I take the words "reasonable" and "reasonableness" mainly but not exclusively to denote material and practical features. Throughout, I use these expressions as largely but not completely interchangeable. Contrast, for example, S. Toulmin's remarks in his *Return to Reason* (Cambridge, MA: Harvard UP, 2001), pp. 24–28 and *passim* with G.G. Granger's quite different views in his *La Raison*, 10th ed. (Paris: PUF, 1993), pp. 41–88. For a recent and searching philosophical and historical account of scientific rationality see B. Saint-Sernin, *Le rationalisme qui vient* (Paris: Gallimard, 2007), especially "Les principes du rationalisme qui vient," pp. 199–260.

47 On what fiction may be able to indicate about what is not fictional, an important element in the considerations here about poetic language and moral intuitions, see M. Sainsbury, *Fiction and Fictionalism* (London: Routledge, 2009) and C. Crittenden, *Unreality: The Metaphysics of Fictional Objects* (Ithaca, N.Y.: Cornell UP, 1991), especially "Real Things in Fiction, Logical Completeness, and Other Forms of Representation," pp. 129–157.

48 Consider the conceptions of what persons are in the context of much contemporary discussion of issues in bioethics. Cf. C. Pelluchon, *La raison du sensible: Entretiens autour de la bioéthique* (Paris: Artège, 2009).

49 For example, some situations on view in the eighteen Polish documentary films presented in Paris, November 12–24, 2009, under the title, "Po-lin – la mémoire de la Shoah dans le cinéma polonais aujourd'hui."

50 On the general notion of value here see J. Raz's 2001 Berkeley Tanner Lectures, *The Practice of Value* (Oxford: OUP, 2002) with critical responses from C. Korsgaard, R. Pippin, and B. Williams; J. Griffin, *Value Judgement* (Oxford: Clarendon Press, 1996); and P. Grice's 1983 Carus Lectures, *The Conception of Value* (Oxford: OUP, 1991).

51 See especially F. Brentano, *Vom Ursprung sittlicher Erkenntnis* (Hambug: Felix Meiner Verlag, 1969), *Grundlegung und Aufbau der Ethik* (Hamburg: Felix Meiner, 1978),

L.M. McAlister, *The Development of Brentano's Ethics* (Amsterdam: Rodopi, 1982), and R. M. Chisholm, *Brentano and Intrinsic Value* (Cambridge: CUP, 1986).

52 For an excellent selection of texts in English from R. Ingarden, W. Tatarkiewicz, T. Czesowski, H. Elzenberg, and Maria Ossowska together with a set of explanatory essays see Cz. Porębski, *Polish Value Theory* (Cracow: Jagiellonian University / Dialogikon, 1995). For more contemporary Polish reflection, among the work of several others see especially the distinguished work in value theory and philosophical ethics of A. Półtawski, W. Stróżewski and K. Wojtyła. The important general historical contexts of this work can be usefully surveyed in J. Lukowski and H. Zawadzki, *A Concise History of Poland* (Cambridge: CUP, 2001), especially in "An Era of Transformation, 1864–1914" and "Independence Regained and Lost, 1914–1945," pp. 155–249.

53 By privileging contemporary English language moral philosophy I have unfortunately not been able to take account of many of the quite pertinent reflections and arguments here from the phenomenological tradition in philosophical ethics generally and especially from Brentano. Cf. *The Cambridge Companion to Brentano*, ed. D. Jaquette (Cambridge: CUP, 2004), and the topics treated in the annual *Brentano Studien: An International Yearbook of Franz Brentano Forschung*, ed. W. Baumgartner, F.-P. Burkard, and F. Wiedmann (Würzburg, 1988–).

54 Two general surveys prove useful here, W.H. Schrader, *Ethik und Anthropologie in der Englischen Aufklärung: Der Wandel der Moral-Sense-Theorie von Shaftesbury bis Hume* (Hamburg: Meiner, 1984), and *Le sens moral: Une historie de la philosophie morale de Locke à Kant*, ed. L. Jaffro (Paris: Presses universitaires de France, 2000).

55 See for example the recent discussions of capacities and capabilities in the contexts of especially Adam Smith's work and generally in English eighteenth-century common sense philosophies in A. Sen, *The Idea of Justice* (London: Allen Lane, 2009), pp. 231–247. See also the related reflections in E. Rothschild, *Economic Sentiments: Adam Smith, Condorcet, and the Enlightenment* (Cambridge, MA.: Harvard UP, 2001), especially "A Fatherless World," pp. 218–252.

56 See M. Richards, *Propositional Attitudes: An Essay on Thoughts and How We Ascribe Them* (Cambridge: CUP, 1990), especially "Structure," pp. 7–57; and S. Schiffer, "Propositional Content," in *The Oxford Handbook of Philosophy of Language*, ed. E. LePore and B. Smith (Oxford: Clarendon, 2006), pp. 267–294.

57 *Ibid.*, p. 197.

58 *Ibid.*

59 Of the many indications of economic and financial breakdown in Europe today see for one example only the International Monetary Fund's bleak scenarios for 2009 and 2010 as reported in France's morning newspaper of record, *Le Figaro*, April 23, 2009. For the notion of a further "ethical rupture," see the extensive confessions and reflections of the millionaire and former Wall Street financial trader, J. Belfort, in his *Le Loup de Wall Street* (Paris: Max Milo, 2009) and in his interview in *Le Monde*, April 23, 2009: "nous allons assister à une 'rupture ethique', avec plus de moral et de partage des richesses. Mais attention, l'histoire se répète."

60 For three articles (with bibliographies) on similar general philosophical problems that arise from reflection on literary fictions, see C. Wilson, "Epistemology of Fiction," W. Iser, "Contemporary Literary Account of the Fictive," and P. McCormick, "Fiction,"

in *Encyclopedia of Aesthetics*, ed. M. Kelly (New York: Oxford University Press, 1998), Vol. 2, pp. 177–185.

61 H. Cappelen and J.Hawthorne, *Relativism and Monadic Truth* (Oxford: OUP, 2009), p. 1. "The Simple View," which the authors take to be "a widespread and mainstream view" today, is the conjunction of the following five assertions. "There are propositions and they instantiate the fundamental monadic properties of truth *simpliciter* and falsity *simpliciter*. The semantic values of declarative sentences relative to contexts of utterance are propositions. Propositions are, unsurprisingly, the objects of propositional attitudes, such as belief, hope, wish, doubt, etc. Propositions are the objects of illocutionary acts; they are, e.g., what we assert and deny. Propositions are the objects of agreement and disagreement." That is, "the contents of sentences are propositions (...) we assert these contents (...) in so far as we are sincere, [and] what we assert is what we believe (...) and in so doing we can agree or disagree with each other" (*Ibid.*, p. 1).

62 *Sources of the Self: The Making of the Modern Identity* (Cambridge, MA: Harvard UP, 1989), Preface, ix; hereafter referred to as "*Sources*." Page numbers in parentheses included in the text unless otherwise indicated refer to Taylor's *Sources*.Taylor uses the cardinal term, "identity," mainly to refer to "the ensemble of (largely unarticulated) understandings of what it is to be a human agent: the senses of inwardness, freedom, individuality, and being embedded in nature which are at home in the modern West" (ix).

63 Durham, N.C.: Duke UP, 2004. See also his *The Ethics of Authenticity* (Cambridge: Harvard UP, 1991) with the important review by A. Ryan in *The New York Times Book Review*, September 27, 1992, and his *Varieties of Religion Today: William James Revisited* (Cambridge: Harvard UP, 2002). All three books are milestones in Taylor's making his way to the general synthesis in his 2007 work, *A Secular Age* (Cambridge: Harvard UP), the greatly expanded version of his Gifford Lectures in 1999 in Edinburgh.

64 My sharp focus here is on *Sources* as currently the most influential of Taylor's many books. Accordingly I would like to limit the concerns here to several only of the many important issues that should be examined thoroughly. In particular, I would like to look more closely at just what Taylor thinks comprises the complex notion of modernity and thereby sketch out the main historical and philosophical backgrounds for the specific concerns here with the European high modernist poetry of suffering.

65 *Sources*, p. 520.

66 Cf. several of the related "intuitions" in L. Dupré, *Passage to Modernity* (New Haven: Yale UP, 1993) which Taylor cites several times in his *Modern Social Imaginaries*, especially on p. 203. See also Taylor's "Die Modernität und die säkulare Zeit," in *Am Ende des Milleniums: Zeit und Modernitäten*, ed. K. Michalski (Stuttgart: Klett, 2000), pp. 28–85.

67 For the requisite backgrounds for Taylor's views on modernity see especially his *Hegel* (Cambridge: CUP, 1975), his *Philosophical Papers*, 2 volumes (Cambridge: CUP, 1985), and, for the latter, several critical reviews such as those by Jonathan Lear in *London Review of Books*, September 19, 1985, and by R. Rorty in the *TLS*, December 6, 1985. Part of the larger critical response can be found in a special Symposium on Taylor's *Sources of the Self* in *Inquiry*, 34 (1991) with papers by Q. Skinner, M. Rosen, S.R.L. Clark, M. Löw-Beer, and W. Kymlicka, together with Taylor's responses.

68 Note that the word, "subjectivation," is unusual. For example, the word does not appear in the two-volume *Shorter Oxford English Dictionary*, 7th edition (Oxford: OUP, 2007).

69 Relativism takes many forms, a point that is often overlooked. With respect to moral philosophy in particular, see for example, R.L. Arrington, *Rationalism, Realism, and Relativism: Perspectives in Contemporary Moral Epistemology* (Ithaca, NY: Cornell UP, 1989), especially pp. 192–247.

70 Taylor cites throughout from the English versions of Rilke's poetry in *The Selected Poetry of Rainer Maria Rilke*, tr. S. Mitchell (New York: Random House, 1982).

71 The contrast here between "internalist" and "externalist" interpretation needs to be situated in the contexts of other uses of this distinction in metaphysics, philosophy of mind, epistemology, and moral philosophy generally. See T. van Gelder, "Internalism / Externalism," in *The Penguin Dictionary of Philosophy*, ed. T. Mautner, 2nd ed. (London: Penguin, 2005), pp. 307–309, with references.

72 The distinction between two kinds of self-reference suggests a further distinction within the general modernist understanding of subjectivation between two different species of subjectivism, one closed the other open. More fundamentally, however, this present distinction derives from a still larger view about changes in eighteenth-century practices of literary representation.

73 Taylor tells this story mainly in Parts II to V of his book.

74 The historical backgrounds in philosophy are readily reviewed by consulting the appropriate chapters of A. Kenny's recent and magisterial four volume *A New History of Western Philosophy* (Oxford: OUP, 2004–2007).

75 Taylor's view here contrasts strongly with the complex and pessimistic vision to be found in L. Kołakowski's collection, *Modernity on Endless Trial* (Chicago: University of Chicago Press, 1990).

76 Consider the very different picture we find of the same period in D.R. Kelley, *Foundations of Modern Historical Scholarship: Language, Law, and History in the French Renaissance* (New York: Columbia University Press, 1970). I am grateful to Frank Peddle for showing me the pertinence of this excellent study.

77 New York: The Free Press, 1990. Unless otherwise indicated, references in this section of the text here refer to Toulmin's 1990 book.

78 Toulmin's historical readings here, just like Taylor's, need careful adjustment in the light of recent historical scholarship such as that on view in such works as A. Grafton, *What Was History? The Art of History in Early Modern Europe* (Cambridge: Cambridge UP, 2009). See the helpful and considered review of K. Thomas, "Fighting Over History," *The New York Review of Books*, December 3, 2009.

79 In fact, the situation was more complicated. See for example the recent essays of J.A. Blair, "The Pertinence of Toulmin and Perelman / Olbrechts-Tyteca for Informal Logic" and H.J. Ribeiro, "Perelman and Toulmin as Philosophers: On the Inalienable Connection Between Philosophy, Rhetoric and Argumentation" in *Rhetoric and Argumentation in the Beginning of the XXI st Century*, ed. H.J. Ribeiro (Coimbra, Portugal: Coimbra UP, 2009), pp. 17–32 and 33–51 respectively.

80 We need to notice immediately that, unlike Taylor, Toulmin places these figures in the careful chronological order of a humanist versus a rationalist intellectual movement, whereas Taylor prefers to juxtapose their respective emphases on different kinds of inwardness.

81 They both cite C. Geertz's highly influential work, *The Interpretation of Cultures* (New York: Basic Books, 1973).

82 See especially H. Putnam, *The Many Faces of Realism* (La Salle, Illinois: Open Court, 1987).

83 In common parlance, according to the *Oxford Dictionary of English*, the English word "discourse" generally means "written or spoken communication or debate." In linguistics, "discourse" means "any continuous stretch of (especially spoken) language larger than a sentence," and the analysis of discourse, "discourse analysis," means the attempt "to discover linguistic regularities in discourses using grammatical, phonological and semantic criteria" (D. Crystal, *A Dictionary of Linguistics and Phonetics*, 5th ed. [Oxford: Blackwell, 2003], s.v.). In philosophy, "discourse" means the same as in linguistics. But "discourse analysis" refers more particularly to the analysis of the meaning of a discourse in terms of the holistic relations between the sentences of the discourse and the discourse as a whole, "for example, the reference of pronouns or other indexical elements [e.g. temporal markers and spatial markers] within a sentence may only be derived from its relation to surrounding sayings" (S. Blackburn, *Oxford Dictionary of Philosophy*, 2nd ed. ([Oxford: Oxford UP, 2005], s.v.). Here, we will use the expressions "discourse" and "discourse analysis" mainly in their philosophical usages.

84 He dedicated the finally finished work to Pound as "*il miglio fabbro*."

85 Cf. J.C.C. Mays, "Early Poems from 'Prufrock' to 'Gerontion,'" in A.D. Moody, ed., *The Cambridge Companion to T.S. Eliot* (Cambridge: Cambridge UP, 1994), pp. 109–10. On some pertinent historical and biographical details concerning Eliot's relations with his first wife, Vivienne Haigh-Wood whose brother, and despite the rumors not Eliot himself, committed her to an asylum in 1938 (cf. the 1984 Michael Hasting play, "Tom and Viv," and the 1994 movie) see among others, L. Menand, "The Women Come and Go: The Love Song of T.S. Eliot," in *The New Yorker*, September 30, 2002. Whether the perplexing fictional conversation I cite from *The Waste Land*, however, is in any way a literarily transposed representation of some fragment of Eliot's personal life with Vivienne must remain speculation only. Accordingly, I will mark this point by sometimes using the expression "the poet" instead of always using "Eliot."

86 T.S. Eliot, *Collected Poems 1909–1962* (London: Faber and Faber, 1963), p. 67. Although I follow here the edition just noted, exactly how Eliot finally intended some of the lines to be spaced and punctuated in a corrected printing remains controversial. As we shall see, these apparently pedantic issues are not inconsequential for understanding the supposedly literal meanings and significance of the lines cited.

87 On the pertinent sense here of a "meaningful situation" see J. Barwise and J. Perry, *Situations and Attitudes* (Cambridge, MA: MIT Press, 1983), pp. 3–26. A situation may be understood as property-possessing individuals "standing in relations at various spatio-temporal locations" (*Ibid.*, p. 7). This notion while technical is important because it can serve as the basis for a semantic theory that captures the specific, which is central in poetic discourse, by contrast with the more usual semantic holism deriving from Frege (1848–1925) that abstracts from the specific.

88 David Jones, *In Parentheses* (New York: Viking, 1963), p. 133. Jones published his extended prose poem about the First World War in 1937. In his Introduction to this work which Eliot highly admired, Eliot called Jones's poem a "work of genius."

89 "Revenge tragedies" were tragic plays produced during the later reign of James I (1603–1625), son of Mary Queen of Scots who inherited the crown of Scotland from

his mother as James VI, and who later as a great grandson of Margaret Tudor inherited the crown of England and Ireland as James I from the Tudor queen, Elizabeth I. Many of these revenge tragedies while marked with extravagant plots exhibit a very rare richness of poetic speech which fascinated Eliot.

90 Eliot takes these lines from one of the Jacobean dramatist Christopher Marlowe's tragedies.

91 This complex, interpersonal exchange, the English poet Stephen Spender writes, is "spoken hysterically by the woman, not answered except by incommunicable and terrible thoughts by the man, [and] is where the poem touches the poet most closely. It is the poem's innermost sanctum. This is the wound, the heart of the suffering. The poet is here brought up against the exhibited conditioned behaviour of the woman who speaks aloud: 'What shall we do tomorrow? / What shall we ever do?' His unspoken comments have that immediacy of speech for which the only possible language is poetry" (*Eliot* [London: Fontana, 1975], p. 108). One need not of course agree with Spender's nonetheless insightful comments.

92 In the passage cited Eliot uses the word "nothing" variously, although mainly as a noun. Generally, the *Shorter Oxford English Dictionary* (*SOED*) reports, that when used as a noun, "nothing" may be paraphrased as "not any (material or abstract) thing." Drawing on the original Old English usage as two words, "no" and "thing," the editors of the *SOED* go on to claim that "nothing" may be paraphrased positively when "followed by an adjective or limiting phrase or clause) [as] not one thing." Technically, on specific issues about what linguists call "the context-change potential of negation," see G. Chierchia and S. McConnell-Ginet, *Meaning and Grammar*, 2nd ed. (Cambridge, MA: MIT Press, 2000), pp. 374–376, and R. Jackendoff, *Foundations of Language: Brain, Meaning, Grammar, Evolution* (Oxford: Oxford UP, 2002), pp. 401 and 403.

93 For a general linguistic overview of different semantic questions about meaning see, for example, "Semantics: The Study of Linguistic Meaning," in A. Akmajian, et al., eds., 5th edition, *Linguistics* (Cambridge, MA: MIT Press, 2001), pp. 227–264. In particular, for a linguistic presentation of the central elements of lexical meaning, sentence meaning and utterance meaning see J. Lyons, *Linguistic Semantics: An Introduction* (Cambridge: Cambridge UP, 1995), especially pp. 234–257.

94 Compare, for example, the 1975 views of H.P. Grice and J. Searle in, respectively, "Logic and Conversation" and "Indirect Speech Acts," reprinted in *The Philosophy of Language*, ed. A.P. Martinich, 5th ed. (New York: Oxford UP, 2008), pp. 171–181 and pp. 182–195.

95 Recall the still celebrated dispute between Carnap and Heidegger from 1929 onwards on what sense if any could be made of such Heideggerean claims as science knows "nothing about nothing" (compare the poet's line: "Is there nothing in your head?"). A good although controversial recent discussion, with full references, can be found in S. Critchley, *Continental Philosophy* (Oxford: Oxford UP, 2001), pp. 90–110.

96 See, for example, W.P. Alston, *Illocutionary Acts and Sentence Meaning* (Ithaca: Cornell UP, 2000), pp. 275–309.

97 Consider, for example, seven "constraints" that P. Horwich explains under the headings of understanding, expression, representation, aprioricity, compositionality, normativity, and use in his *Meaning* (Oxford: Clarendon Press, 1998), pp. 12–42. Note however that Horwich has repeatedly revised his work. A thorough critical assessment of Horwich's rich and influential work can be found in A. Gibbard, "Horwich on Meaning," *Mind*, 117 (2008), 141–166 (with bibliography).

98 See, for example, A. Cruse, "Paradigmatic Sense Relations of Inclusion and Identity," in his *Meaning in Language* (Oxford: Oxford UP Press, 2000), pp. 146–160.

99 See, for example, K. Bach and R.M. Harnish, "Linguistic Communication: A Schema for Speech Acts," in S. Davis, ed., *Pragmatics: A Reader* (New York: Oxford UP, 1991), pp. 231–241.

100 With respect to substantives (nouns) or items functioning as substantives in figurative expressions, see M. Reimer and E. Camp, "Metaphor," *The Oxford Handbook of Philosophy of Language*, ed. E. Lepore and B. Smith (Oxford: Clarendon Press, 2006), pp. 845–863; and, with respect to sentences involving figurative utterances, see D. Boivert and K. Ludwig, "Semantics for Non-declaratives," *The Oxford Handbook of Philosophy of Language*, ed. E. Lepore and B. Smith (Oxford: Clarendon Press, 2006), pp. 864–892.

101 For the contemporary philosophical contexts of discussions of literal meaning see R.M. Sainsbury, *Reference without Referents* (Oxford: Oxford UP, 2005), especially pp. 47–85. On literal meaning see F. Recanati, *Literal Meaning* (Cambridge: Cambridge UP, 2004) and, more particularly, S.C. Levinson's discussion of the literal-force hypothesis versus figurative meaning in his *Pragmatics* (Cambridge: Cambridge UP, 1983), pp. 165–166, 263–265, and 274–276.

102 Just before his death Davidson finished editing in five volumes for Oxford's Clarendon Press most of his previous work that had appeared earlier in essay form only. These volumes include the originally published and now expanded *Essays on Actions and Events* (1980) and *Inquiries into Truth and Interpretation* (1984), as well as the later *Subjective, Intersubjective, Objective* (2001), *Problems of Rationality* (2004), and *Truth, Language and History* (2005). He also finished his first "real book," *Truth and Predication* (Cambridge, MA: Harvard Belknap, 2005) which includes his late reflections on the interpretation of literal meaning (see especially pp. 61–75). For backgrounds and documentation see the "Intellectual Autobiography of Donald Davidson," "Bibliography of Donald Davidson," and replies to his critics in *The Philosophy of Donald Davidson*, ed. L.E. Hahn (Chicago: Open Court, 1999). See especially in this volume R.W. Dasenbrock, "Locating Donald Davidson and Literary Language" and Davidson's "Reply to R.W. Dasenbrock," pp. 361–377 and 378–380 respectively.

103 See, for example, the essays in R.W. Dasenbrock, ed., *Literary Theory after Davidson* (University Park, PA: Penn State UP, 1993), especially the Introduction, pp. 1–17. For an excellent discussion of Davidson's work on both interpretation and translation see M. Montminy, *Les fondements empiriques de la signification* (Montreal: Bellarmin, 1998), pp. 97–152.

104 On Davidson and Quine see L. Bergstrom, "Davidson's Objections to Quine's Empiricism," and F. Tersman, "Davidson and Quine's Empiricism" in *Interpreting Davidson*, ed. P. Kotatko, P. Pagin, and G. Segal (Stanford: CSLI, 2001), pp. 17–36 and 269–284 respectively. Davidson replies to each in the same volume on pp. 290–292.

105 For a more formal treatment of Davidson's "compositional meaning theory" see E. LePore and K. Ludwig, "What is Logical Form?" in Kotako et al, eds., *Interpreting Davidson* (Stanford: CSLI, 2001), esp. pp. 117–122.

106 Note that the many volume *Oxford English Dictionary* (OED) is not the same as the much more recent and more comprehensively based one-volume *Oxford Dictionary of*

English (*ODE*). The latest editions of the *Shorter Oxford Dictionary of English (SODE)* in two volumes rely on the same extraordinarily extensive data base as the *ODE*.

107 By contrast with the uses of the word "holism" in the physical and social sciences, "holism" or "meaning-holism" in the work of Davidson, Quine and others in the philosophy of language "is the view that the meaning of any term depends on the meaning of every term or sentence in the language" (*Dictionary of Philosophy*, ed. T. Mautner, 2nd ed. [London: Penguin, 2005], s.v.). Cf. C. Peacocke, "Holism," in *A Companion to the Philosophy of Language*, ed. B. Hale and C. Wright (Oxford: Blackwell, 1997), pp. 227–247.

108 *Truth and Interpretation* (Oxford: Oxford UP, 1984), p. xiii.

109 Alfred Tarski (1902–1983), a Polish mathematician and logician, worked mainly at Berkeley. For his most important papers see his *Logic, Semantics, and Mathematics*, 2nd ed. (Indianapolis: Hackett, 1983).

110 In *Truth and Interpretation: Perspectives in the Philosophy of Donald Davidson*, ed. E. LePore (New York: Blackwell, 1986), pp. 433–444. This much remarked essay is republished in Volume Five of Davidson's essays, *Truth, Language, and History*, pp. 89–107. There, Davidson follows this essay interestingly in a special section with other later essays on similar issues in the following order: "The Social Aspect of Language" (1994), "Seeing Through Language" (1997), "Joyce and Humpty Dumpty" (1989), "The Third Man" (1992), and "Locating Literary Language" (1993). Davidson's original title alludes to the eighteenth-century English dramatist and politician, Richard Sheridan's character, Mrs. Malaprop, and to what the *SOED* calls her "ludicrous misuse of words, especially in mistaking a word for another resembling it" in Sheridan's 1775 play, *The Rivals*. Perhaps we may say that, in the play, the fictional character Mrs. Malaprop has ludicrously misused words by mistaking the words "arrangement" for "derangement" and "epithets" for "epitaphs," thereby mistaking the phrase "a nice arrangement of epithets" for "a nice derangement of epitaphs."

111 For a scrupulous collation of the manuscripts, editing, and glossing of the complete sonnet in a modern-spelling text, see *The Complete Sonnets and Poems*, ed. C. Burrow (Oxford: Oxford UP, 2002), pp. 486–487. Davidson cites lines 9 to 11, which grammatically make up an incomplete sentence in the text. Line 12, "And you in every blessed shape we know," which Davidson does not cite, completes the sentence in the text. Burrow glosses the expression, "foison," in line 9 from the OED as "plentiful crop or harvest." He takes line 10, "The one doth shadow of your beauty show," as: "the spring is merely an image of your beauty." He takes line 11, "The other as your bounty doth appear," as: "the bountiful harvest seems like your generosity." And he takes "know" in the line Davidson does not cite as: "recognize." Note that, after substitutions, we are left with a complete sentence in the text, but of course no more than Burrow's doggerel.

> "Speak of the spring and [plentiful crop] of the year,
> [the spring is merely an image of your beauty,]
> [the bountiful harvest seems like your generosity,]
> And you in very blessed shape we know."

112 Davidson's is a tall order. See, however, A. Schmidt, *Shakespeare Lexicon and Quotation Dictionary*, 3rd ed., 2 vols. (Berlin, 1902); and A.C. Partridge, *A Substantive Grammar of Shakespeare's Non-dramatic Texts* (Charlottesville: University of Virginia Press, 1976).

113 S. Spender, p. 42.

114 See, for example, A. Tarski's 1944 paper, "The Semantic Conception of Truth and the Foundations of Semantics," reprinted in *The Philosophy of Language*, ed. A.P. Martinich, 5th ed. (Oxford: Oxford UP, 2008), pp. 85–107.

115 "A recursive definition of an expression," E.J. Lowe writes in *The Oxford Companion to Philosophy*, ed. T. Honderich, 2nd ed. (Oxford: Oxford UP, 2005), p. 792, "proceeds by first specifying a special subclass of the items it applies to and then specifying the remaining items it applies to in terms of a relation which any such item bears to an item to which the expression already applies."

116 The pertinent discussions here for Davidson's talk of "holism" can be found in J. Fodor and E. LePore, *Holism: A Shopper's Guide* (Oxford: Blackwells, 1992). On the details of "meaning holism" see P. Pagin, "Meaning Holism," *The Oxford Handbook of Philosophy of Language*, ed. E. LePore and B. Smith (Oxford: Clarendon Press, 2006), pp. 213–232.

117 These are the approaches on view in some of the work cited earlier, for example in that of E. Marlier, A.B. Atkinson, B. Cantillon, and B. Nolan, *The EU and Social Inclusion: Facing the Challenges* (Bristol: The Policy Press, 2007), especially, pp. 197–236), and of O. Galland and Y. Lemel, *Valeurs et cultures en Europe* (Paris: La Découverte, 2007), especially pp. 97–112.

118 See P.M. Bauleo and J.R. Martino, "The Dawn of the Particle Astronomy Era in Ultra-High-Energy Cosmic Rays," *Nature*, 458 (16 April 2009), 847–851. Note that a brief news report in *Le Monde*, accompanied by a colour picture from the European Space Organisation, announced that on 23 April 2009 the Burst Alert Telescope on NASA's American Swift satellite detected in the Lion Constellation an extraordinary long-duration gamma ray burst and its infrared afterglow caused by the collapse of the heart of a massive progenitor star transforming itself at the end of its life into a black hole. The automated giant visual telescopes of the European Organisation for Astronomical Research in the Southern Hemisphere at both La Silla and le Paranal Observatories in Chile were rapidly able to determine that this gamma ray burst lasted ten seconds and had occurred more than 13 billion years ago, roughly 600 million years after the occurrence of the Big Bang, in the cosmic dark ages when the universe had reached only 5% of its present age. This is the oldest and thus the farthest cosmic event and astronomical object yet detected. See N. R. Tanvir *et al.*, "A g-ray Burst at a Redshift of z =~ 8.2," *Nature*, 461 (2009), 1254–1257 and R. Salvaterra, *et al.* "GRB 090423 at a Redshift of z =~ 8.1," *Nature*, 461 (2009), 1258–1260. Discrepancies await further investigation.

119 Valéry's earlier reflections are especially interesting. They can be found in the manuscript collections of the *Bibliothèque Nationale* in Paris, especially here and there in the manuscript volumes entitled "Proses Anciennes 1887–1995," "Proses Anciennes: Articles 1897–1900," and "Articles 1897–1900." I am grateful to the BN for permission to consult these and other manuscripts, and especially for the help I received from the former curator of the Paul Valéry papers, Mme. F. de Lussy. A good example of the early reflections on language is Valéry's article "La Sémantique" which appeared in the January 1898 issue of *Mercure de France* (see the manuscript in "Articles Projets d'articles et Textes Divers 1897–1900," 12–28). Valéry's hesitations can be observed by studying the different drafts of several pages of the manuscript text of the article. For an idea of his speculative views on the language of literature see in the same manuscript the draft of an article, "A propos de Riemann," especially p. 81.

120 We will rely especially on *Thomas Reid: An Inquiry into the Human Mind on the Principles of Common Sense*, ed. D.R. Brookes (University Park, PA: Pennsylvania State UP, 1997), especially "Of Seeing," pp. 77–202.

121 The fullest account of Valéry's life and works can be found in the exhaustive 1366 page biography of M. Jarrety, *Paul Valéry* (Paris: Fayard, 2008). Full further references to the primary and those older secondary materials noted in abbreviated form only in what follows (see examples in the following note) are to be found in Jarrety and in the Pleiade editions of Valéry's *Oeuvres* (Paris: Gallimard).Valéry's published work is still but a fraction of the immense materials still to be edited in the coming decades. For some of the unpublished works see the "*La Valeryareum de la Bibliothèque littéraire Jacques Doucet*" ed. G.K. Hall. The basic resource materials are to be found in the *Départment des manuscrits, Bibliothèque Nationale* (BN. Mss), in the *Cahiers*, in the *Correspondence Gide-Valéry* (Mallet 1955), in the *Correspondence Valéry-Fourment* (Nochal: 1957), in Paul Valéry's *Lettres à quelques uns* (Valéry 1952), the *Oeuvres* (Hytier, Paris: Gallimard 1957 and 1960), and in the *Valéryanum*. But some material remains widely dispersed in such places as Austin, Texas, and Tokyo.

122 For the general background of Valéry's poetics see J. Hytier, *Le poétique de Valéry*, Paris 1953 and W.N. Ince, *The Poetic Theory of Paul Valéry* (Leicester: Leicester UP), 1961.

123 In general, my citations are from the unabridged facsimile edition of the *Cahiers* in 29 volumes (Paris: Éditions CNRS, 1957–1961) rather than from the shorter version that Judith Robinson edited in the Pleiade edition (Paris: Gallimard, 1973 and 1974). The references incorporated directly in my text to the volume and the page of the unabridged edition.

124 Here and throughout for all passages from Valéry's Notebooks the rough English translations are mine. The translations are "rough" in the sense that often I have not been able to capture the poetic resonances of Valéry's extraordinary uses of French.

125 For standard twentieth-century views on topics in the philosophy of language that Valéry often touches on see the now classical articles collected in for example *The Philosophy of Language*, ed. A. P. Martinich, 5th ed. (Oxford: Oxford UP, 2008). For much more recent contemporary philosophical views on many of these issues see especially the 41 freshly commissioned articles, each with lengthy bibliographies, in *The Oxford Handbook of Philosophy of Language*, ed. E. LePore and B. Smith (Oxford: Clarendon Press, 2006) and the earlier collection, *A Companion to the Philosophy of Language*, ed. B. Hale and C. Wright (Oxford: Blackwell, 1997). Many of these articles are on linguistic matters and not just exclusively on matters in the philosophy of language. Here, I do not try to confront Valéry's views in any detail with today's views on similar matters.

126 This issue touches on the disputed matter as to whether all perceptual experience is conceptualized. See for example H. Putnam's discussion in his *The Threefold Cord: Mind, Body, and World* (New York: Columbia UP, 1999), pp. 154–159. See also some of the papers collected in *Conceivability and Possibility*, ed. T.S. Gendler and J. Hawthorne (Oxford: Clarendon Press, 2002), especially the comprehensive Introduction, pp. 1–70.

127 Scientific images abound in Valéry's work. See for example Virtanen, 1974. *The Scientific Images of Paul Valéry* (Lincoln: Nebraska UP), any come from his early readings. Valéry bought the translation of Kelvin's *Conférences scientifiques et allocutions* when it appeared in Paris in 1893, a book he referred to again when he met Lord Kelvin in

London the next year. Further details can be found in the National Library of Scotland catalogue, *Paul Valéry* (Edinburgh, 1976). This catalogue also includes J. Middleton Murray's review from the *TLS*, 23 August 1917 of Valéry's great modernist poem which I do not discuss here, "La Jeune Parque."

128 See BN Manuscript, "Monsieur Teste," two volumes, Vol. 1, f. 22.

129 The emphasis here and in all other citations is Valéry's unless otherwise noted. Many of Valéry's most interesting comments on method can be found in the two volumes of the "Leonardo" manuscript. See for example vol. 2, pp. 64–65.

130 Walzer 1964, p. 65.

131 Some of these interests can be seen at work in the early period of his *Cahiers*, roughly between 1887 and 1897, a period also covered partly in his correspondence with Gide. See for example the French translation of Clerk Maxwell in two volumes (Paris: 1885–1887) which was presented to Paul Valéry and signed by Gide, in *Paul Valéry: Pré-Teste: Manuscript Inédits. Edition Originale. Université de Paris: Bibliothèque Littéraire Jacques Doucet, 3–23 Décember 1956*, item #144; hereafter referred to as "*Catalogue*."

132 See C. Travis, "Pragmatics," in *A Companion to the Philosophy of Language*, ed. B. Hale and C. Wright (Oxford: Blackwell, 1997), pp. 87–107. The citation is from p. 87. See also Z. G. Szabó, "The Distinction between Semantics and Pragmatics," in *The Oxford Handbook of Philosophy of Language*, ed. E. LePore and B. Smith (Oxford: Oxford UP, 2006), pp. 361–389.

133 *Oeuvres* I: 864.

134 On this "trinity" see especially his course at the *Collège de France*, "Corps, Monde, Esprit."

135 *Oeuvres* I: 1323.

136 In the course of his thoughtful review of Jaretty's monumental book ("*Valéry, personnage balzacien*," *Le Monde*, May 9, 2008), the distinguished French critic M. Fumaroli has usefully summarized much of the knowledge so far about these "others" in Valéry's complicated personal life.

137 Cf. A. Rouart-Valéry (1964 and 1966). In the 1956 Catalogue cited in note 12, see item #93, "Gênes-Octobre," version of "Nuit de gênes" which A. Rouart-Valéry published in facisimile *Valéry à Gênes* (Torino 1964). Quite strikingly, after Genoa, Valéry wrote no poetry for almost twenty years until he published "*La Jeune Parque*" in 1917 (see F. de Lussy, *La genèse da "La Jeune Parque"*, Paris, 1975).

138 *Oeuvres* I: 19–20.

139 See BN Manuscript, "Proses Anciennes 1887–1895," 265ff. for some probably related reflections on these difficulties of living solely intellectually. In his now authoritative biography Jarrety provides much new material on the identites of both the extraordinary woman in Montpellier and the various "others" in Valéry's life. See Catherine Pozzi, *Journal*, ed. C. Paulhan (Paris: Phébus, 2005) and especially M. Diaz-Florian, *Catherine Pozzi: La Vocation à la nuit* (Paris: Aden, 2008).

140 Valéry describes what led up to the writing of "M. Teste" in his "Préface pour la traduction suédoise de la soirée avec Monsieur Teste," dated September 1934.

141 *Oeuvres* I: 1301.

142 *Oeuvres* I: 1172.

143 *Oeuvres* I: 1174.

144 *Oeuvres* I: 1361. An excellent very recent English translation of Mallarmé together with parallel French texts can be found in *Stéphane Mallarmé: Collected Poems and Other Verse*, tr. E.H. and A.M. Blackmore (Oxford: Oxford UP, 2008) with explanatory notes, chronology, and selected bibliography.

145 Cf. Reimer and E. Camp, "Metaphor," in *The Oxford Handbook of Philosophy of Language*, ed. E. LePore and B. Smith (Oxford: Clarendon Press, 2006), 843–863, with extensive references to much contemporary work. See also R. Moral, "Metaphor," in *A Companion to the Philosophy of Language*, ed. B. Hale and C. Wright (Oxford: Blackwell, 1997), pp. 248–268.

146 *Oeuvres* I: 1159.

147 *Oeuvres* I: 1387.

148 *Loc. cit.*

149 *Oeuvres* I: 538.

150 "Alain" was the pen name of Émile Chartier (1868–1951) whose teaching of philosophy in France's elite schools as well as his five volumes of *Propos* were widely influential between the two world wars. Importantly, Alain wrote in the tradition of the aphoristic writings of such works of the French moralists as La Rochefoucauld's 1664 *Maximes*.

151 *Oeuvres* I: 165.

152 I take a different approach here to the topic of moral knowledge than the one I elaborated with respect to Tolstoy's *Anna Karenina* in the chapter on moral knowledge in P. McCormick, *Fictions, Philosophies and the Problems of Poetics* (Ithaca, NY: Cornell UP, 1988).

153 Note that just as in the previous chapter, by way of insuring a non-idiosyncratic, proper representativeness for the general philosophical views I am reporting on, I will continue to cite relevant articles from the most recent general reference works in English language philosophy. The views which distinguished contemporary English-language philosophers express in these reference works I will consider here to be "standard." Some such views of course while standard may still not be true, as continuing work continues to investigate. Where the matter under discussion may require, I will cite the often less widely held views of certain individual philosophers' works including my own.

154 We need not here go into the difficult subject of the nature and number and kinds of basic things, what is often called today in English, "ontology." For a succinct and important recent account see E.J. Lowe, *The Four Category Ontology: A Metaphysical Foundation for Natural Science* (Oxford: OUP, 2006), and especially H. Robinson, "The Ontology of the Mental," in *The Oxford Handbook of Metaphysics*, ed. M.J. Loux and D. W. Zimmerman (Oxford: Oxford UP, 2003), pp. 527–555. Hereafter, I cite this work as *OHM*. For the basic things of the mind, see H. Steward, *The Ontology of the Mind: Events, Processes and States* (Oxford: Oxford UP, 1997), and articles in *Agency and Self-Awareness*, ed. J. Roessler and N. Eilan (Oxford: Clarendon Press, 2003) and *Mental Action*, ed. M. Soteriou and L. O'Brien (Oxford: Oxford UP, 2009).

155 Cf. F. Dretske, "Perception," in *The Oxford Companion to Philosophy*, ed. T. Honderich, 2nd ed. (Oxford: Oxford UP, 2005), p. 688. Hereafter, I cite this work as *OCP*. Cf. A. Noë, *Action in Perception* (Cambridge, MA: MIT Press, 2004).

156 *Ibid.*, p. 688. For a more empirical and strictly psychological view of perception see the standard account of R.L. Gregory, "Perception," in *The Oxford Companion to the Mind*, ed. R.L. Gregory, 2nd ed. (Oxford: Oxford UP, 2004), pp. 707–710. Hereafter, I cite this reference work as *OCM*.

157 A. Lacey, "Intuition," in *OCP*, p. 442.

158 For some of the important nuances here see R.M. Chisholm's classical study, *Perceiving: A Philosophical Study* (Ithaca: Cornell UP, 1957).

159 Cf. many of the recent articles in *Perceptual Experience*, ed. T.S. Gendler and J. Hawthorne (Oxford: Oxford UP, 2005).

160 See for example *Essays on Moral Realism*, ed. G. Sayre-McCord (Ithaca, NY: Cornell UP, 1988), D.O. Brink, *Moral Realism and the Foundations of Ethics* (Cambridge: Cambridge UP, 1989), and R. Shafer-Landau, *Moral Realism: A Defense* (Oxford: Oxford UP, 2003).

161 S. Blackburn, "Moral Scepticism," in his *Oxford Dictionary of Philosophy*, 2nd ed. (Oxford: Oxford UP, 2006), p. 242. Hereafter, I cite this reference work as *ODP*.

162 W. Sinnott-Armstrong, "Moral Skepticism," in *The Cambridge Dictionary of Philosophy*, ed. R. Audi, 2nd ed. (Cambridge: Cambridge UP, 1999), pp. 589–590. Hereafter, I cite this reference work as *CDP*.

163 See K. Jones, "Moral Epistemology," in *The Oxford Handbook of Contemporary Philosophy*, ed. F. Jackson and M. Smith (Oxford: Oxford UP, 2005), pp. 63–85, especially pp. 70–73 on "Intuitionism." Hereafter, I cite this reference work as *HCP*.

164 M.G. Singer, "Moral Epistemology," *CDP*, pp. 584–586.

165 Plato's understanding of knowledge in his *Theaetetus* as "justified true belief" has required modifications in the light of epistemological work in the 1960's. The American philosopher E.L. Gettier demonstrated that some beliefs may well be true, and the person justified in holding these beliefs to be true, and yet the person's justification turns out to be accidental or lucky and hence not essential in the sense of being intrinsically related to the beliefs' truth. Discussion continues today as to what a less unsatisfactory working definition of knowledge might be. See E.L. Gettier, "Is Justified True Belief Knowledge?" *Analysis* 23 (1963), 121–123, and three responses to Gettier by A.I. Goldman, K. Lehrer and T.D. Paxson, and F. Dretske reprinted in *Knowledge: Readings in Contemporary Epistemology*, ed. S. Bernecker and F. Dretske (Oxford: Oxford UP, 2000), pp. 18–62.

166 See for example J.M. Doris and S.P. Stich, "As A Matter of Fact: Empirical Perspectives on Ethics," in *HCP*, pp. 739–766 with an excellent bibliography, and K.A. Appiah, *Experiments in Ethics* (Cambridge, MA: Harvard UP, 2008), especially "The Case Against Intuition," pp. 73–120. See also J. Waldron's critical review of Appiah, "Right and Wrong: Psychologists vs. Philosophers," *The New York Review of Books*, 8 October 2009, pp. 39–41.

167 C. Wilson, "Moral Knowledge," in *The Oxford Companion to Philosophy*, 2nd ed. (Oxford: Oxford UP, 2005), p. 621.

168 For an important recent review of just what may arguably be taken as common across the variety of human cultures today see D. Jones, "Human Nature: the Remix," *Nature*, 457 (12 February 2009), 780–783. The article includes many useful further references.

169 V. Hope, "Reid, Thomas," *The Oxford Companion to Philosophy*, ed. T. Honderich, 2nd ed. (Oxford: Oxford UP, 2005), p. 798, hereafter cited as *OCP* 2005.

170 Molyneux wrote to Locke about the even today still puzzling ways that persons integrate visual and tactile space in perception. Locke quoted the letter in his 1694 philosophical masterpiece, *Essay Concerning Human Understanding* (Bk 2, chapter 9, section 8): "Suppose a Man born blind, and now adult, and taught by his touch to distinguish a Cube, and a Sphere of the same metal, and nighly of the same bigness, so as to tell, when he felt one and t'other, which is the Cube, which the Sphere. Suppose then the Cube and Sphere placed on a Table, and the Blind Man to be made to see. *Quaere*, Whether by his sight, before he touch'd them, he could now distinguish, and tell, which is the Globe and, which the Cube." Cf. G. Evans 1985 paper, "Molyneux's Question," reprinted in *Vision and Mind: Selected Readings in the Philosophy of Perception*, ed. A. Noë and E. Thompson (Cambridge, MA: MIT Press, 2002), pp. 319–350, especially the figure on p. 331.

171 Cf. N. Cheng *et al.* "Intrinsic Light Response of Retinal Horizontal Cells of Teleosts," *Nature*, 460 (2009), 899–903; and M. Tri H. Do *et al.*, "Photon Capture and Signalling by Melanopsin Retinal Ganglion Cells," *Nature* 457 (15 January 2009), 232, and 281–287.

172 Eugenio Montale, *Bones of the Cuttlefish*, tr. A. Mazza (Oakville, Ontario: Mosaic Press, 1984), pp. 57–58. Other English translations of Montale's poetry are to be found in *Eugenio Montale: Collected Poems, 1920–1954*, tr. J. Galassi (New York: Farrar Straus and Giroux, 2000), *The Coastguard's House: English Versions of the Poetry of Eugenio Montale*, tr. J. Reed (Newcastle upon Tyne: Bloodaxe Books, 1990), *Poets in Our Time*, tr. A. Hamilton (New York: Urizen Books, 1976), *Eugenio Montale: New Poems*, tr. G. Singh (New York: New Directions, 1972), and in four separate volumes of Montale's four major books of poetry, *Ossi di seppia* (1925), *Le occasioni* (1939), *La bufera e altro* (1956), and *Satura 1962–1970* (1971), each translated by W. Arrowsmith (New York: Norton).

173 Compare here and throughout the translations by different hands in *Poems: Montale*, ed. H. Thomas (London: Penguin, 2002), with introduction, chronology, and further reading. See also T. Parks, "A Prisoner's Dream: Eugenio Montale in Translation," *The New York Review of Books*, 4 February 1999. One of the first scholars to bring Montale's work to the attention of the English language world was the celebrated journalist and Romanist, Samuel Putnam, whose influential article, "A Miniature Anthology of Italian Poetry" in *This Quarter*, 2 (1930) H. Thomas cites and whose translation of "Cuttle Bones" Thomas reprints. Samuel Putnam (1892–1950) was the father of the distinguished American philosopher, Hilary Putnam.

174 Many of the most important of these literary backgrounds can be found in some of Montale's prose writings. See especially *Eugenio Montale: Selected Essays*, tr. G. Singh (Manchester: Carcanet, 1978) and *Eugenio Montale: The Second Life of Art: Selected Essays*, ed. and tr. J. Galassi (New York: Ecco Press, 1982).

175 Montale's collected poetry appeared in 1980 as *L'opera in versi*.

176 Tr. Mazza, p. 44. Cited by Arrowsmith in *E. Montale, Cuttlefish Bones* (1920–1927), tr. W. Arrowsmith (New York: Norton, 1993), pp. 214–221. Hereafter I cite this work as "Montale1993."

177 For a standard and more recent empirical account see I.P. Howard, "Spatial Coordination," in *The Oxford Companion to the Mind*, ed. R.L. Gregory, 2nd ed. (Oxford: Oxford UP, 2004), pp. 855–861, with bibliography.

178 See "L'eroismo," in Montale's *Quaderno di quattro anni*.

179 See the commentary of G. Almansi and B. Merry, *Eugenio Montale: The Private Language of Poetry* (Edinburgh: Edinburgh UP, 1977), pp. 37–38, cited in Montale 1993, p. 221.

180 Montale 1993, p. 69.

181 On the notions of rationality and reason particularly in the domain of values see R. Boudon, *La Rationalité* (Paris: Presses universitaires de France, 2009), especially "La rationalité ordinaire des croyances normatives," pp. 77–99.

182 R. Foley, *The Theory of Epistemic Rationality* (Cambridge, MA.: Harvard UP, 1989), p. 169.

183 Standardly, fallibilism is a philosophical view about knowledge deriving from the American philosopher, C.S. Peirce (1839–1914) that represents a middle ground between dogmatism (knowledge requires the attainment of certainty) and skepticism (the attainment of certainty and even the assignment of probabilities are impossible). On this view, "it is not necessary that beliefs be certain, or grounded on certainty. We may justifiably rest content with beliefs in circumstances in which further evidence, forcing us to revise our opinion, may yet come in" (S. Blackburn, "Fallibilism," in his *Oxford Dictionary of Philosophy*, 2nd ed. [Oxford: Oxford UP, 2005], p. 130).

184 Cf. R. Feldman, "Foley's Subjective Foundationalism," *Phenomenology and Philosophical Research*, 50 (1989–1990), 156.

185 See the *Shorter Oxford English Dictionary on Historical Principles*, ed. A. Stevenson, 6th ed. (Oxford: Oxford UP, 2007); hereafter cited as *SOED* 2007.

186 The classical view of moral motivation in modern moral philosophy is to be found in David Hume's, *A Treatise of Human Nature*, ed. L.A. Selby-Bigge and P.H. Nidditch (Oxford: Clarendon Press, 1978), 2.3.3. N. Sinhababu provides a recent re-articulation of Hume's view in his paper, "The Humean Theory of Motivation Reformulated and Defended," *The Philosophical Review*, 118 (2009), 465–500.

187 S. Darwell, "Ethical Intuitionism and the Motivation Problem," in *Ethical Intuitionism: Re-evaluations*, ed. P. Stratton-Lake (Oxford: Clarendon Press, 2002), pp. 248–270.

188 B. Rundle, "Motives and Motivation," in *OCP* 2005, p. 633.

189 For example, see M. Slote, "Moral Sentimentalism and Moral Psychology," in *The Oxford Handbook of Ethical Theory*, ed. D. Copp (Oxford: Oxford UP, 2006), pp. 219–239; hereafter cited as *HET* 2006.

190 R. Jay Wallace, "Moral Psychology," in *The Oxford Handbook of Contemporary Philosophy*, ed. F. Jackson and M. Smith (Oxford: Oxford UP, 2005), p. 95; hereafter cited as *HCP* 2005.

191 *Ibid.*, p. 96.

192 Montale 1993, pp. 151, 153.

193 Almansi and Merry 1977, p. 56; cited by Arrowsmith in Montale 1993, pp. 258.

194 Almansi and Merry 1977, pp. 57–59; cited by Arrowsmith in Montale 1993, pp. 259–260.

195 *Ibid.*

196 "Translator's Preface," in *Eugenio Montale: The Occasions*, tr. W. Arrowsmith (New York: Norton, 1987), p. 15.

197 In France, for example, one of the most affluent countries in the EU, the United Nations Committee on the Rights of Children, after interviewing high government French officials in the Spring of 2009, concluded that France had several expanding grey zones in its policies concerning children, including guaranteeing the access of poor and isolated children to proper health care.

198 On the developments of the EU debates about a European social inclusion policy and the place of general access to health care see E. Marlier, A.B. Atkinson, B. Cantillon, and B. Nolan, *The EU and Social Inclusion: Facing the Challenges* (Bristol: The Policy Press, 2007), pp. 1–11 and pp. 17–57; hereafter referred to as "Marlier *et al.*, 2007."

199 For the conclusions of the regular European Council meetings see the website, http://www.consilium.europa.eu

200 Cited in Marlier *et al.*, 2007, p. 6.

201 For text and commentary with bibliography see the UNICEF-France publication by F. Martinetti, *Les Droits de l'enfant* (Paris: E.J.L. / Librio, 2002), especially pp. 58–60 on children's rights to proper health care. For the important backgrounds to the 1989 UN Convention on Children Rights see the discussion in A. Bhalla and P. McCormick, *Poverty Among Immigrant Children in Europe* (London: Macmillan / Palgrave, 2009), pp. 18–23, which I draw on here. See also F. Dekeuwer-Défossez, *Les Droits de l'enfant*, 7th ed. (Paris: Presses universitaires de France, 2006), especially pp. 77–121.

202 See the UNICEF twentieth anniversary report on children published on November 20, 2009 in Paris. Unicef reports that roughly 1 billion children worldwide continue to be deprived of their basic human rights, including about 150 million children who live in the streets.

203 Cited in C. Vincent, "Les droits d'un milliard d'enfants restent bafoués," *Le Monde*, November 20, 2009.

204 Because of the complicated publishing history of Eliot's works, in what follows to simplify I italicize the titles of Eliot's poems regardless of whether they originally appeared in separate book form or as parts only of separate books.

205 *Collected Poems 1909–1962* (London: Faber, 1963), p. 189.

206 *Murder in the Cathedral* (London: Faber, 1968), p. 83.

207 *Ibid.*

208 For an instance of informed comment on recent productions see Frank Kermode's review of the 1993 Stratford-upon-Avon production in the *TLS*, May 28, 1993. See however R. Grove's discussion of the interpretive advantages in viewing Eliot's 1935 play from our present perspectives in his "Pereira and After: The Cures of Eliot's Theatre," in A.D. Moody, ed., *The Cambridge Companion to T.S. Eliot* (Cambridge: Cambridge University Press, 1994), pp. 159–60.

209 H. Gardner, *The Art of T.S. Eliot* (London: Faber, 1968), p. 137.

210 See the summaries and the Figure, "L'évolution du virus," in *The New England Journal of Medicine*, cited in the four-page dossier by F. Aizicovici *et al.*, *Le Monde*, November 5, 2009, which I rely on for these remarks.

211 Dr Chan was reported to have made this observation on April 25, 2009. Cited in *Le Monde's* dossier noted above.

212 *Le Monde*, November 12, 2009.

213 E. Hirsch, *Pandémie grippale: l'ordre de mobilisation* (Paris: Cerf, 2009), cited in *Le Monde*, November 5, 2009.

214 Cf. "Motivate," etc. in *Shorter Oxford English Dictionary*, 2007.

215 "Liberate," etc. in *Ibid.*

216 In what follows I draw partly on some of my previous work on Kant in my book, *The Negative Sublime: Ethics, Warfare, and the Dark Borders of Reason* (Heidelberg: Universitätsverlag Winter, 2003).

217 Tr. J.T. Goldthwait (Berkeley: University of California Press, 1960, reprinted 1991), pp. 47–48.

218 Standardly, to posit something is to put something forward "as a useful assumption or starting-point, but not [as something] necessarily regarded as known to be true" (S. Blackburn in his *The Oxford Dictionary of Philosophy*, 2nd ed. [Oxford: Oxford UP, 2005], p. 284).

219 Tr. G. Treash (New York: Abaris Books, 1979), p. 73.

220 E. Foerster, "Kant's *Selbstsetzungslehre*," in *Kant's Transcendental Deductions* (Stanford: Stanford UP, 1989), p. 217.

221 Foerster 1989, p. 229.

222 Kant, A 600-601 / B 628-629; cited in Foerster 1989, p. 265, note 15.

223 "Non rifugiarti nell'ombra," in E. Montale, *Cuttlefish Bones*, tr. W. Arrowsmith (New York: Norton, 1993), pp. 42–43; translation slightly modified.

224 Cf. E. Montale, *The Second Life of Art: Selected Essays of Eugenio Montale*, ed. and tr. J. Galassi (New York: Ecco Press, 1982), pp. 3–18, 12–19.

225 From "Intenzioni (Intervista imaginaria)" (1946), cited in E. Montale, *Cuttlefish Bones* (1920–1927), tr. W. Arrowsmith (New York: Norton, 1993), p. xvi.

226 Cf. G.-P. Biasin, *Montale, Debussy, and Modernism* (Princeton: Princeton UP, 1990).

227 Tr. A. Mazza 1983, p. 44.

228 Tr. W. Arrowsmith 19932, p. 67.

229 Cf. P. McCormick, *Fictions, Philosophies, and the Problems of Poetics* (Ithaca: Cornell UP, 1988), Chapter Seven, "Real Fictions," pp. 256–301.

230 William Arrowsmith, "Translator's Preface," in Montale 1993, p. xxiii.

231 Recall the eighteenth-century sentimentalists and their commitment to the existence of a specific "moral sense."

232 Cf. M. Slote, "Moral Sentimentalism and Moral Psychology," in the *Oxford Handbook of Ethical Theory* (Oxford: OUP, 2006), pp. 219–239. Hereafter, I cite this reference work as *HET*.

233 Cf. C. McGinn, *Mental Content* (Oxford: Blackwell, 1989), especially pp. 169–208.

234 But among others see R. Audi, "Intuitionism, Pluralism and the Foundations of Ethics," in *Foundations of Ethics*, ed. R. Shafer-Landau and T. Cuneo (Oxford: Blackwell, 2007), pp. 402–419.

235 *Oeuvres* I.

236 *Oeuvres* I: 633.

237 Valéry describes what led up to the writing of "M. Teste" in his "Préface pour la traduction suédoise de la soirée avec Monsieur Teste," dated September 1934. See BN Manscript "Monsieur Teste," vol. 2, p. 139 *bis*.

238 Among the many prefaces Valéry wrote to exhibitions of paintings, see in particular *Berthe Morisot (1841–1895). Catalogue. Préface de Paul Valéry*. Paris: Musée de l'Orangerie, 1941. Recall also his passionate interest in Degas whom he dared to describe only after Degas's death (Valéry 1936). For some of Valéry's own work, see de Man 1948, especially the water colour, "M. Teste à l'Opéra" with Valéry's inscription, "Il ne regardait que la salle." An excellent collection of Valéry's drawings and paintings is on permanent exhibit at the Musée Paul Valéry in Sète, France, the site of his poetic masterpiece, *Le cimetière marin*.

239 See note 177.

240 Letter to Valéry Larbaud 1887.

241 *Ephemerides*; cited in A. Rouart-Valéry.

242 The force of this resistance is underestimated in the much discussed essay of J. Derrida in his *Marges de la philosophie* (Paris: Minuit, 1972). Note the very different approach in Genette 1979.

243 *Cahiers* 19: 538. Hereafter, I include references to the *Cahiers* directly in the text in parentheses.

244 Ince 1968.

245 *Oeuvres* I: 927.

246 *Ibid.*

247 The Narcissus theme in Valéry's works is closely linked with actual events in his childhood. See Aigresse 1970.

248 *Oeuvres* I: 928.

249 *Oeuvres* I: 929.

250 *Oeuvres* I: 931; emphasis omitted.

251 *Oeuvres* I: 930.

252 *Mélanges*, 105.

253 See Robinson, *L'analyse de l'espont dans les "Cahiers" de Paul Valéry*, Paris 1963 and Celeyrette-Pietri, *Valéry et le moi*, Paris 1979. The latter has an excellent bibliography and index. It also includes many references to the unpublished manuscripts.

254 *Oeuvres* I: 1219.

255 Much philosophical work continues on the various problems associated with consciousness. An outstanding contemporary and extensive collection of 49 articles can be found in *The Nature of Consciousness*, ed. N. Block, O. Flanigan, and G. Güzeldere (Cambridge, MA: MIT Press, 1997). The basic book in the revival of contemporary philosophical work on consciousness is probably D.J. Chalmers, *The Conscious Mind: In Search of a Fundamental Theory* (Oxford: Oxford UP, 1996). See also the papers collected in *Mind and Cognition*, ed. W.G. Lycan, 2nd ed. (Oxford: Blackwell, 1999. Once again, I do not try here to engage Valéry's views with any of these contemporary discussions which serve, nonetheless, as necessary backgrounds for taking the critical measure of Valéry's views.

256 1950: 92.

257 *Oeuvres* I: 1488.

258 *Oeuvres* I: 1489.

259 Crow 1972a and 1972b.

260 Du Bos (1965) makes the point well. See BN, 76.

261 *Ibid.*

262 *Oeuvres* I: 1275.

263 *Oeuvres* I: 1310.

264 *Oeuvres* I: 1292.

265 *Oeuvres* I: 1207.

266 *Oeuvres* I: 1121.

267 *Oeuvres* I: 1207.

268 *Oeuvres* I: 1215–1216.

269 *Oeuvres* I: 1214.

270 *Oeuvres* I: 1403.

271 *Oeuvres* I: 1408–1409.

272 *Oeuvres* I: 1403.

273 *Oeuvres* I: 1407.

274 *Oeuvres* I: 1387.

275 *Oeuvres* I: 1262.

276 *Oeuvres* I: 1321.

277 *Oeuvres* I: 1337.

278 *Oeuvres* II: 547.

279 *Oeuvres* I: 1338.

280 *Oeuvres* I: 1320–1321.

281 *Oeuvres* I: 1363.

282 *Oeuvres* I: 1378.

283 *Oeuvres* I: 1349–1350.

284 For a more detailed discussion see for example the 16 papers collected in *Properties*, ed. D.H. Mellow and A. Oliver (Oxford: Oxford UP, 1997), especially the "Introduction," pp. 1–33 and the extensive bibliography, pp. 270–274.

285 This summary phrase is A. Kenny's in his discussion Reid's "common sense views" in A. Kenny, *The Rise of Modern Philosophy* (Oxford: Clarendon Press, 2006), p. 89. For a much fuller treatment see N. Rescher, *Common Sense: A New Look at Old Tradition* (Milwaukee, Wisconsin: Marquette UP, 2005).

286 For historical backgrounds, bibliography and analyses see the recent articles in *The Cambridge Companion to Thomas Reid*, ed. T. Cuneo and R. van Woudenberg (Cambridge: Cambridge UP, 2004). On perception and epistemology see especially R. Nichols, *Thomas Reid's Theory of Perception* (Oxford: Clarendon Press, 2007), F. Van Cleve, "Reid's Theory of Perception," in *The Cambridge Companion to Thomas Reid*,

tated bibliography together with the introductions and notes to the selections in *The Gadamer Reader*, ed. and trans. R.E. Palmer [Evanston: ILL: Northwestern UP, 2007, pp. 429–432], an expanded version of a selection that Gadamer himself made from his writings edited by J. Grondin, *Gadamer Lesebuch* [Tübingen: J.C.B. Mohr, 1997]). For a bibliography of Gadamer's work together with replies to some of his critics see the essays collected in *The Philosophy of H.-G. Gadamer*, ed. L.E. Hahn (Chicago: Open Court, 1997).

308 In reflecting on Gadamer's very extensive work it is important to remember that Gadamer sometimes uses the word "truth" not just in traditional classical and contemporary ways but especially in the contexts of Heidegger's unconventional reflections on the idea of truth as *aletheia* or "truth as unconcealedness." For a brief, standard overview see M. Suhr, "Aletheia," in the *Metzler Philosophie Lexikon: Begriffe und Definitionen*, 2nd ed. (Stuttgart: Metzler, 1999), ed. P. Prechtl and F.-P. Burkard, pp. 16–17.

309 To situate Gadamer's hermeneutic themes with respect to contemporary Anglo-American work in aesthetics see the recent extensive collection of 48 essays in *The Oxford Handbook of Aesthetics*, ed. J. Levinson (Oxford: OUP, 2003), especially A. Neill's, "Poetry," pp. 605–613, with bibliography.

310 H.-G. Gadamer, *The Relevance of the Beautiful and Other Essays*, tr. N. Walker (Cambridge: Cambridge University Press, 1986), pp. 140–154. Note that Gadamer himself did not himself publish this work as a collection of some of his essays. Since nonetheless this work gathers together in one place a number of quite important pieces about literary art, I will focus mainly but not exclusively on this collection here.

311 Gadamer 1986, p. 143. Hereafter unless otherwise indicated references in the text are to Gadamer's 1986 collection.

312 Note that some have wrongly taken Roman Ingarden's very extensive phenomenological work on the literary arts as exclusively formal. In fact while formal to some extent, this work is, while not hermeneutic, still mainly epistemological and metaphysical and not just ontological. Cf. *Roman Ingarden: Selected Papers in Aesthetics*, ed. P. McCormick (Munich: Philosophia Verlag, 1985).

313 Gadamer 1986, pp. 1–53.

314 "Facticity" here is a technical word usually found in existentialist, phenomenological, and hermeneutic contexts. Cf. R. Solomon's brief entry, "Facticity," in *The Penguin Dictionary of Philosophy*, 2nd ed., ed. T. Mautner (London: Penguin, 2005, pp. 213–214. Solomon writes: "Facticity is the name that these philosophers [he mentions earlier Heidegger and Sartre] give to that aspect of human existence that is defined by the situations in which we find ourselves, the 'fact' we are forced to confront. Facticity includes all of those factual details over which one has no control (...) but it also includes the nature and limits of being human as such (...)."

315 Gadamer 1986, pp. 105–115. Cf. E. Grassi, *Kunst und Mythos*, rev. ed. (Frankfurt: Suhrkamp, 1990), p. 122.

316 For an excellent recent selection of pieces from Ricoeur's voluminous work organized around the three major themes of language and the world, the subject of narratives, and actions and institutions see *Paul Ricoeur: Anthologie*, ed. M. Foessel and F. Lamouche (Paris: Seuil, 2007), with chronology and a selected bibliography both of Ricoeur's works and of some works about Ricoeur. For a full bibliography of Ricoeur's

voluminous work see F.D. Vansina (Leuwen: Peeters, 1985 ff.). See also the essays about his work with Ricoeur's replies in *The Philosophy of Paul Ricoeur*, ed. L.E. Hahn (Chicago: Open Court, 1995), the March–April, 2006 special issue of *Esprit* and the special issue of *Revue de métaphysique et de morale*, 50 (2006).

317 Paul Ricoeur, *Temps et récit*. 3 vols. (Paris: Seuil, 1983–1985); my translations throughout. Hereafter unless otherwise indicated references in the text are to these volumes.

318 I set aside here his two later major works, *Soi-même comme un autre* (Paris: Seuil, 1990) and *La Mémoire, l'histoire, l'oubli* (Paris: Seuil, 2000) since they do not deal centrally with literary works of art. See however Ricoeur's own discussion of the unity in his earlier work in *Réflexion faite. Autobiographie intellectuelle* (Paris: Éditions Esprit, 1995), his extended interviews, *La Critique et la Conviction: Entretiens avec François Azouvi et Marc de Launay* (Paris: Calmann-Lévy, 1995), and his last work, *Parcours de la reconnaissance. Trois études* (Paris: Stock, 2004).

319 Ricoeur's more extensive reflections on action and action theory may be found in his collection of articles, *Du texte à l'action* (Paris: Seuil, 1986).

320 Cf. E. Cassirer, *The Philosophy of Symbolic Forms*, 3 vols. (New Haven: Yale UP, 1953–1957). Casirer first published this major and still influential work in German from 1923–1931.

321 Vol. 2, 43–44. Ricoeur's discussion of the symbolism of evil goes back to his very rich reflections on some of the imagery of evil in religious and mythic texts in his *Finitude et culpabilité*, vol. 2, *La symbolique du mal* (Paris: Aubier, 1960), especially pp. 11–30 and 323–332. See also his collaborative work with the biblical theologian, A. Lacoque, *Penser la Bible* (Paris: Seuil, 1998).

322 This hermeneutic reflection on past truths in terms of the notion of "tradition" may be contrasted with the importantly different reflection on past truths in the Anglo-American tradition. See for example Michael Dummett's three John Dewey lectures first presented at Columbia University during the Spring Semester in 2002 and now published in revised and extended form as, *Truth and the Past* (New York: Columbia UP, 2004), especially "The Concept of Truth," and "The Metaphysics of Time," respectively pp. 1–28 and pp. 73–96.

323 Ricoeur nuances and extends his views about historical narrative especially in his later major work, *La Mémoire, l'histoire, l'oubli* (Paris: Seuil, 2000).

324 Many of the standard papers in Anglo-American philosophical reflection on reference may be found in the collection of six papers on reference and descriptions together with references to further readings in *The Philosophy of Language*, ed. A.P. Martinich, 5th ed. (Oxford: OUP, 20089), pp. 209–278. See also the five more recent papers on reference collected in *The Oxford Handbook of Philosophy of Language*, ed. E. LePore and B. Smith (Oxford: Clarendon Press, 2006), pp. 393–554 with bibliographies.

325 Contrast Ricoeur's view here with that of Dummett's in *Truth and the Past* (New York: Columbia UP, 2004), pp. 87–90. More generally, see the debate between D.W. Zimmerman, "The Privileged Present: Defending an 'A-Theory' of Time," and J.J.C. Smart, "The Tenseless Theory of Time," in *Contemporary Debates in Metaphysics*, ed. T. Sider, J. Hawthorne, and D.W. Zimmerman (Oxford: Blackwell, 2008), pp. 209–238.

326 Tr. S. Mitchell (New York: Random House, 1984), p. 193.

327 See the detailed table of times, places, and fragments in U. Fülleborn and M. Engle, eds., *Materialien zu R.M. Rilkes* "Duineser Elegien," Vol. 1 (Frankfurt: Suhrkamp, 1980), pp. 376–77.

328 See for example A. S. Bhalla, *Royal Tombs of India: 13th to 18th Century* (Ahmedabad: Mapin Publishing, 2009).

329 The World Food Organization of the United Nations meeting in Rome from November 16–18, 2009 estimated that currently there are more than one billion people in the world who are suffering from hunger and malnutrition. Since June 2008 after the earlier food riots in numerous countries agricultural prices have declined precipitously thereby marginalizing the small subsistence farmers' families and leading to massive rural exodus. Cf. the interview with the United Nations specialist, O. de Schutter in *Le Monde*, November 17, 2009.

330 See especially the empirical data with many tables and charts in C. Brousse, J.-M. Firdion, and M. Marpsat, *Les sans-domicile* (Paris: La Découverte, 2008), especially Table 1, "Éléments de chronologie autour des sans-domicile," pp. 8–10. See also I. Christensen and I. Koch-Nielsen, *Danish Research on Homelessness with a Focus on Hidden Homelessness*, www.cuhp.org.

331 J. Gadrey and F. Jany-Catrice, *Les nouveaux indicateurs de richesse*, 2nd ed. (Paris: La Découverte, 2007), especially "Évaluer les indicateurs," pp. 92–98, and Table 8, "Évaluation des aspects relativement techniques des indicateurs," pp. 96–97.

332 Cf. "Social Network Characteristics Associated with Risky Behaviours Among Runaway and Homeless Youth," *Journal of Health and Social Behavior*, n° 40 (1999), 63–78; and T. Amossé *et al.*, "Vie et santé des jeunes sans domicile ou en situation précaire," *Rapport de l'Institut de recherche et de documentation en économie de la santé*, n° 1355 (2001).

333 In general see *Child Poverty in Perspective: An Overview of Child Well-Being in Rich Countries* (Florence: UNICEF Innocenti Research Centre, 2007), especially "Material Well-Being" and "Subjective Well-Being," pp. 5–11 and 34–38 respectively.

334 For statistics on social exclusion within Europe see especially the Internet site, http://ec.europa.eu/employment_social/spsi/common_indicators_fr.htm, especially B. Edgar, *et al.*, "Measurement of Homelessness at European Union Level." More generally for Europe see the standard Eurostat data at http://epp.eurostat.ec.europa.eu. For France in particular see the very recent two comprehensive reports of the French government's specially established *Comité pour la mesure des performances économiques et du progrès social*, both authored by a blue-ribbon panel led by the Nobel laureats, J. Stiglitz and A. Sen, and by J.P. Fitoussi, *et al.* The first volume is entitled, *Richesse des nations et bien-être des individus*, and the second, *Vers de nouveaux systèmes de mesure* (Paris: Odile Jacob, 2009). In the first volume see especially "Bien-être social," pp. 98–125, and in the second see especially "Qualité de la vie," pp. 141–296, both with bibliographies. See also the statistics and their analyses in the November 2009 volume of the French national office for statistics (INSEE), *France. Portrait social* (Paris: La documentation française, 2009), especially the definitions and tables on "La protection sociale" together with the comparative tables on social protection in the other 26 EU countries on pp. 270–271 and pp. 304–305 respectively.

335 P. Kourilsky, *Le Temps de L'altruisme* (Paris: Odile Jacob, 2009), pp. 23–29.

336 C. Altieri 1984.

337 Cf. C. Hosek and P. Parker, eds., *Lyric Poetry: Beyond New Criticism* (Ithaca: Cornell University Press, 1985).

338 On the pertinent notions of self and subjectivity here see P. Ricoeur, *Soi-même comme un autre* (Paris: Seuil, 1990), pp. 167–198.

339 Montale 1992, p. 61. Translation slightly modified.

340 Johannes Bobrowski, *Shadow Lands*, tr. R. and M. Mead (New York: New Directions, 1994), p. 148.

341 The phrase is Hans Magnus Enzensburger's.

342 Johannes Bobrowski, *The White Mirror*, tr. M. Nagel (Orono, Maine: Puckerbrush Press, 1993), p. 25; translation slightly modified.

343 *The Shorter Oxford English Dictionary*, 6th edition (Oxford, 2007), or *SOED*, describes "literal" as "designating or pertaining to a sense or interpretation of a text, orig., esp. the Bible, obtained by taking words in their primary or customary meaning and applying the ordinary rules of grammar, without mysticism, allegory, or metaphor (...)."

344 See for example C. Swoyer, "Abstract Entities," and C. Dorr, "There Are No Abstract Entities" in *Contemporary Debates in Metaphysics*, ed. T. Sider, J. Hawthorne, and D.W. Zimmerman (Oxford: Blackwell, 2008), pp. 9–31 and 32–63 respectively.